One-Eyed Science

Occupational Health and Women Workers

■ ■ ■

In the series
Labor and Social Change
edited by Paula Rayman
and Carmen Sirianni

One-Eyed Science

Occupational Health and Women Workers

■ ■ ■

Karen Messing

FOREWORD BY JEANNE MAGER STELLMAN

TEMPLE UNIVERSITY PRESS

PHILADELPHIA

Temple University Press, Philadelphia 19122
Copyright © 1998 by Karen Messing. All rights reserved
Published 1998
Printed in the United States of America

Text design by Erin Kirk New

Poem quoted on pp. 36–37, "Recipe for a Sidewalk," by Kate Braid, was originally
published in *Covering Rough Ground* (Victoria, British Columbia: Polestar Book
Publishers, 1991). Reprinted with permission.

Library of Congress Cataloging-in-Publication Data

Messing, Karen.
    One-eyed science : occupational health and women workers / Karen
Messing ; foreword by Jeanne Mager Stellman.
        p.   cm.—(Labor and social change)
    Includes bibliographical references and index.
    ISBN 1-56639-597-6 (cloth : alk. paper). — ISBN 1-56639-598-4
(paper : alk. paper)
        1. Women—Employment—Health aspects.   2. Occupational diseases—
Sex factors.   3. Sex discrimination against women.   4. Sexism in
medicine.   I. Title.
    RC963.6.W65M47   1998
    616.9'803*'082—dc21   97-26885

To Beverly, Mrs. Smith, Andrée, Ginette, Nina,
Guylaine, Nicole, and the others who explained to us
about women's work

■ ■ ■

Contents

■ ■ ■

Foreword

■ ■ ■

JEANNE MAGER STELLMAN

There is no room for argument about the true length of an inch. There may be sociopolitical discussions about whether its usage is to be abandoned in favor of the metric system, but its size, as well as the precision with which any specified measuring instrument can measure length, cannot be questioned. Similarly, we can use a variety of scales for measuring temperature, but everyone who uses them knows what they mean and how to convert from one scale to another. Meters, degrees Centigrade, liters, and cups are units for specifying physical attributes that do not vary with the political climate or the philosophy of the measurer.

When we enter the world of biology and medicine, these truisms vanish. Biological measures ought to be accompanied by cautionary statements providing the data needed for determining just what the measures mean and just how good they are. Even the most straightforward measures are susceptible to inherent biases: height (measured at which part of the day and during which stage of the lifecycle?), weight (for women, at what stage and specific point in the menstrual cycle?), blood pressure (was the measure repeated? was the person standing or sitting or under stress?). Anyone doubting this need only open Karen Messing's book at random to come up with appropriate examples.

Biological measurements are inherently inaccurate and imprecise. The inaccuracy stems from the inadequacy of the model and the imprecision from the difficulties in the measurement itself. Why the inaccuracy? At least two basic explanations exist. First, there is much that we do not know about biological mechanisms. Estimating the goodness-of-fit of any measure requires specific knowledge of the true value. But for most biological phenomena we can only make "guesstimates," at best, of what the expected values are. Second, there may in fact be no "true value." The universe is ultimately controlled by statistics: from bouncing and colliding particles on up to bouncing and colliding societies, we all seem to be randomly moving about, and what we measure as "behavior" is the average bounce under specified conditions.

Now, when we are talking in colossally large terms, such as the numbers of atoms or molecules, the average is a pretty darned good measure, the conditions under which we are operating can be pretty well specified, and voilà, we have a measurement in which we can believe, or at least for which we can state the inherent accuracy and precision with great confidence. We will continue to buy thermometers and yardsticks without any qualms.

But biological populations, or biological phenomena in which we may be interested, do not occur in the absurdly large numbers in which atoms and molecules exist. The entire population of the earth and all the living creatures on it—from the tiniest virus to the tallest basketball player or grizzly bear—are far fewer in number than the quantity of atoms in a cup of tea (with or without sugar)! Thus the sample we take becomes very important—and it sometimes may *not* be generalizable to the whole. (That is, populations and cultures have some differing characteristics that may limit the ability to draw a sample representative of all humans across all groups.)

Compounding the problem of the inadequate number of people, bugs, or attributes for truly accurate and precise measures based on average values is another troubling aspect of biological measurement. If you go back three paragraphs, you will see that most important expression: "under specified conditions." When you measure temperature, you really need to know external pressure. (Water boils at different temperatures depending on where you are with respect to sea level.) Biological behavior is remarkably susceptible to external conditions. On the molecular level, environmental conditions can determine form and function; on the social level, even the most casual observer can cite endless examples of how who we are, how we feel, and certainly how we function is dependent on environment—the old nature versus nurture argument applied to both genetic and whole organism levels. For a biological measurement to be meaningful—whether it be as simple a measure as blood pressure or as difficult as an epidemiological evaluation of human risk—the operative conditions must be specified. And, most of the time, they are not—or cannot be—specified.

Specifying the operative conditions is the essence of Karen Messing's work and of her genius. Throughout this book—and so much of her other writing and thinking—she has an uncanny ability to define the conditions that may have led to the observed result; and far too often these conditions are not exactly what the researcher had in mind! Knowledge of the operative conditions defines the limits of generalizability of the observations. It helps us to understand the inherent biases in the measurement. It helps us to understand what actually may be going on in any given situation.

What does this have to do with women's health—and particularly women's ability to function as full working members of society? First, it gives us a perspective for answering that most fundamental question: when is something a women's health problem and when is it a health problem for women? Can we determine whether results of experiments or epidemiological studies have found a women's problem because the "specified conditions" included working environments that were different for men than for women? Is the measure of women's health really a proxy measure for the different conditions under which women labored? Or is there some operative combination of gender and environment? The same criteria apply to studies that omit women. How generalizable to women are the effects observed for men?

Awareness of the limits of measurements and causal models is the underpinning of science itself, and *One-Eyed Science* discloses just how unaware and lacking in humility are those who have created the data and the policies on occupational health and safety and on women's health, in general, and how ignorant of the limitations of their work and of the social models and policies that have both influenced and been derived from that work.

This book is a keen analysis of the problems of science and women's health: where we have been, and the directions we should take for a better understanding of the nature of women's work, women's health, and the well-being of society. In 1946 Anna Baetjer wrote *Health and Efficiency of Women in Industry*. In 1978, I wrote *Women's Work,*

Women's Health: Myths and Realities. Now, 50 years after Baetjer, Karen Messing finds that many of the same problems persist—in science and in the workplace. But the fact that these problems have persisted for a half-century is not a cause for despair—major heartburn will do—because we now have a much clearer picture of the problem, and there are more of us carrying on the struggle. With books like these in our armamentarium, we have a strong tactical advantage, as well. Now we need to maintain the momentum to go on.

Preface

■ ■ ■

Ten years ago, my colleague Donna Mergler and I were asked to be resources in a training session on "women's occupational health" for health care workers. We had each given sessions in occupational health before, although never on this topic. We usually began by asking all workers to describe their jobs and identify what they thought were their health risks. We would write the list of problems on a transparency, asking questions to stimulate participants to examine their work environment.

In the usual session involving 30 workers, this exercise would last about an hour. We would then explain the scientific bases for the various categories of health problems, using the workers' examples. Our presentation usually took a couple of hours, and then trainers from the unions would take over and explain the legal and regulatory context and how problems could be prevented.

This time, we ran into trouble. The session started at 9:30; when we broke for lunch, we had not finished going around the room. In fact, we had not gotten halfway. We were barely able to finish hearing all the workers had to say by the end of the day, and we never got to give our presentation at all. They talked about lifting heavy patients, working around toxic chemicals and radiation, and slipping on icy steps. Hospital janitors described exhaustion from cleaning their ever-expanding areas, home care workers told of efforts to turn disabled patients in slippery bathtubs, and radiology technicians told hair-raising stories of exposure when X-ray machines were accidentally turned on by young interns. A good 90 percent of their grievances concerned stress. How could receptionists deal with patients who threw things at them when the doctor was late? What should cleaners say to the nurse who dropped a bag of urine and refused to clean it up?

And, above all, how could workers deal with time pressure? How could nurses' aides fit patient care into standards that provided a given number of seconds for feeding a patient who might be recalcitrant or sleepy? What should a night orderly do, alone with 300 elderly semi-autonomous residents, when three wake up at once? How could laboratory technicians cope with the threat of catching hepatitis and other diseases when handling hundreds of blood tubes every day? How could a nurse finish her reports in time to pick up her daughter at day care? Donna and I came out of the session shaken. It was as if we had opened a valve and stories were pouring through. Neither we nor the union trainers had foreseen the depth of the women's needs.

Ten years later, a member of a committee that determines grants in occupational health explained to me, "In occupational health, there are central problems and peripheral problems." Asked for examples of each type, he offered "construction workers falling off scaffolding" as central and "stress" as peripheral.

If women have so many occupational health problems, why do they not interest those responsible for research and intervention in occupational health? This book was written to answer that question.

Occupational health science and intervention have not often been about women. There is legislation on the length of the workday, but none for the combination of paid and unpaid work. There are standards for how much weight a stevedore can lift and how often, but none for how many shirts a woman can sew on a shift. There is a threshold limit value for exposure to asbestos for miners, but no limit to the number of insults a receptionist may hear per hour without a break. Scientists have not produced information on which to base this sort of standard. In fact, occupational health scientists have not perceived these problems as part of their field.

It must also be said that women's health activism has not, by and large, been about workers. Breast cancer activists do not worry about flight attendants' exposure to cosmic rays,[1] scientists who do research on osteoporosis do not ask whether women on their feet all day are more or less likely to suffer from it, feminists who question hormone replacement therapy for menopause do not seem to know about the relation between chemical exposures and premature menopause.

This is not the fault of the activists: the scientists are just as ignorant. A scientist who was planning a large study of osteoporosis among women who worked at an electric company refused to include occupational factors because there was no previous evidence that they were relevant. When I pointed out to her that exercise was known to be a determinant of bone density, she replied that she would include recreational exercise but that her questionnaire items had been worked out and did not include any on physical activity on the job.

In this I book ask, *why has there been little or no fruitful dialogue between those interested in women's health and those interested in occupational health?*

This book has been influenced by a need to make other scientists aware of the effects of their indifference to women's suffering. Recently, my colleague Nicole Vézina testified at the hearing of a mail sorter. Nicole had studied the workplace and compared it to a vision of hell: extremely noisy and uncomfortable, with some workers handling about 12,000 kilograms of packages per day.[2] The flavor of employee–employer relations can be captured in the events surrounding the noise reduction program. The employer had been put on notice that the workplace noise was over the regulated 90 decibels, and consultants had suggested putting ball bearings on the conveyor belts to diminish it. The employer therefore installed just enough bearings to bring the noise level below 90 decibels and then stopped, leaving about half the conveyor belts without any noise reduction device.

The workers had a claim before the compensation board involving problems with the elbow joint caused by repetitive work.[3] Nicole analyzed the work and found that extremely repetitive movements put stress on the elbow joint. A professor from another university testified that the worker's injuries were not related to her work. Although he accepted Nicole's description of the movements, he quoted from the scientific literature purporting to show that repeated movements could not produce injury below a specific weight manipulated. He also described his own laboratory tests, which, he held, showed that this type of work was not dangerous.

When the worker lost her case, Nicole was extremely upset. She kept thinking about the arm and shoulder pain suffered by the mail sorters she had met. She could not understand why the other scientist seemed not to be bothered by the workers' suffering. Although she did not agree with his interpretations of the scientific literature, she had to admit that no researcher had examined the exact situation in which the mail sorter found herself. No study had considered such a high number of repetitions or the awkward position that the worker maintained. Nicole asked other researchers in our group, CINBIOSE, to think about the case and explain why it had been lost. (CINBIOSE is an interdisciplinary research center. The abbreviation stands [in French] for the Center for the Study of Biological Interactions in Environmental Health [*Centre pour l'étude des interactions biologiques entre la santé et l'environnement*]. It is composed of 9 [women] professors from the biology, legal sciences, sociology, psychology, and kinesthesiology departments of the University of Québec and about 30 student and paid researchers from North and South America, mostly women.)

So this book was written to ask, *how do scientists decide whom and what to study in the occupational health field?*

This book is about scientists' perceptions and how they are molded by their position and their own working conditions. It is about women workers and the discounting and invalidation of their perceptions. It is about some ways that women workers and scientists can be brought together to make occupational health studies more accurate and effective in improving working conditions.

The book is also my attempt to resolve my own difficulties in understanding the interactions of biological and social factors. Pursuing a bachelor's degree in social relations, a combination of sociology, psychology, and anthropology, at an Ivy League university, I was uncomfortable with the theories being advanced there, especially since they seemed somewhat classist, racist, and sexist (I was taught that people remain poor because they have not learned to save for tomorrow, that blacks are poor because they have a matriarchal tradition, that women have penis envy because that is natural). Because I wanted evidence-based theories, I turned to the natural sciences, receiving my doctorate from McGill University in the field of genetics, one of the more deterministic sciences.

Armed with these quite disparate tools, I tried to understand where nature ends and nurture begins when dealing with socially relevant characteristics of diverse populations. Like other biologists before me and with their help (especially Ruth Hubbard, Richard Lewontin, and Anne Fausto-Sterling), I came to understand that it is not a good idea to start by thinking about people's characteristics. The question is not:

are those in the biological category "women" intrinsically weak, are "blacks" genetically musical, and so forth. It is essential to recognize from the outset that these supposed biological categories are really social definitions. If one black grandparent or great-grandparent is enough to make a person black, we are certainly not dealing with genetics when we compare blacks and whites. And the definition of people with the chromosomal abnormality Turner syndrome[4] as women because they do not have a penis (they don't have a uterus, ovaries, or breasts either, but that doesn't seem to count) leaves me wondering about the biological basis of our definitions of sex as well.[5]

I also realized, with help, that environment channels the performance and well-being of biologically divergent populations.[6] Door openings allow some to pass easily and cause others to bump their heads. But doors can be made big enough for all; the door size is a political decision. For a feminist, it was enabling and enriching to realize that politics determined the weight of flour sacks that preferentially excluded women from good jobs in a cake factory. The sacks weighed 40 kilograms, a weight that only able-bodied males could lift. They were not made to weigh 100 kilograms, because then no one could have lifted them. So why not have them weigh five or 10 kilograms, so that most people could lift them? Only because no one in a decision-making position needed them to be smaller than 40 kilograms.

This realization sent me back to school to study ergonomics at the Conservatoire national des arts et métiers in Paris. I had to learn how to analyze situations in order to suggest ways to make work environments less restrictive. Ghislaine Doniol, François Daniellou, and Catherine Teiger taught me that environments are almost totally plastic if the right questions are asked. When I returned to Québec after this training, I learned that finding the right solution was not enough. It was no use suggesting that cleaning would be organized more efficiently if men were no longer defined into "heavy" cleaning and women into "light" cleaning; someone important had to agree. The partnership program of the Québec Council of Social Research allowed CINBIOSE researchers to get together with some important people: the women's committees of the three major Québec unions. With them, we could hope to create a political context to improve the health of women workers. They helped us understand the grave consequences of treating sick workers as though they were malingerers and cheaters. In this book, class analysis of occupational health issues has not been explicitly developed, as other authors such as Dan

Berman, Steve Fox, and Asa Christina Laurell, have done. I leave the theoretical analysis of the relation of gender, class, and race in occupational health science to someone else.

In this book, I explain how we have applied the three fields of biology, ergonomics, and social relations to a single political challenge: making the field of occupational health more gender-sensitive. I begin with the question I am most often asked: why is this necessary? Why should women's occupational health be any different from men's? The first three chapters address this issue by describing male/female differences in jobs, health, and basic biology.

Chapters 4 to 6 concern science as a social institution. Why are scientists unresponsive to the needs of women workers? Is there some incompatibility there, or is it just that scientists are no more feminist than most people in our culture? This section explains how the scientific milieu works: who gets in, how scientific research projects originate, and how they turn into scientific knowledge.

Through case studies, Chapters 7 to 10 detail the scientific treatment of issues important to women workers: musculoskeletal disease, office work, emotional stress, and reproductive hazards. These chapters illustrate Ruth Colker's statement: "The prevailing pattern . . . is that women are treated with respect to their biology in ways that perpetuate their subordination in society."[7] Their differences from men can be emphasized or ignored by scientists, but the result of both procedures is the neglect of problems experienced by women workers.

In the final section I make some proposals for change. Chapter 11 presents ways to minimize the consequences of past approaches to occupational health for women workers. It suggests how women, their concerns, and their work can be included in labor standards, compensation programs for occupational accidents and illnesses, and workplace policies. The last chapter proposes alternative ways of doing research, some of which have already been developed around the world and in our research center, CINBIOSE, at the University of Québec at Montréal. I end with some suggestions on how to do reliable research that will provide women workers and policymakers with the information they need to improve women's workplaces.

Most of the examples in this book are taken from my experiences in Québec, where I have lived since 1965. But growing up in Springfield, Massachusetts, I saw nothing very different. One of my earliest memories is of being taken through a factory where women assembled radio parts during the late forties, a job CINBIOSE studied in Québec in 1994. Women in both factories worked with rapid hand movements, bent over tiny components, but neither of the employers could see any reason for them to complain about their working conditions. U.S. readers may find some differences in the context for funding scientific research, but since we all publish in the same journals and compete with each other for the same jobs, these should be few. The Québec legal system has made some useful innovations, such as protective reassignment for pregnant workers and a healthier union context, but more and more we copy our labor standards from the United States. (I point out some differences within the North American context.)

One major difference should be noted here. In Québec, racial differences are dwarfed by the great ethno-linguistic division (French versus English). This is not to say that racism does not exist in Québec, but only that we have encountered few people of color since they are rare in the French-speaking workplaces we have studied. Much remains to be said about the way colonialism and ethnocentrism affect workers and the union movement in Québec.

I count more than 20 researchers at CINBIOSE who have contributed to the research results and the thinking presented in this book: Donna Mergler, Nicole Vézina, Suzanne Bélanger, Katherine Lippel, Louise Vandelac, Julie Courville, Céline Chatigny, France Tissot, Carole Brabant, Sylvie Champoux, Johanne Leduc, Sylvie Bédard, Sylvie de Grosbois, Susanne Deguire, Johane Prévost, Yves St-Jacques, Alain Lajoie, Evelin Escalona, Micheline Boucher, Lucie Dumais, Sophie Boutin, and Serge Daneault. Ana Maria Seifert, in addition to her full-time job as the heart and soul of CINBIOSE, has been my partner and collaborator in almost all the investigations.

This book is at the confluence of three fields studied by feminists, and I have been influenced by all three. For the study of women and science I am particularly indebted to Ruth Hubbard and Abby Lippman; for the study of women and health I am indebted to Patrizia Romito, Marie-Josèphe Saurel-Cubizolles, Maria De Koninck, and Francine Saillant; for the study of women and work I am indebted to Catherine Teiger, Danièle Kergoat, and Joan Stevenson. I learned about how to do science from Catherine, Marie-Josèphe, and Ted Bradley. And I am very grateful to our union partners Carole Gingras, Gisèle Bourret, Nicole Lepage, Danièle Hébert, and Ghyslaine Fleury and to countless workers who have shared their experiences with us. My conscience allows me to write this book in the first person singular only because it would have taken too much time for us all to do it together (although it would have been fun) and my co-workers all have other important things to do.

The Conseil québécois de la recherche sociale, the Social Science and Humanities Research Council of Canada, the Fonds FCAR, and the Institut de recherche en santé et en sécurité du travail du Québec supported most of the research presented here.

Unless otherwise noted, the quotations from union health and safety representatives are taken from my translation of the transcript of a meeting held on April 29, 1995, organized by the research team L'invisible qui fait mal.

Finally, I thank the people who read parts or all of the manuscript, even though I was too stubborn to follow all of their suggestions: Pierre Sormany, Katherine Lippel, Jeanne Stellman, Steve Stellman, Mary Baldwin, Leonor Cedillo, Åsa Kilbom, Susan Stock, Dorothy Wigmore, Angelo Soares, and Mario Richard. Lesley Doyal gave me a good suggestion for the last chapter. Daood Aidroos, Nathalie Gignac, Karine Escobar, and France Tissot were able research assistants. Michael Ames, Jane Barry, and Paula Rayman at Temple University Press were particularly helpful in putting a name to some of the flaws in the manuscript. And Pierre, Daood, Mikail, and of course Edgar and Pauline provided emotional support.

1

Women Workers
and Their Working Conditions

■ ■ ■

Since occupational health is intimately linked to the jobs people do, we need to know what work women do before considering its effects on health. When feminist sociologists looked at jobs, they discovered that most women work in very different environments from most men.[1] In fact, women and men occupy such totally different niches in the labor market that we can almost talk of separate work forces. In order for men and women to be evenly distributed across the job market, about three-quarters of women would have to change jobs. A recent study of North Carolina workers puts the figure for gender segregation (76 percent) even higher than that for racial segregation (55 percent).[2] This is the most important reason to focus specifically on women's occupational health.

The differences are of two general types: employment conditions (salaries, hours, length of contracts) and job content.

Employment Conditions

The most striking fact about women's employment conditions is still that women have lower salaries than men. In 1993, women in Canada who worked full-time during the whole year earned 72 percent of the salary of the average man.[3] In the United States, the comparable figure is about 76 percent.[4]

Part of the male/female difference comes from the fact that

women hold the lower-paying jobs, but there is also a difference in pay rate for the same jobs. In the United States in 1995, for example, full-time women sales representatives earned 69 percent as much as men in their profession, female cleaners earned 84 percent as much, female computer operators earned 74 percent as much, and female factory inspectors 65 percent as much.[5]

The male/female difference in income is significant because income is an important health determinant, and it shows the low value put on women's work, the "vertical segregation" of the job market that affects women's health a bit less directly. Hierarchical position is also an important health determinant, directly and indirectly—directly, because workers' physical and mental health are better when they are more autonomous; indirectly, because the more power workers have, the more easily they can make their workplaces healthier. If we look at the list of women's and men's top jobs (Table 1) we notice that women are 66 percent of sales workers but only 35 percent of sales supervisors. In a bank studied by CINBIOSE, 88 percent of tellers were women, but only 16 percent of branch managers were.[6]

Compared to men, women also are paid for less of the time they work. In other words, a smaller proportion of women's work time belongs to the professional work day. Since, in occupational health, hours worked per week correspond to the duration of exposure to occupational hazards, it would appear that women are generally less exposed at their jobs than men. In Canada for example, 52 percent of women over 14 and 65 percent of men held jobs.[7] The average male worker put in 37.6 hours a week, and the average female worker, 34.4 (based on a 50-week working year).[8] Women are three times as likely as men to work part-time and three times as likely to be temporary workers.[9] More than a quarter of women work part-time, while fewer than 10 percent of men do.[10]

When we consider women's work day, the paid work day is just half the picture. Women's work day does not end when they leave the office or factory; it just changes. Studies done by Statistics Canada show that Canadian married men with children under five work 18.2 hours per week at domestic tasks and child care, compared with 32.2 hours per week for married women with children under five and 23.8 for single mothers of children under five.[11] The extra 14 hours per week more than makes up for the slight difference in average hours of paid work. Walters and colleagues found that female registered nurses (with or without children) reported 24 hours a week spent on homemaking

TABLE 1: Top Twenty Professions for Women, U.S.A., 1992

Workers	Number of women (thousands)	% women
1 Secretaries/stenographers/typists	4,246	98
2 Teachers, preschool–high school	3,154	75
3 Records processing clerks (esp. bookkeepers, accounting clerks)	2,891	88
4 Sales workers, personal and retail (except cashiers)	2016	66
5 Cashiers	1,998	79
6 Registered nurses	1,702	94
7 Nursing aides, orderlies, attendants	1,574	89
8 Information clerks (esp. receptionists)	1,466	89
9 Sales supervisors	1,352	35
10 Waitresses	1,090	80
11 Textile machine operators (esp. sewing machine operators)	917	76
12 Sales representatives, business and financial (esp. real estate)	899	40
13 Cooks	865	46
14 Hairdressers and cosmetologists	688	91
15 Janitors and cleaners	635	30
16 Fabricators, assemblers, and hand workers (esp. assemblers)	632	33
17 General office clerks	599	84
18 Mail and message distributors (esp. postal clerks)	546	37
19 Social, recreation, and religious workers (esp. social workers)	540	50
20 Maids	525	82

Source: Compiled from information from the U.S. Bureau of Labor Statistics and from Stellman, J. (1994). Where women work and the hazards they may face on the job. Journal of Occupational Medicine 36 (8): 814–825.

Note: As noted in the original article, detailed titles were not listed fot the following classes of occupations: secretaries, stenographers and typists; information clerks; records processing clerks; sales supervisors; sales representatives, business and financial; fabricators, assemblers, and hand workers, mail and message distributors; social, recreation, and religious workers. However, within these categories I have listed the occupation, if any, that accounted for most of the women.

tasks (including car repairs and outdoor tasks), compared with 16 hours for male nurses.[12] Women are also responsible for 70 to 80 percent of elder care. Half of the women now between 35 and 64 will have to care for an older relative at some time.[13]

This difference in family responsibilities has several consequences. First, employment is affected. As mentioned above, women are more likely than men to be found in part-time jobs. Of women who work part-time, one-third do so because they were unable to find full-time work, but 11 percent work part-time because of personal or family obligations.[14] Women work shorter periods before being interrupted: (an average of 81 months at their present job compared with 108 for men).[15]

Second, women's family responsibilities have consequences for their fertility and health. Several studies have identified teachers as particularly likely to contract breast cancer. This has been explained as a result of delayed childbirth among this occupational group.[16] Interviews with teachers show that they have trouble responding to their own children after a long working day with other children.[17] This points up the necessity to examine the whole issue of delayed childbirth as an occupational health issue with effects both on certain cancers and on fertility. It may be that in some occupations childbirth is delayed because of an incompatibility between professional and family responsibilities.

Third, there are consequences on the level of extraprofessional activities required to meet family and professional responsibilities. Women are much more often absent from work because of family or personal obligations than men (6.4 days per year versus 0.9 for men). [18] Not only does this level of absence affect the perception of women's dedication to their jobs; it also results in their being unable to take sick days for their own illnesses.

Job Content: Different Job Titles

Women are segregated into specific industrial sectors and into female-majority jobs within these sectors. This seems to be true all over the world. In 1983, the Confederation of National Trade Unions, with help from the Canadian government, sponsored a conference on women's occupational health.[19] Each report was presented jointly by a scientist and a worker who had been involved in the research. Women came to the conference from four continents and 15 countries, including Thailand, Brazil, and South Africa. We North Americans were astonished to find that women from the third world did most of the same jobs we did: the Thai, Swedish, and French reports were on garment workers; the Québec report on food processing workers aroused interest among the Latin Americans, since women in those countries also worked in food processing plants.

Even more surprisingly, the division of labor within factories was similar. Women did packing and inspection, repetitive jobs and cleaning. Men did heavy lifting, truck loading and driving, and supervision.

As CINBIOSE researchers have had increasing contact with European, African, and South American women, the similarities have struck us as often as the differences. In Brazil, the United States, France, and Québec, women are the cashiers in the supermarkets and men are the meat cutters. On all four continents the primary school teachers are usually women, while university professors are usually men.

Of course, there are important differences. In Brazil and France the cashiers work sitting down while in North America they stand all day.[20] Primary school classes contain 20–40 children in North America, often 50 or more in South America, and up to 100 in Africa. Women are much more often street vendors in Asia and Africa than in North America. But the sexual division of labor seems to be a fact of life around the world.

In North America, the services sector accounts for an increasing proportion of all jobs, while women are still overrepresented in services and underrepresented in manufacturing and in food and resource generation. Women are often found in office work, personal services and the caring professions: in the top professions of Table 1, there are five office professions (secretaries, etc.), five personal service professions (waitresses, etc.) and four caring professions (teachers etc.). The picture is similar in Canada, although job titles are grouped somewhat differently.[21]

A nonnegligible proportion of women do factory work, concentrated in specific factories and parts of factories. In the clothing industry, women sewing machine operators make women's clothes, while men usually sew men's coats. Cutters are almost always men, while pressers are sometimes women. In the auto industry, women sew seat covers and men install engines. In metallurgy, men tend the furnaces and women do the office work.

Until recently, occupational health research has concentrated on the sectors and departments where men work. This work has been thought to be "heavier" and more dangerous, so it has been better regulated. In Québec, for example 85 percent of jobs fully covered by health and safety legislation are occupied by men.[22]

Even though we do not think of women as doing heavy physical labor, many women's jobs have an important physical component, which can produce aches and pains and eventually even cripple. Secretaries type thousands of characters per hour, repeatedly sliding the same tendons over the same joints. Day care center workers pick up 20-pound children over and over again. Pressers lift heavy irons. Cleaners scrub to remove grime. Primary school teachers bend over little children's desks for long periods in one of the most taxing positions for the human back. These and other women's jobs involve stresses that can lead to health problems, and the fact that their physical component is often unrecognized means that workers' health is unprotected by the usual health and safety norms and practices.

In order to see how the physical demands on women and men differ, consider, as we did, the assembly line in a cake factory.[23] At the beginning of the process, men mixed the batter, poured it out, put it into the baking trays, and put the trays in the oven. They took out the trays with the baked cakes and dumped the cakes on a tray, whereupon the women took over. They lined up the cakes in neat rows, put them on cardboard plates, and ran them through the wrapping machines. They then packed them in little boxes with labels, put the little boxes into bigger boxes, and handed them over to the men, who loaded them into trucks and drove away to deliver them. The sexual division of labor was almost absolute. The rare women who took men's jobs felt or were made to feel quite uncomfortable.

Poultry processing, in Québec and in France, works the same way.[24] Men kill the turkeys and cut them into large pieces; then women cut off the smaller bits and trim them. Women label and pack individual turkeys, but men load and drive the trucks that take them away.

These divisions correspond to different physical requirements. Women's jobs often demand rapid hand movements, visual acuity, and standing in a fixed position. We have seen that rapid movements are necessary in most assembly-line positions. Service jobs such as data entry and cleaning also require rapid, repetitive movements.

Visual acuity is necessary in many jobs requiring fine work: sewing, microelectronics, work with Video display terminals (VDTs). Endurance, particularly the ability to maintain a fixed position, is a stressor more often found in women's jobs, particularly in North America. Supermarket clerks, bank tellers, and department store salespeople are among the workers, mostly women, who stand all day with no access to a seat even during slack periods.[25]

Job Content: Same Job Title

When we started observing work, we were astonished at the difference in job content between women and men who had the same job title. After many hours of observation, we are convinced that it is impossible to extrapolate the risks in, say, a male cleaner's job to those of a woman cleaner.

Cleaning in Québec hospitals is divided into "light" and "heavy" categories, once known more openly as "Housekeeping (women)" and "Housekeeping (men)," with men earning more than women.[26] This is a partial list of the tasks done by each:

Heavy work
   He [*sic*] uses mop at least 24" wide, vacuum cleaner, polishing machine,
   floor-stripping machine
   He washes the vents, windows
   He washes the walls and ceilings
   He takes down, hangs up draperies and curtains

Light work
   She [*sic*] uses mop at least 18" wide, "light" vacuum cleaner for furniture
   She dusts
   She washes the wastebaskets, ashtrays, doors, mirrors, toilets
   She fills dispensers (paper, soap)[27]

Similar job assignments are found in industrial cleaning. Women dust and wash bathrooms, and men dry-mop, wash, wax, and vacuum floors. In this less unionized area, the light/heavy pay differential has persisted. The "light cleaning" job title, by government regulation, pays 40 cents per hour less than "heavy cleaning."

We heard many justifications for the sexual division of manual labor. When asked to distinguish heavy from light cleaning, the men in one hospital said: "Women aren't made to do heavy work. They couldn't use the floor polisher. If you make a false move, bang!" They went on at some length to convey the total impossibility of a woman's using the floor polisher. Most women agreed that certain operations were impossible for them. One woman explained to us that it was lucky for her that her husband was the heavy worker on her route. That way, he could do any jobs that were too heavy for her. On the other hand, some women told us that handling the floor polisher was just a trick that anyone could learn.[28]

In Chapter 3 I examine critically some of the scientific justifications given for dividing jobs in this way.

Mental and Emotional Requirements in Women's Jobs

Several researchers have examined the emotional aspects of work done by women. Finnish researchers found that women's jobs involved less autonomy and more repetition and also required more social skills.[29] Similar results were found in studies by the European Foundation for the Improvement of Living and Working Conditions.[30] These little-recognized requirements of women's jobs may be responsible for some mental health problems.

To do an ergonomic analysis of the cognitive aspects of several jobs done by women, Teiger observed women sewing gloves. The employer wanted to know why no worker stayed past the age of 26. The answer was found in the job requirements. Workers received the two halves of the glove from a cutter and sewed them together. This sounded like an easy task to the employer, who did not know that the cutters frequently made minor errors so that the two halves did not fit together correctly. The sewing machine operators had to compensate for the errors in cutting by making small adjustments in the fit of the two halves while sewing at high speed. It required enormous concentration to "marry" the two halves,[31] and the workers were not able to keep up this job for very long—they were superannuated at 26!

The same requirements—speed and concentration—were found in jobs done by women in turkey processing.[32] The woman who trims turkey wings has six seconds to pick up the wing from a conveyor belt and remove bits of fat, skin, bone, cartilage, and any blood clots. If the wing is not perfectly trimmed, it is she who will be criticized by the person responsible for quality control. The work requires not only mental alertness but also physical dexterity and endurance. Nevertheless, this job was called "light work" by the employer. In fact, until ergonomists protested, employers used this job for workers recovering from work accidents.

Some large studies relating heart disease to stress have inspired scientists to think about workers' emotions. Karasek and his colleagues found that workers experienced "job strain" when demands were high and decision latitude low.[33] That is, workers can cope with hard job requirements if they have the power to do things the way they see fit, but become distressed and ill when they lose this discretionary power. In general, women's jobs have more "job strain" than men's,[34] although, the concept applies to men's jobs as well. Some emotional aspects of jobs are assigned almost exclusively to women. Perhaps because it applies to few men's jobs, the concept of emotional labor has only recently been developed to describe the requirements of some jobs in the service sector. Hochschild defines emotional labor as "the management of feeling to produce a publicly observable facial and bodily display . . . sold for a wage." She describes how airline flight attendants are explicitly paid to manage their own and the passengers' emotions, to prevent fear and create customer loyalty. Women airline attendants, she notes are much more likely to be required to perform this type of emotional labor than men.[35]

Entering Nontraditional Jobs

Even women entering a well-established existing male job often encounter differences in physical, mental, and emotional job content. One would think that a male gardener and a female gardener would both do the same tasks. We found the opposite when we studied gardeners and other blue-collar workers employed by a large Canadian city.[36] Women had been integrated into municipal blue-collar jobs following pressure from feminist groups. At the time of our study, women were still in only 22 of the 201 blue-collar job categories, and they made up only 5 percent of the more senior permanent employees and 39 percent of temporary employees. We interviewed 106 women and men, paired for seniority and for job title at the time of hiring, about their jobs and about the teams in which they worked.

Several indications led us to the conclusion that women and men with the same seniority and job title did not in fact perform the same tasks. First, fewer than half of the paired workers gave similar job descriptions. Second, workers were specifically asked whether men and women who worked with them were assigned to the same tasks. Just over half the women reported that they did not do the same tasks as their male colleagues.[37] The reasons given were varied: choice of the supervisor, the colleagues, or the individual, or lack of appropriate-sized equipment. The principle constituting this gendered division of labour was characterized in two ways: 10 women (mostly cleaners) said women did work that required more care or had to be done to a higher standard, and 17 (mostly gardeners) said that men did the jobs requiring more physical strength. Women were more likely to do weeding, planting, and pruning bushes, and men were more likely to do "heavier" tasks, such as pushing loaded wheelbarrows uphill, pruning trees, and using forks and picks. Men were also more likely to use machines such as the cultivator. Using machines was a privilege often reserved for the gardening team leader, almost always a man.

Women in other blue-collar municipal jobs also said they had trouble getting to use machines. The first woman cleaner assigned to a sports arena, "Marie," told us about her struggle to get to use a cleaning machine. Although these municipal cleaners were not officially segregated into "light" and "heavy" work, she (and the female co-workers who joined her later) were often assigned to cleaning offices and other places where it was important to be meticulous, while men cleaned the corridors and gyms. In larger spaces, floors were not mopped but were washed with a cleaning machine. The machine had a seat so that the worker could ride up and down the corridor or the gym. Since it was much more fun to ride the machine than to scrub in corners with a mop, a rotation was established so that all workers had a chance at it. When Marie's turn came, the supervisor passed her over and assigned the machine to a man. Marie protested and threatened to make a fuss. The supervisor finally allowed her to use the machine, but refused to explain how it worked, and gave her a nearly impossible task to do with it. He appeared disappointed when she succeeded, and she was never again allowed to use the machine.

This kind of task segregation affects health in two ways. First, since men and women do not do the same jobs, they do not have the same health risks. Second, discrimination can affect mental health. Cynthia Cockburn[38] and Ann Stafford[39] have described the humiliations and violence experienced by women in training for nontraditional jobs. Others have revealed the sufferings of women in these jobs, exposed to wearing criticism, harassment, homophobic attacks, and even physical violence.[40]

Discrimination also exists in more traditional jobs. During collective interviews with a group of six bank tellers chosen to represent different working conditions,[41] "David" illustrated for us the different male/female relationships with the bank management. He and "Suzanne" were sitting side by side at their computers with their backs to the window. They had closed their respective blinds because of glare from the sun. A visiting bank executive walked in and yelled at Suzanne for closing her blinds. He explained that people outside had to be able to see in, as a protection against bank robbery. He forced Suzanne to open her blinds but said nothing to David. As soon as the executive left the branch, Suzanne closed her blinds, since otherwise she could not read her screen. When the executive revisited the bank a few weeks later, he was furious to see that Suzanne's blinds were closed. He threatened her with dismissal, but still said nothing to David, whose blinds were also closed.

Asked to comment on this tale, the women bank tellers made comments like: "I don't like to think about it," "If you get angry every time, you'd be angry all the time," "I just don't pay attention." In other words, they saw discrimination against women as part of their working conditions and met it with resignation.

Ann Robinson interviewed women teachers and found that they were subject to discriminatory remarks from pupils, parents, colleagues, and supervisors. A secondary school teacher "Just last week, I was in the secretary's office and I said something to another teacher. He said 'You're so aggressive! Are you on the rag?' Another teacher next to him said 'No she's not on the rag, she just isn't getting enough.' All in front of a bunch of students." All 72 women Robinson interviewed spoke of the persistence of sexist stereotypes.[42]

We can conclude from this rapid look at the workplace that women and men often face different task requirements and physical and emotional stresses. This is true even when they have the same job title and even when they are officially assigned to the same tasks. When scientists compare women and men or extrapolate studies on male workers to women with similar job titles, they may be missing important information. By and large, women's health is subject to different workplace effects from those of men.

2

Is There a Women's
Occupational Health Problem?

■ ■ ■

Perhaps because women are not thought of as workers or because women's jobs seem safe and healthy, people do not often worry about women's occupational health. Those who reflect on women's health have not automatically included the effects of working conditions, despite the fact that most women now have paid jobs. The public health policy of my government talks about women's health and about occupational health as separate entities with no overlap. Even the feminist health advocacy community rarely mentions occupational health problems.

It is very unusual for a researcher to specialize in women's occupational health as I do, and people have trouble imagining what I could possibly study. I recently was invited to give a talk at a university gathering of women health professionals. When I called the organizer to see how to orient my talk, she started by saying that she really did not know what I could talk about, since she did not know what was meant by "women's occupational health." It may seem strange that a feminist health specialist would express such ignorance, but in fact her reaction was quite typical and understandable. People just do not think of women's jobs in connection with occupational health.

There are several reasons for this, which I discuss in this chapter. One is that women do not emerge from the tables produced by the various workers' compensation boards. When we examine statistics on compensation for occupational illness and injury, we see that men have from three to ten times more compensated industrial accidents and injuries per worker, with a ratio depending on the jurisdiction, industry, and year.[1] In the United States, the occupational fatality rate for men is 12 times as high as that for women.[2] These statistics have often been interpreted to mean that women's jobs are safer than men's. In fact, when workers in a job have many accidents, this obvious, perceptible danger may be invoked as a reason to keep women out. For example, women in many countries have been forbidden by law to work in mines because of the risks involved.

In this chapter I ask: Do men really have more accidents? Apart from accidents, do men have more health problems relating to their jobs? Are occupational health statistics a good way to judge whether women's jobs are dangerous? In the following discussion, I present some of the steps we at CINBIOSE took toward answering these questions and some of our (and others') results.

Two different theories can be formulated. The conventional theory says that women have fewer compensated injuries and illnesses because their jobs are safer. According to this theory, job segregation has kept women out of dangerous jobs, and thereby protected their health. The alternative argument, which I will develop here, is that women have fewer compensated injuries and illnesses because the compensation system has been set up in response to problems in jobs traditionally held by men. The types of health problems women have are not recognized or compensated, creating a vicious circle where women's occupational health problems are not taken seriously, therefore not recognized, therefore do not cost enough to matter.

Do Men Really Have More Accidents?

Examining the theory that men have more accidents than women because their traditional jobs are more dangerous, CINBIOSE researchers wanted to see whether men and women in jobs traditionally assigned to men would have the same number of accidents. We therefore did a study to find out whether women entering nontraditional jobs had more or fewer accidents than men. Our results did not give a clear answer, but they alerted us to some pitfalls in comparing men's and women's accident rates.

We tried to compare the accidents of the blue-collar municipal workers described in Chapter 1. If we were to calculate accident rates for women and men from the resulting table (Table 2, we would think

TABLE 2: Municipal Workers' Accident Claims by Sex and
Employment Status, 1989–1990

	Permanent		Temporary	
	Number (and %) of accidents	*Number (and %) of employees**	*Number (and %) of accidents*	*Number (and %) of employees**
Women	40 (6.1)	97 (4.9)	74 (32.2)	239 (39.3)
Men	619 (93.9)	1808 (95.1)	156 (67.8)	369 (60.7)
Total	659 (100.0)	1905 (100.0)	230 (100.0)	608 (100.0)

*Number of employees normally assigned to the 14 job titles on November 11, 1990.

at first that women temporary workers have less than their share of
accidents and that women permanent workers have more. When we
thought about it a little longer, we realized that we could not in fact
compare accident rates between the sexes, or at least that comparing
accident rates would not tell us very much about the relative safety of
women's and men's jobs.

This difficulty arose because men and women workers were not
comparable in this municipality. Women were younger and had less
seniority because most were hired after the beginning of an affirmative action program in 1987. They started as temporary workers
and became permanent later on. Since temporary workers were
called in by the city as the need arose, according to seniority, temporary women workers probably worked many fewer hours than
men. The municipality could not supply us with the distribution of
hours worked according to the sex of the worker. So we could not
calculate the number of accidents per hour worked.

The fact that women were less senior probably had another effect
on comparative accident rates. In general, more senior workers had
fewer accidents than less senior workers, a tendency that has also
been found by other researchers.[3] This is probably because workers
learn by experience how to avoid accidents. Therefore, permanent
women workers' slightly higher accident rate in proportion to their
number may have been due to their having less seniority than the
permanent men workers.

The reason for going into all this detail about the work situations of women and men blue-collar workers is to show the problems researchers face if they compare accident rates between the sexes without thinking about the different positions they occupy in the workplace. Of the 15 papers comparing male and female accident rates that we found in the scientific literature, only three controlled for age/seniority in their analyses, although men in the workplace average eight years more seniority than women.[4] Only five papers controlled for hours worked, despite the fact that women do three-quarters of all part-time work. These omissions tend to mislead us into thinking the numbers given are comparable.

Does this mean that overall, women really do not have fewer accidents than men, considering the hours worked and the relative seniority? Probably not. But the answer also depends on how we examine the accident rates.

Comparing Women and Men within the Same Industry: Are Women Safer Workers?

While it is true that men work more often in jobs with many accidents, men do not always have more work-related injuries than women when comparisons are made within the same industry. Results of studies are variable: sometimes women have more accidents than men, sometimes fewer.[5]

We did an approximate calculation of work accidents and industrial illnesses by industrial sector in Québec for 1992 (see Table 3. The sectors are listed in six groups corresponding to those used by the Québec Occupational Health and Safety Commission to organize its prevention efforts.

It can be seen from the table that the groups vary widely in the rates of compensation. This is because accidents are more often recognized among construction workers, for example, than among social workers. We also note that there are about 10 times more accidents than industrial diseases. This is because it is easier to relate an injury to the workplace (as when a chemical worker is injured in an explosion) than an illness (such as a cancer developing over many years). These figures probably underestimate industrial disease, since many industrial diseases go unrecognized. Women have more recognized industrial disease than men, but fewer accidents.

TABLE 3 : Approximate Rates of Compensation for Accidents and Industrial Diseases, Québec, 1992

Sectors* (% women in the sectors)	Compensated work accidents per hundred workers			Compensated industrial disease per thousand workers		
	F	M	F/M	F	M	F/M
1. Construction, Chemicals (15%)	1.00	6.60	0.15	0.91	1.52	0.60
2. Wood, metallurgy (15%)	4.44	10.67	0.42	5.67	2.55	2.22
3. Public admin- istration, transpor- tation (31%)	1.82	6.33	0.29	2.28	1.54	1.49
4. Commerce, textiles (42%)	2.00	6.41	0.31	1.62	0.90	1.80
5. Personal and commercial services, communications (48%)	1.63	3.48	0.47	0.97	0.45	2.16
6. Medical, social, educational services (64%)	2.48	3.40	0.73	1.12	0.44	2.53

Source: The numerators (work accidents, industrial disease) are from the Commission de la santé et de la sécurité du travail (CSST), Service de la statistique, data from December 31, 1993. 31, 1993. The denominators are from Statistics Canada, *Canada Census 1991*, table 1. No. 93-326. Statistics Canada, Ottawa.

Note: Data may underestimate accidents during 1992 because some cases had not been adjudicated when the table was made. Census data were not available for 1992, and accidents and disease by sex were not available for 1991.

*We show only the two sectors that account for the largest numbers of workers in each group.

Other Ways of Comparing Women's and Men's Occupational Health

These official statistics may not be the best way of comparing men's and women's occupational health. Official statistics reflect claims that have been accepted by the Occupational Health and Safety Commission, often against fierce opposition. Getting recognition for accidents and occupational illnesses requires that the worker make a claim for compensation based on lost time and succeed in having that claim recognized. Lippel and colleagues have looked at the success of women's claims for compensation and have found dis-crimination: women found it more difficult to prove that their

TABLE 4: Principal Causes of Death for Women and Men,
Ages 45–64, in the United States, 1992

Cause of death	Rank for women (Deaths per 100,000 population)	Rank for men (Deaths per 100,000 population)*
Cancer	1 (245)	2 (306)
Heart disease	2 (123)	1 (314)
Cerebrovascular disease	3 (27)	4 (34)
Respiratory disease	4 (23)	6 (29)
Life expectancy at birth (years)	79.1	72.3

*Third place for U.S. men is held by accidents.

Source: Adapted from Centers for Disease Control, National Center for Health Statistics (1994)
Advance report of final mortality statistics, 1992. Monthly Vital Statistics Report 43 (6):
Supplement, pp. 1–73.

Note: Data in this table are not exactly comparable to the Canadian data, which are rates for
the entire population, of all ages, incorporating a correction for age.

TABLE 5: Age-Standardized Death Rates for Women and Men
in Canada, 1992

Cause of death	Rank for women (Deaths per 100,000 population)	Rank for men (Deaths per 100,000 population)
Cancer	1 (153)	2 (244)
Heart diseases	2 (141)	1 (256)
Cerebrovascular disease	3 (67)	3 (85)
Respiratory disease	4 (32)	4 (54)
Life expectancy at birth (years)	80.9	74.6

Adapted from Statistics Canada. Women in Canada. Catalogue No. 89-503, 1995, 41–42.
Statistics Canada, Ottawa. Statistics Canada information is used with the permission of the
Minister of Industry, as Minister responsible for Statistics Canada. Information on the
availability of the wide range of data from Statistics Canada can be obtained from Statistics
Canada's regional offices, its World Wide Web site at http://www.statcan.ca, and its toll-free
access number 1-800-263-1136.

stress-based illnesses were work-related.[6] It may be that decision-
makers are reluctant to believe that women's jobs can make them
ill, so that their occupational illnesses are not recognized as such. We
will therefore examine patterns of health and illness among women
to see whether they could be related to their work.

    In general, women live longer but have a generally poorer state
of health. Women and men die of somewhat different illnesses (Tables 4 and 5. The difference in longevity has been attributed to
"lifestyle" factors such as smoking, drinking, and risk-taking. In

TABLE 6: Chronic Conditions Limiting Activity among
Men and Women in the United States, aged 45–69

Health problem	Rate/1000 women	Rate/1000, men
Arthritis	84*	45
High blood pressure	53	40
Diabetes	27	21
Deformity/orthopedic impairment—back	26	25
Chronic obstructive lung disease (bronchitis, etc.)	22	27
Heart disease except ischemic and arrhythmias	21	25
Ischemic heart disease	21	40
Deformity/orthopedic impairment—legs and feet	17	21
Intervertebral disc disorders	16	18
Visual impairment	17	21

Source: Adapted for Verbrugge, L. M. and Patrick, D. L. (1995) Seven chronic conditions: their impact on US adults' activity levels and use of medical services. American Journal of Public Health 85 (2): 17 3–182.

Information on chronic health problems is also available in Canada, and there also, muscle and joint problems are important. U.S. rates are based on physician visits and the Canadian (see Table 7) on self-reports. More women suffer from arthritis than see a physician about it, so Canada's rates appear higher.

fact, women still smoke and drink much less than men.[7] Employed women live longer than unemployed women and housewives, so the fact of being employed is probably a positive factor for women's health.[8] However, mortality varies by occupation. Most studies of occupational deaths, unfortunately, provide little data on women.

Although women live longer than men, women and men in many countries can expect to live a similar number of years *in good health*.[9] Put differently, women spend about twice as long as men being disabled, often due to muscle and joint problems (Tables 6 and 7). In the United States, Canada, and Québec, several studies reveal that women are especially likely to have arthritis, "rheumatism," carpal tunnel syndrome, and inflammations of various joints (tendinitis, bursitis, epicondylitis).[10] Chapter 7 shows that these aches and pains may very well be related to women's working conditions.

Also found more frequently among women are "mental health problems."[11] Whether women really have more such problems or not (see Chapters 7 and 9), it is undeniable that women consult more health practitioners, have more acute hospital admissions, and take more medication for mental problems than men.[12] Again, some

TABLE 7: Persons over 15 Reporting Health Problems, Canada, 1992

Health problem	Women %	Men %
Arthritis/rheumatism	25	16
Skin or other allergies	25	16
Hypertension	16	16
Migraines	13	5
Any health problem	66	59

Adapted from Statistics Canada. *Women in Canada.* Catalogue No. 89–503, 1995, p. 45. Statistics Canada, Ottawa.

mental health problems may be due to working conditions, but it has been very hard for women to prove that their symptoms are related to the workplace. This difficulty in believing that women's jobs can cause health problems can create a vicious circle: researchers do not think of looking for an occupational cause of women's health problems, such causes are not demonstrated, so the problems are attributed to women's biological or psychological "nature."

Many other problems suffered more often by women have at least a possible link with their working conditions. Women more often have skin problems and allergies; these problems may be associated with some tasks commonly done by women, such as cleaning. Other health problems specific to women that may have an occupational base are cancers of the breast, ovaries, uterus, cervix, and vagina, as well as other disorders of the female reproductive system. Menstrual problems such as irregular or painful periods are quite common among women, and our research group has found occupational factors to be involved in these disorders.

How can we find out whether any of these problems can be attributed in part to occupation? Several researchers have looked into these issues. One approach has been to examine health problems reported by women according to the sector of the economy where they work.[13] Although employment sector is not the best indicator of job content, this type of gross analysis does suggest a need to study women's jobs. Musculoskeletal problems emerged as a specific risk associated with sales, restaurant, and cleaning work. Psychological distress was found among those in sales, restaurant work, and teaching. Allergies and skin conditions were common in white-collar work, especially teaching,[14] and also in personal services such as hairdressing.

TABLE 8: Municipal Employee Time Lost during 1989–1990, by Activity and Sex

Activity	Sex	Number of Accidents	Mean Days Lost	Mean Age of Workers with Lost Time
Cleaning streets	Women	4	23.5	30.7
	Men	105	32.6	43.1
Garbage collection	Women	17	28.6	33.9
	Men	149	20.8	33.8
Gardening	Women	12	8.3	30.6
	Men	25	24.4	45.1
Indoor cleaning	Women	6	23.5	44.8
	Men	27	52.6	47.8
Horticulture	Women	17	17.4	32.3
	Men	27	52.6	37.2
Outside maintenance	Women	28	21.3	31.5
	Men	110	27.6	40.5

Another indicator that might be used to identify occupational health problems among women is sick leave. Women are more often absent from work than men, and only part of the absence can be explained by family responsibilities.[15] Bourbonnais and colleagues have suggested that sick leave certified by a doctor could be a reasonable measure of occupational hazards.[16] They found that nurses exposed to certain working conditions were more apt to be absent. This indicator may work well with populations whose access to sick leave is well regulated or guaranteed by a collective agreement. Within the same jobs, we do not find that women and men differ in the length of time on sick leave.

We also examined how long blue-collar municipal workers assigned to the same tasks were absent after a work accident (Table 8). (The comparison is not perfect because the women and men may have been assigned to different parts of the tasks or attacked them in different ways.)

Men were absent longer, averaging 29.4 days of absence per accident compared with 20.4 days for women. However, men with accidents were older than women (average of 43 versus 37 years), in keeping with the fact that women had been hired more recently. Women's shorter absences are thus probably explained by the difference in age, since older workers take longer to recover from work

TABLE 9: Pain Sites Reported by Male and Female
Blue-Collar Workers

Group	N	Number (and %) reporting pain, any site	Number (and %) with pain in upper limbs	Number (and %) with pain in lower limbs	Number (and %) with pain in back
Gardeners					
Women	25	19 (76%)	8 (32%)	6 (24%)	13 (52%)
Men	18	12 (67%)	1 (6%)	6 (33%)	8 (44%)
Total sample					
Women	58	39 (67%)	15 (26%)	12 (21%)	28 (48%)
Men	55	27 (49%)	3 (5%)	10 (18%)	17 (31%)

Note: Percentages do not add to 100 because individuals reported multiple symptoms.

accidents. No evidence could be found in this study to show that women were "fragile" or more at risk than men.

Statistics on work accidents, even when combined with sick leave statistics, give only a partial view of occupational health problems. Not all illness leads to absence, and it is important that occupational health science also address human suffering not associated with loss of work time. A worker can continue to work in pain for years.[17] During our interviews, we asked blue-collar workers to show us on a drawing of the human body the sites where they felt pain after work. Women showed us more pain and fatigue in all jobs and within specific job titles, and more sites of pain and fatigue (Table 9.) They showed us more pain in the upper limbs and back, but the same level of pain as men in the lower limbs. Among gardeners, the largest occupational group, women and men had differences in the pattern of pain. This may have been due to their different work assignments.

We can see that women and men have distinctive patterns of health problems, some of which could be due to their work. In saying that, we have not really explained these differences. In order to understand the health problems of working women and men, we have to go back to where and how they work. We have seen that most women in North America are in specific areas of the labor market, usually hired for particular types of jobs. They are often assigned to distinct tasks within the same job title, and they may be treated quite differently by supervisors, co-workers, and clients.

Therefore, as I mentioned in Chapter 1, women and men, even

those in the same jobs, are not necessarily exposed to the same health risks. Women and men in this study (and in the workplace) not only have different biology, they also have different seniority, average age, task assignments, work techniques, and lives outside work.

The following chapter considers one explanation of the differences between women's and men's occupational health problems: biological differences between women and men. I ask, are women and men assigned to different jobs because of their biological differences? In other words, does the gendered division of labor protect women's health?

3

Are Women Biologically Fit for Jobs?
Are Jobs Fit for Women?

■ ■ ■

Sometimes it appears that a sexual division of labor is unavoidable. In a poultry processing plant studied by my colleague Nicole Vézina, the employer decided to minimize the physical and mental damage of repetitive work by introducing job rotation. Cutting up turkeys had previously been divided into 17 operations, each one assigned to a different worker. About half the jobs were traditionally assigned to women. With the new system, workers would rotate through the 17 jobs. Because we were studying the health of women in nontraditional jobs, we were eager to see how men and women would react to being in each other's jobs in poultry processing.

We were in for a disappointment. When Nicole observed the work, she found that the rotation was not complete. By common agreement, women rotated through about half of the operations and men through the other half. No operation was done by a majority of both sexes. Worse, each sex was concentrated in jobs which shared a particular type of movement, increasing the repetition. Men made forceful, large, single strokes, and women used quicker, shorter movements.[1] It seemed as though a kind of natural selection had forced the women and men apart, re-creating the gendered division of labor. The women said some jobs were too hard for them, and the men said some

Source: Much of the material in this chapter has been adapted from Messing, K. and Stevenson, J. (1996) Women in procrustean beds: Strength testing and the workplace. Gender, Work and Organization 3 (3): 156–167.

jobs were too repetitive for them. Was natural selection indeed at work? Again, two theories of the gendered division of labor can be advanced. The theory of natural selection (square pegs in square holes, round pegs in round holes) would say that men and women have very different biological make-up and are "naturally" suited for different jobs. According to a crude version of this theory, men are stronger physically and more stable mentally. Being put into men's jobs is therefore dangerous for women, the more fragile sex. A theory of social determination (clay pegs in square or round holes) would suggest, on the contrary, that women and men could do each other's jobs but are channeled separately by social forces such as stereotyping.

The alternative theory I present here is more complicated. It accepts some of the premises of the other two but presents a more dynamic view of the workplace (clay pegs in clay holes). This theory of mutual adaptation says that: (1) The average woman and man have somewhat different physical characteristics, although there is considerable overlap. At work stations designed for the average man, therefore, many women and some men will be at a disadvantage. In poultry processing, the turkeys were strung up so high that it was hard for a woman of average size to reach them. (2) If given the chance, workers usually adapt their work stations, equipment, tools, and procedures to their own capacities. When men are considered to be the "normal" occupants of a workplace, women are discouraged from adapting the environment in ways most suitable for them. Blue-collar women have told us they are afraid to ask for special treatment such as smaller tools. (3) Women are assigned to jobs that are very demanding on a physical and mental level, such as trimming tiny pieces of fat from turkey breasts. However, not much value is attributed to the types of demands found in these jobs. Neither employers nor workers consider the ability to do these jobs as a specific qualification, and it is assumed that anyone can do them. Women are thought to be in these jobs because they are unable to do anything else; therefore they do not get much money for doing these jobs. Men express their inability to do these tasks as lack of interest or boredom. (4) Men and women in this factory suffer 75 work-related injuries per 100 workers *per year*.[2] We cannot speak of natural selection in an environment that is so disadvantageous for all workers. The fact that a biologically diverse population finds itself divided into two different job categories cannot be attributed to fitness when clearly neither group is anywhere near fit enough for the heavy requirements of its job.

If we do not accept biological or social determinism, the gendered division of labor in poultry processing and elsewhere must be explained in more complex ways, related to interactions among social, biological, and political factors in the historical context of particular factories and services. Harriet Bradley has demonstrated in a fascinating book that jobs restricted to women in one time and place were often reserved for men a few years later or a few miles away.[3] In consequence, the division of labor cannot be seen as a way to protect health by assigning jobs according to women's and men's capacities.

Moreover, jobs can *never* be perfectly assigned according to employee characteristics, because no one can predict how they will need to be performed in practice. Even the most regimented, standardized assembly-line jobs are done differently by each new worker. To promote health and efficiency, a much better policy for job assignment is to make sure that workplaces are designed so that workers can be given discretionary power and means to adapt their work stations and their methods to their own abilities and to the rapidly changing requirements of their work.

In this chapter, I give evidence for this alternative "clay-clay" theory, limiting myself to the physical aspects of jobs. I discuss what employers think are important physical qualifications for doing a job. I next examine the biological characteristics of the average man or woman: size and strength, as shown by standard testing methods. I show how strength testing can keep women from entering nontraditional jobs. I then question whether the strength tests are an appropriate way to judge whether women should enter nontraditional jobs. I present some data on whether nontraditional jobs are really dangerous for the average woman. Finally, I question two ideas that are at the origin of discussions of women's "fitness" to enter certain jobs. First, I look at the prejudices that limit the notion of fitness to the types of requirements in men's jobs and discuss some of the physical requirements of women's traditional jobs. Second, I propose a model for biology–job interactions that should supersede the notion of fitness and center on the promotion of health in the workplace.

Selection Tests and Health Protection

Pre-employment selection tests are a good way to examine employer representations. In the past, employers screened with their eyes, using such informal genetic and physiological testing to eliminate smaller men, women, blacks, older workers, and other groups thought to lack aptitudes for specific jobs. More recently, scientific tests have taken the place of the employers' eyeball approach. Feminists welcomed human rights legislation that prohibited older forms of discrimination against specific groups. In Québec, a series of cases brought before human rights tribunals by feminists and unions established that maleness cannot be made a hiring or transfer requirement for a job requiring the worker to lift weights, because average differences between the two sexes cannot be presumed to apply to individuals.[4] Similar jurisprudence in the United States has diminished outright elimination of women based on prejudices concerning women's physical strength. Women in North America have increased access to jobs requiring them to lift weights, subdue angry or insane people, or manipulate heavy equipment.

However, some research shows that an industrial accident is more likely when job requirements exceed the worker's strength.[5] Feminists may experience conflict between their wish to promote access to employment and a desire to protect women workers' health. Many feminists suggested judging the ability to do the job by testing applicants, a strategy that is widely used in industry.

Differences in Size and Shape

Differences between men's and women's performance on strength tests are related to biological differences between the sexes. Some general explanations must be given before venturing into this perilous territory.[6] First, it is useful and important to distinguish between genetics, biology, and capacity to perform a task. A biological phenomenon may or may not be due in part to genes. Height is a biological characteristic, whatever its origin. The variation in height between people is determined by an interaction between genes and environmental factors such as nutrition and high-heeled shoes. Performance, or the ability to reach objects on high shelves, depends on shelf height, availability of step stools, and the like.

Thus, even when a biological characteristic has an important genetic component, it can be changed by altering the environment. The capacity to lift weights or become pregnant is determined only in part by genes. Exercise, nutrition, stress, and working conditions are important modifiers of both capacities. Environments can make some genetic characteristics disappear. Diet can entirely prevent some genetic diseases from affecting health. People genetically underendowed with the ability to lift heavy wooden boxes can become fitter if the boxes are made from light plastic. It would be most accurate to say that those human characteristics that are important to the workplace result from gene–environment interactions that can be consciously manipulated. So genes do not really *determine* an individual's capacity, although they can limit it in certain environments.[7]

Gene–environment interactions are relevant to the study of male–female differences because women and men differ by a small chunk of their genetic material: one chromosome. Women have 23 pairs of chromosomes, including two copies of chromosome X, and men have 23 pairs of chromosomes, including an XY pair. One X chromosome contains 2 to 3 percent of human genes. Genes on the X chromosome (which men also have) affect vision, blood clotting, digestion, and many other functions unrelated to sex or sexuality. There are also a few genes affecting hormone action. The Y chromosome, which only men have, contains fewer than 20 genes, all of which seem to be involved with sexual characteristics. Thus, the Y chromosome is a tiny part of human heredity.

The mechanics of sex determination have not all been worked out, but it appears that the number of X and Y chromosomes in a fetus is related to the appearance of external genitals and the secretion of certain hormones, starting at about the sixth week of fetal life. Hormone secretions, particularly after puberty, influence height, muscle fibers, and body fat distribution; with nutrition and exercise, they play an important role in the difference in appearance between women and men. Still, the relationship of chromosomes to any specific behavior or capacity of mature individuals remains variable and hard to define, since there are so many differences between the environments of women and men.[8]

Therefore, the following discussion deals *only* with biological differences found in contemporary populations of female and male workers and with their influence on occupational health. It does not discuss the origins of those differences or the degree to which they could be changed by training or education. It considers how political decisions taken in the workplace affect the impact of workplace design on workers with different shapes, sizes, and strengths.

Women and men come in many shapes and sizes, but the average man and the average woman are different. When we did our study

TABLE 10: Approximate Measurements of U.S. Adults in Inches

	Percentile* for men			Percentile for women		
Dimension	5th	50th	95th	5th	50th	95th
Height	65	69	74	60	64	68
Distance reached up	77	82	87	71	76	81
Sitting height	34	36	38	31	34	36
Arm length	29	30	33	26	28	31
Hand breadth	3	3.5	4	2.5	3	3.5

Source: This table is extracted from data presented by Pheasant, S., (1986). *Bodyspace*, p. 111. Taylor & Francis, London.

*Half of US men are taller than the 50th percentile for men; 5 percent are taller than the 95th percentile, etc.

of 113 blue-collar workers, we found that not one of the 58 women was taller than the average man, and none of the 55 men were shorter than the average woman. In other words, although there was overlap, the tallest 28 people were all men and the shortest 29 people were all women. In this, these workers did not differ from other human populations.

The data in Table 10 show percentile values for some measurements of U.S. adults. In general, for most dimensions, the average woman is smaller than 95 percent of men, and the average man is bigger than 95 percent of women. It has been calculated that, in random encounters between a woman and a man, the man will be taller than the woman 92 percent of the time.[9]

For weight, the differences are somewhat smaller. In 25 percent of chance encounters between a woman and a man, the woman will be heavier. A larger proportion of women's body weight is fat (about 25 percent, compared with 15 percent for men), and a smaller proportion is muscle. Men and women are also shaped differently. Women's feet are proportionately smaller, the upper leg and lower leg are in different proportions, the hip joint is constructed somewhat differently, and young women's joints are somewhat more flexible.[10]

These differences refer to averages, but the average person probably does not exist. Many women can be found with the average characteristics of men, and vice versa, so it makes no sense to keep all women or all men out of certain jobs. It does become relevant to ask whether physical differences are at the source of the sexual division of labor. As mentioned, the conventional way to examine this question is through strength tests.

Differences in Strength

With biomechanics expert Joan Stevenson, I have reviewed women's performance on some strength tests, some of which are used in pre-employment screening and some in developing labor standards. We also examined the tests themselves and their relevance to the workplace. Some of our conclusions are reproduced here.[11]

Men's and women's strength is usually compared on specific tasks. Test strategies have been developed using three approaches. In *psychophysiological* tests, subjects are asked to lift increasing weights. They adjust the load to reach the maximum they can accept. *Physiological* tests examine body functions such as oxygen consumption and heart rate during exercise. *Biomechanical* tests calculate muscular effort at a task, which is compared with databases. These three fields of study have served to generate the widely used lifting guidelines of the U.S. National Institutes of Occupational Safety and Health (NIOSH). These guidelines are very important in occupational health because they are used in designing jobs and are also referred to when deciding whether injury compensation claims will be accepted. In general, if the physical requirements of a job fall within the guidelines, judges tend to consider that the job is safe and the injury must have been caused by something else in the worker's life.

I discuss the three types of tests separately, showing how specific characteristics of each put women at a disadvantage.

PSYCHOPHYSIOLOGICAL TESTS

The best-known psychophysiological databases for manual handling tasks performed by women and men were compiled by Snook and Ciriello.[12] Subjects (68 men and 51 women) were asked to lift boxes to which weights were added until the subject refused to go on lifting. All other parameters were controlled by the investigators: box size, lift "envelope" (floor to knuckle or knuckle to shoulder height), movement (push, pull), distance, and others. Overall, men lifted/lowered about twice as much weight as women. Gender differences were much smaller for push/pull performance, with far greater overlap in test scores. Gender differences were also reduced for tasks involving faster lifting rates, smaller boxes, and lifts involving more lower body strength. For example, at one lift every five seconds, women perform 65 percent as well as men, dropping off to 50 percent at one lift every five minutes.

Another researcher asked men and women to execute a psychophysiological test for 40 minutes. Then the subjects tried to predict the weight they could lift for a full day.[13] Testing for longer periods showed that the men had overestimated their ability by about twice as much as the women. This result may imply that the psychophysiological database underestimates women's strength because women may be more prudent about accepting heavy loads.

PHYSIOLOGICAL TESTS

Physiological testing has focused on the ability of the cardiovascular system to deliver oxygen and food to the muscles during work. Assessment of cardiovascular capacity and efficiency is determined by measuring the amount of oxygen consumed and waste carbon dioxide produced during physical activity. For example, subjects are asked to exercise in the laboratory while hooked up to equipment that measures their oxygen consumption, heart rate, cardiac output, etc. Since this equipment is too cumbersome for industrial use, indirect measures such as heart rate are often used to assess work demands in the real workplace. In absolute terms (irrespective of body size, fitness, or dimensions of the cardiovascular system), men consume 40 to 60 percent more oxygen than women.[14] When consumption rates are expressed per unit of body weight, the difference diminishes to 20 to 30 percent, and when expressed per unit of body weight after correction for women's higher proportion of fat, the difference in oxygen consumption drops off and may even disappear.[15]

The tendency in physiological testing is to report absolute measures of oxygen consumption (without any corrections) because of the assumption that the workload of tasks is fixed, regardless of who is doing it. Since the methods have been designed to use the same protocol for both genders, no one has studied the ways in which men and women manage their workload for a given task. For example, a man with greater upper-body strength may choose a lifting strategy that profits from this strength. He will use a simple one-stage lift with his arms while a woman might lift in two movements, or use other parts of her body to help her arms lift, or use leverage of some kind. If a woman is forced into the same protocol as the man, apparent gender differences in energy expenditure will be magnified. To the extent that techniques are imposed, physiological measures will tend to exaggerate true gender differences.

BIOMECHANICAL TESTS

Biomechanical testing is based on the measurement of muscular effort required at each joint involved in a given task. Using video techniques to record worker posture, and knowing the subject's body weight and the weight of the load lifted, it is possible to estimate the force exerted at each joint. Typically, these tests show that women average 60 percent of the strength of men.[16] The female–male difference in physical force is largest for the upper limbs and smallest for the lower limbs, with other muscles in between (see Table 11).[17]

However, there is always overlap between women's and men's performance. The degree of overlap varies with the test used. Task protocols also can increase apparent gender differences. Since skeletal anatomy and (according to some researchers) muscle characteristics differ between women and men, and these combine with the differences in body proportions and the pattern of muscular development, male–female comparisons vary depending on the task studied. Fothergill and co-workers studied a variety of positions and movements and showed that male–female differences in strength for a given task depended on the direction in which force was exerted.[18] Men and women differed more when pulling or pushing at some angles than at others. Other researchers found that the impact of sex differences on grip strength varies with the distance between the handles of a pair of pliers. Because women's hands are smaller, their grip weakens when the handles are too far apart.[19]

Biomechanical assessments of task strategies as performed by men are often used as the model for task performance by both genders. This approach may not be appropriate, since there are many differences in the way that the average woman and man perform strength-based tasks.[20] Reported differences include the following observations: men lift larger weights less often, while women use lighter loads with more repetition; men use the upper body more, and women accentuate the lower body, for example by suspending weights from their hips rather than carrying them in their arms.

TABLE 11 : Relative Strength of Women and Men

Movement involved	Average woman's maximum as a percent of man's	Range over several studies
Push or pull with arms	56%	35–79
Push or pull with legs	72%	57–86
Push or pull with torso	64%	59–84

Note: These figures are based on Laubach's review of the literature: Laubach, L. (1976) Comparative muscular strength of men and women. Aviation, Space and Environmental Medicine 47: 534–542. Reprinted with permission of the Aerospace Medical Association.

Joan Stevenson has carefully examined one widely used biomechanical test, the incremental lifting machine (ILM).[21] The subjects were asked to lift a weight in a single motion from a starting height of 30 cm to a target height of 180 cm. Under these conditions, the 126 women succeeded in lifting 48 percent of the weight lifted by the 143 men.

Stevenson compared ILM performance to a task designed to reflect a typical real-life lifting situation (lifting a box from the floor to a height of 135 cm).[22] She found that performance on the ILM was a much poorer predictor of women's eventual performance on the box lifting task than of men's. Women did proportionately better on the box lifting task if they were allowed some freedom in designing their own ways to perform the task: they then lifted 63 percent of the weight lifted by the men. When women were given the opportunity to redesign the task, they accomplished it differently. They tended to lift in two distinct moves rather than in the one continuous lifting movement selected by men.

Another reason for the difference in performance between the ILM and box lifting was the nature of the movement pattern the ILM imposed. Because women are, on average, shorter, a greater proportion of the women's lifting time was passed with the arms above waist level, a position in which it is more difficult to exert strength. The inferiority of the ILM as a predictor of women's performance was hidden in the original study of the machine because female and male populations were combined.[23]

Women's strength relative to men's seems to be undervalued by all these types of tests. They were all developed first with men and then applied to women, so it is not surprising that they are not well adapted to measuring women's abilities. Stevenson suggests developing tests that would be better predictors of women's performance as well as being more closely related to real-life lifting tasks.

How to Pick People

Would women have better access to jobs if strength testing were improved? We must admit that, even under the most favorable conditions, most women lift less weight than most men. To quote the authors of one test used for screening firefighter applications, "females scored well below the male mean values. . . . We have been able to identify a select group of females [36 out of 1087] who have higher body weight, higher fat-free weight and a relatively low percentage of body fat who compare favorably with males on specific physical performance tests which are related to firefighting. . . they are currently employed as firefighters in the City of Chicago." [24] Strength testing therefore kept 96.7 percent of women applicants out of the firefighter jobs, retaining only those whose bodies most closely resembled those of men. Changing the tests might allow a few more women in, but the majority of women would probably still be screened out. Would this be wise?

CINBIOSE was once consulted by a municipality where the firefighters were terrified by the prospect of being overcome by smoke in a burning building, with a woman partner too weak to carry them out. Firefighters admitted that many of their male colleagues had grown too old and out of shape to carry them, but insisted that this was not a reason to hire new less-fit workers. We could only sympathize with this fear, since we ourselves would want to be rescued by people with the closest possible resemblance to Superman or Wonder Woman. On the other hand, hiring those who perform best on strength tests may not select those who could best find the way out of a burning building or keep from becoming overcome by smoke. Stevenson suggests that screening for physical strength be used not to select the strongest applicants, who will probably all be men, but just to screen out those who are too weak to do the given job. After this minimum is reached, other job characteristics should come into play, such as those requiring intellectual skills and emotional stability. If this were done, the percentage of women firefighters would be considerably higher than it is now.

The firefighter's job is typical of traditionally male jobs with a physical component. Most cases of physical barriers to employing women workers involve single operations that require a large degree of strength but that occur infrequently during job performance. In many cases the requirement for extreme strength could be circumvented. One example of this was the brakeman's job at the Canadian National Railway. Applicants were required to pick up a heavy 83-pound (38-kg) coupling device and carry it 80 feet (24 m). Most women failed the test. The Canadian Human Rights Commission heard testimony that the task was unrelated to most of the content of the job and that the coupling device could be carried in partnership, reducing the weight carried by half. The commission found the brakeman test to be discriminatory. Another example was the job of mixer at the cake factory we studied, mentioned in the Preface. Two or three times an hour, the man assigned to mixing would lift a 40-kg bag of sugar and pour it into a mixing machine. Women were not assigned to this job because they could not lift the bag. Asked why the bag could not be divided into two or four lighter portions, management replied that they did not see the need for this, since the man had no trouble lifting it.

We are not so sure that the man would have no trouble lifting heavy weights day after day. Québec men have 3.3 times as many compensated accidents to their backs as women.[25] These data suggest that the jobs of very many men are beyond their strength. We cannot conclude from the available evidence that keeping women out of jobs in which they are required to lift weights is a good way to protect the health of either sex. It seems more likely that the exclusion of women allows employers to require men to do dangerous jobs, on pain of being regarded as sissies if they refuse.

How Do Biological Differences Interact with the Workplace?

We can now answer the question of whether the gendered division of labor in manual jobs can be attributed to biological differences between women and men. The question should be divided up. First, are women now able to do nontraditional jobs without injury? Second, could nontraditional jobs be made more accessible so that women could do them without injury?

As shown in the previous chapter, we have trouble answering the first question. Women in nontraditional jobs do not necessarily do exactly the same tasks as men in those jobs, so that comparisons of injury and illness rates are difficult. Also, women may be entirely excluded from jobs with especially heavy physical demands. In the municipality we studied, women had entered only 22 of the 201 job titles; many people thought women could not do the other 179 jobs.

It is likely that some traditional men's jobs are dangerous for more women than men. We came across one workplace that seemed to be specifically dangerous for women.[26] The proportion of women in a package-sorting job, decreased with seniority, although the job had been integrated for a long time. The few women at this job (14 percent) had 63 percent of the work accidents in recent years. The job involved picking up one package every three seconds (7,000 per day) and finding and entering its code into a computer. Packages weighed almost two kilograms each, and the total weight handled in a day with the left hand was 12,000 kg. We asked whether women could have been preferentially eliminated by the requirement for lifting weights in an awkward position. When we observed the job, we also noticed that the work station imposed an extra burden on shorter workers, who had to handle the packages with the left shoulder joint quite distorted. It is possible that women were also being eliminated through a bad fit between the average woman's body and the work station.

Thus, it is hard to separate discussions of fitness from issues in workplace design. The answer to our second question seems to be that, yes, nontraditional jobs can and should be made more accessible. Many workplaces seem to have been designed by a sort of latter-day Procrustes[27] so that women have to distort their bodies to fit. The women blue-collar workers told us of too-large boots and gloves, too-big shovels, and clippers with too-wide intervals between the handles. A supervisor told us he could not assign women to prune trees because the belt of the device that hoisted pruners into the air was too large for most women, and they could slip through and fall.

Thus, part of the risk of manual, materials-handling jobs stems from unwillingness to abandon the approach of finding the worker to fit the job rather than making the job accessible to the workers. We have found many jobs assigned to men because of isolated operations that could be corrected to make the job accessible to more people: laundry bags that were too heavy and had to be pitched into a very high-rimmed receptacle (why not reduce the size of the bags or lower the receptacle or eliminate the operation altogether?), wastebaskets that were too large (why?), mirrors placed too high to be washed (or looked into?).

When we read the ergonomics literature, we find that women are often excluded without a backward look when spaces and equipment are designed.[28] Danielle Chabaud-Rychter has described how women are excluded at every stage of development of kitchen devices, both as housewives and as workers.[29] In fact, this appears to be a well-accepted practice among ergonomists. The learned British journal *Applied Ergonomics* ran an article on design considerations thoughtfully entitled "Anthropometry [the science of measuring people] for a mix of different populations." The author produced measurements of 19 body dimensions of 408 subjects to demonstrate human diversity, concluding, "Anthropometrists should address the users of the intended system irrespective of their ethnic background." In presenting his methods, the author mentioned in passing: "One of the contributing factors to variations in anthropometric data is sex. This source of variation was controlled by sampling from the male population only. The reason for ruling out females is that the academic buildings [where the study was done] are restricted to males." None of the reviewers or editors appears to have jibbed at the implied discrimination or required that the article's title be corrected.[30]

"Fitness"

RECIPE FOR A SIDEWALK

Pouring concrete is just like baking a cake.
The main difference is
that first you build the pans. Call them forms.
Think grand.
Mix the batter with a few simple ingredients:
        one shovel of sand
                one shovel of gravel
                        a pinch of cement.

Add water until it looks right.
Depends how you like it.
Can be mixed by hand or with a beater called
a Readi-Mix truck.
Pour into forms and smooth off.
Adjust the heat so it's not too cold,
not too hot. Protect from rain.

Let cook until tomorrow.
Remove the forms and walk on it.

There is one big difference from cakes.
This one will never disappear.
For the rest of your life your kids
will run on the same sidewalk, singing
My mom baked this!   —Kate Braid[31]

We think that fitness for a job must be considered as an interaction between individuals (with all their possibilities for change) and a plastic, adaptable work environment. But when a woman wants to take a nontraditional job, people regard fitness as a static characteristic of the woman alone. They ask whether she is strong enough, stable enough, etc.

We thought about fitness when talking to a woman who had been refused transfer to a man's job in a factory. The employer said she was not physically capable of doing the job. She asked at least to be allowed to try out, but was turned down and sent back to the assembly line. She told us wistfully, "I wish I'd gotten the job, I'd be less tired when I get home." We wondered what kind of fitness the employer was thinking of. What is strength, anyway? Are men really stronger than women, or does the answer depend on our definition of strength?

Women's segregated work has its own physical demands, not usually recognized in the workplace. Strength testing as usually done has been almost exclusively based on the types of movements used in traditional men's work. The psychophysiological and biomechanical tests involve discrete displacements of objects weighing over 10 kilograms, repeated with rest periods in between. The physiological measurements require a large expenditure of energy over a relatively short period of time. Other types of physical requirements, such as standing for a long time, have not been the subject of pre-employment testing.

We recently interviewed a group of male and female hospital cleaners about the physical difficulties encountered in their work. The women complained to us that women who wish to be assigned to "heavy" cleaning (now 100 percent male) must take a strength test, while men who wish to be assigned to "light" cleaning (now 80 percent female) are not tested in any way. We observed the physical requirements of "light" cleaning, which involved constant bending and stooping, picking up and dusting small objects, very quick scrubbing movements with the arms and hands, and nearly constant

motion over a long work day. We also observed the physical requirements of the men's jobs: slower and somewhat less frequent
movements, often against greater resistance, usually carried out
while walking, with more rest breaks.[32] The physical requirements
of both jobs were considerable, but quite different. Only one of the
two types of jobs was considered by the employer to require
strength that could be tested by a pre-employment test.

Physical requirements of some tasks traditionally done by women
are quite heavy. For example, sewing machine operators sew one pant
leg every 6 to 10 seconds. They must pick up the pant leg, run it
through the machine, and put it on a rack. Over a typical work day,
Nicole Vézina and her colleagues found that one group of sewing machine operators exerted a total of 3,500 kilograms of force with their
arms and 16,000 kilograms with their legs.[33] This kind of highly
repetitive task is typical of women's work in industry.

Other physical requirements for women's work include the ability to work without stopping over a long period of time. The sewing
machine operators were not able to take even tiny (less than five second) breaks: 93 percent of their time was taken up by their actual
work, compared with only 50 percent for a traditionally male me-
chanic's job, whether done by a man or a woman.[34] In poultry processing, women have fewer rest breaks than men.[35]

Sales clerks and bank tellers (usually women) must be able to
stand for long periods. Grocery cashiers in North America must
move (lift or slide) one article every 10 seconds while standing in a
fixed position so that they can enter the price in the cash register.[36]
Bank tellers stand more than 90 percent of the time.[37] In poultry
slaughterhouses and canneries, women are much more likely than
men to state that they work standing in one place.[38] Other types of
traditional jobs require maintaining an effort for long periods;
many cleaning jobs involve stretching or scrubbing in a cramped or
stooped position. People are never given a pre-employment test on
how long they can stand or bend or hold their arms in the air.

Other types of strength required in women's traditional work include: the agility to handle many different-sized and -shaped
weights at once, some of which may squirm or be asymmetrical (babies or grocery packages); the ability to change rapidly from one position to another all day long (cleaning toilets in trains).[39] Laundry
workers' heart rates resemble those of miners because of the combination of incessant lifting of wet sheets with hot temperatures.[40]

These capacities are rarely the subject of pre-employment strength screening. And, of course, no pre-employment test requires workers to continue for over 10 hours without stopping (the average Canadian woman's combined domestic and professional work day).

We further questioned the notion of fitness when we realized that many of the stereotypes about women's and men's abilities have nothing to do with real, demonstrated differences between the average man and woman. For example, in many Québec hospitals women cleaners are not allowed to climb ladders. One woman complained that her job description required her to clean high areas but forbade her to use even a stepstool, so she ended up cleaning on tiptoe. Another woman told us that her supervisor had explained to her that if a woman used a stepladder and fell, insurance would not cover it. Although this information was false, we heard this story in several workplaces. Workers were told (and some believed) that women were unable to climb ladders. This belief is not backed by any research results.

With cleaners, a perceived difference in ability by sex has resulted in sex-typed job descriptions, thought to correspond to the abilities of each sex (see Chapter 1). In fact, only the requirements for men are thought of as "fitness." The qualities required of women are thought of negatively, as disqualifications from doing the activities men are required to do. This disqualification then becomes a prohibition, so that women are not allowed to use cleaning machines or climb stepladders. The prohibition is no longer related to the physical requirements of the job that may have led to the gendered division of labor in the first place. It becomes an independent prejudice and takes on a life of its own.

Conclusion

The scientific field of pre-employment strength testing has been modeled on the male body and on the type of strength required in jobs done most often by men. Many of the obstacles to women in nontraditional jobs come from stereotyping; if the will were there, all jobs that can comfortably be done by most men could be adapted fairly easily so that most women could do them. Many different talents and capacities are required by every job, even those that look to be the most routine and simple. Valuing and testing only those capacities that are more common among men is a result of sexism. Looking at the health risks only in those tasks usually done by men ignores the insidious damage done to women by repetition, cramped postures, and long hours.

The whole idea of pre-employment testing seems to be based on a misunderstanding of how workers interact dynamically with their jobs while trying to protect their health. This misconception results in strength tests that are not related to real-life job requirements and do not meet the needs of any workers. They do, however, serve effectively to support discrimination against women.

All these problems make one wonder how it is that scientific fields arise in isolation from or even in contradiction to the needs of workers, especially women workers. Why are there so many more studies of lifting weights than of standing? Why are the parameters for tool design so limited? How could the editors and reviewers of a learned journal not notice that women had been excluded from a study on "a mix of different populations"? Wondering about these phenomena leads us to look at how scientists are selected and trained.

4

Who Are Scientists?

■ ■ ■

The relationship between occupational health scientists and women workers has been quite simple: until very recently, women and women's jobs were almost completely absent from occupational health studies. Women's sufferings from prolonged standing were not given the attention that men received when they wrenched their backs while lifting heavy loads. Women's cancers and disorders of the female reproductive system were not studied as occupational health problems. Collective stress reactions were ascribed to "mass hysteria." Labor standards were usually based on the needs, jobs, and bodies of the average man. Even now, women's occupational health does not fit well into the framework traditionally used for setting priorities in occupational health. Very few areas of concern to women have been explored by occupational traditionally health and safety researchers.

Many feminist researchers have examined how women are treated by medical scientists. Ruth Hubbard, Gena Corea, and Anne Fausto-Sterling, and others began this inquiry in the 1970s; Londa Schiebinger, Donna Haraway, and many more have continued it. Feminists have also examined how women *do* science, whether they are recognized as scientists (Margaret Rossiter, Evelyn Fox-Keller, and Marianne Ainley) or when they are outsiders (Lorraine Code). There is also a growing tradition of women insisting that their knowledge and experience be considered seriously by scientists: I think, for example, of Lois Gibbs and Love Canal and of Judy Norsigian and the Boston Women's Health Book Collective, as well as countless trade union activists. Here I base myself on their work in occupational health.

Chapters 7 to 10 show in detail how scientists treat women's occupational health problems. In the next three chapters, I want to explain where these scientists are coming from. Who are scientists? How are they trained, and by whom? How do they decide on their research subjects? Where does the money come from? How does a research project turn into scientific knowledge? This information will shed light on why scientists have some trouble understanding women's occupational health problems. I have not concluded that scientists are mean people or even that they are particularly sexist. Rather, occupational health scientists are trained and molded by scientific institutions whose evolution has not equipped them to meet the needs of women workers.

Who Scientists Are

Scientists who study occupational health can come from several fields. Some study the effects of workplace conditions on physical and mental health: those who see patients (physicians and clinical psychologists), those who make statistical links between exposures on the job and illnesses (epidemiologists), and those who study the mechanisms by which chemicals and radiation produce biological changes (toxicologists). Others study the workplace to characterize exposures: those who look for chemical and physical hazards (industrial hygienists), those who look for conditions that produce mental and emotional damage (sociologists and psychologists), and those who examine work activity in order to discover constraints on the worker (ergonomists).

Women are a minority in all of the above occupations and especially the natural and biomedical sciences. Women encounter barriers at several points on their way to a position of influence in science. First, anyone who wants to direct her/his own research program must obtain a Ph.D. or M.D. degree. The Ph.D. represents at least nine years of study after high school and the M.D. from eight (Québec) to 10 or more years (United States and Canada), depending on the program chosen.

To get the necessary degrees, scientists and physicians must overcome obstacles that eliminate many women, minorities, and people with working-class origins. As Ruth Hubbard puts it: "What are the social or group characteristics of people who are allowed to make scientific facts? Above all, they must have a particular kind of education, which includes graduate and postgraduate training. Until the 1960s, youngsters mainly from the upper-middle and upper classes, most of them male and white, had access to that kind of education. Since then, more white women and people of color (both women and men) have been able to gain access, but the class origins of scientists have not changed appreciably."[1] Spending long years in school full-time is impossible for most women with children or people from the working class, but there are very few part-time Ph.D. programs in science and none in medicine. M.D.'s and science Ph.D.'s impose rigid schedules; they require the student to be physically present in the laboratory or in the field at hours that depend on the life cycles of animals or the last-minute emergencies of workplaces or study populations, while physicians must be available for very long hours in hospitals. These schedules are hard to reconcile with the responsibility for young children or with the necessity to hold a part-time job.

Since the years spent in graduate study coincide with those when most women have children, women (but not usually men) are forced to choose between school and children. The fellowships that support students have inadequate provisions for maternity and parental leave. Some programs allow several months' (unpaid) leave after childbirth, but none allow for parental leave. Québec's provincial scholarship program, for example, allows students to take a one-year unpaid maternity leave, but does not allow them to pro-rate their scholarships for part-time study.

An informal inquiry in one U.S. department showed that three times as many women as men left Ph.D. programs without a degree after two years of study.[2] Several of my own very promising students have stopped before getting their Ph.D.'s because of conflicts between childrearing demands, financial pressure, and the requirements of a Ph.D. program. As the divorced mother of young children, I myself was only able to finish my degree thanks to unlimited and unquestioning financial sacrifices by my upper-middle-class parents, combined with an ability to coerce my friends into doing a lot of unpaid babysitting. A colleague in a similar situation, but from a working-class family, survived her student years because of exceptional support from CINBIOSE faculty, staff, and other students, almost all women, and her mother's availability for babysitting.

Such support for women with children is unusual. Most departments have very few women, and their absence also discourages women students. One study discovered that young women found it difficult to do graduate work in departments where there were few women. The isolated women faculty members were less supportive of young women and their family responsibilities and more apt to require them to behave like men.[3]

Those few women and working-class people who get the necessary degrees then come up against obstacles to getting hired. No data are available on the sex, ethnicity, or social class of occupational health scientists, but male domination in medical and scientific research and teaching is easy to document. Historically, doctors in the U.S. and Canada have been white men;[4] even though the number of women doctors is growing rapidly, they are not building research careers. The same is true of scientists generally:[5] women make up only 20 percent of Ph.D. scientists in the United States and only 6 percent of the 120,000 listed in the "Who's Who" of science, *American Men and Women of Science*.[6] Many books and papers have been written about the paucity of women in science, in the United States[7] and Canada.[8]

The shortage of women scientists is not entirely due to a lack of trained personnel. Women are much less common among practicing scientists than among people who have finished Ph.D.'s in science. That is, many women Ph.D.'s do not have jobs as scientists. Two kinds of explanations have been given for this phenomenon: bias and structural factors.[9]

Bias has certainly been important in my own experience. I have observed some mechanisms that militate against women's getting hired for academic positions. The first incident occurred when I was in graduate school. My supervisor was a woman who had been hired as an assistant professor, the initial rank in academia. She worked closely with a male colleague who had been hired at the same time at the same level. During their first three years, they published the same numbers of papers, including two in collaboration, one of these in her field and one in his. She was an excellent teacher and organizer and was given a large course to run. Despite having a baby during the period, she was so successful and popular that students put forward her name first when consulted on who should be made dean of students. The male professor was by his own admission a terrible teacher and was asked to teach one advanced course with few students. Student evaluations of his teaching were awful. At the end of the period of probation, he was promoted and she was not, although she was offered another appointment at the same level. She refused in anger, and the last I heard of her, she had moved to another city and was outside the academic stream.

Years later, in a biology department where I was a professor, a similar situation arose. The university had, after many discussions, adopted an affirmative action policy providing that if a man and a woman had equal qualifications, the woman would be hired. We received applications for the position of substitute professor from two candidates who had started their doctoral work in the same laboratory at the same time. The woman had gotten her Ph.D. and had done two years of additional research in another laboratory. The man had not yet finished his degree. The woman had published several scientific papers, and the man had not yet published. Both had successfully taught courses in our department. Even though a Ph.D. was a written requirement for being hired as a professor, the department hired the man. When a permanent position became available, the women in the department decided that a fairer decision would have to be made. After several meetings in which the question was hotly debated, we were able to hire the woman by invoking the affirmative action policy. It seemed ironic to us that a policy providing for a woman to be hired when qualifications were *equal* should need to be invoked when the qualifications were so obviously unequal.

I got a clue to interpreting this situation when one of my male colleagues, exasperated with me, exploded: "You know very well that (the male candidate) would make a more agreeable colleague, don't you? Go on your intuition!" In fact, *my* intuition told *me* the woman would make a better colleague. She in fact went on to become a well-respected chair of our department. The men in my department just were not listening to the same signals as I. Despite their abilities, both women described above seemed to lack some indefinable attribute that was important to my colleagues.

It may not just be their sex. Women, working-class people, or people of color may express themselves in somewhat different language, which may be perceived as ambiguous, inaccurate, or sloppy.[10] Hesitation or prudence may be misperceived as incompetence. Women who combine childrearing with scientific training, or people who need to earn money while studying, may be misperceived as not serious about science. Thus, people responsible for hiring academics may be governed by stereotyped notions of what scientists are like.

Structural factors are also important. When bias is absent, hiring is based on the curriculum vitae (CV), a list of the applicant's publications and grants. It has been pointed out that the childbearing years keep many women from producing an impressive CV.[11] Some granting institutions in Canada now provide a place in their grant applications to mention factors that may interfere with a researcher's "productivity." Although this section allows women who have young children to describe the influence of their situation on their publication record, not all "peers" will take these responses into account. We were recently told by the director of a granting agency to "get rid of" one of our researchers who had trouble meeting deadlines for reports. We pointed out that she was a superb researcher, working more than 40 hours a week despite the constant sickness of one or another of her young children (three months, 18 months, six and 8 years old) during the Montréal winter. In response, he repeated several times that she was not serious about her work and we should not keep her.

How Grants Are Obtained

Once scientists have succeeded in getting a Ph.D. and being hired at a job where research is possible, they must get money for the research. Especially in the biomedical sciences, researchers need great sums of money. According to their annual reports, the average operating grant (exclusive of major equipment purchases) from the U.S. National Institutes of Health in 1994 was $69,251 a year (U.S.); the average grant from the Medical Research Council of Canada in 1994–95 was $65,300 (CAD).[12] These grants are usually given for three years. The 1995 report of the Québec Institute for Occupational Health and Safety puts the average total grant at $128,700 (CAD). Depending on the type of research, the money is used to pay for personnel, operating equipment, chemicals, and publication costs. A study of mutation rates in the cells of 60 nuclear power plant workers cost us about $200,000, mostly for chemicals and technical assistance. An ergonomic study of four groups of women workers cost $216,000 for technical assistance, filming equipment and supplies, and office supplies.

The requirement for money means that scientists must be able to persuade some institution with money to part with it. The institutions with money are government, private nonprofit foundations such as the Canadian or American Cancer Society, and businesses. With few exceptions, community groups and unions do not have access to enough money to fund serious biomedical research.

Some scientists are employed directly by industry and obtain all their research money from their employer. Academics can also get money from industry for research: 59 percent of 210 U.S. companies doing life-science research supported university-based research, spending an estimated total of $1.5 billion in 1994. [13] Much of this research is pharmaceutical, but occupational health studies may also be supported. For example, I once attended a presentation where a representative from a large metal refinery described, with slides, the pioneering work the company had sponsored on heart disease and cancer among its own workers. For some reason not entirely clear to me, the company was proud of the exceptional research opportunities provided by the chemical and physical aggressors in their plant.

Employers, particularly large corporations, often fund research on their own workers. Although the credibility of such research is frequently questioned, accepting funds from employers seems to be a good career move. In Québec, McGill University has the most respected medical school and the most funding for medical research.[14] Three successive chairs of the McGill Medical School's Department of Epidemiology and Biostatistics received funding or were hired respectively by the asbestos mineowners, a synthetic textile plant associated with a higher incidence of colon cancer, and an explosives plant where many workers have died. A head of McGill's School of Occupational Health was regularly asked by an aluminum producer to testify against workers who claim they have occupational cancers. An editor of the learned journal *Mutagenesis* was funded by an employer of radiation-exposed workers. Meetings of the Environmental Mutagenesis Society are funded in part by chemical companies. Such relationships with employers keep scientific institutions alive in a time of budgetary restrictions and are encouraged by universities.

Funds not provided by employers can be requested from government, private, or university funding agencies. The latter sources employ peer review in the form of a panel of scientific experts who determine whose research will be funded. We once examined determinants of our own success in getting grants and found that for the same researcher, grant proposals were more likely to be accepted if the project involved nonhumans or human cells in culture rather than live humans, if the work was done in a laboratory rather than in the field, if there was a woman on the peer-review committee, and if there was no visible worker input at any level of the project.[15] Projects refused even though other proposals from the same researcher were accepted at the same time by the same granting agency included: a questionnaire-based study of reproductive problems of health care workers (a study of their cells was accepted); a study of neurotoxic effects suffered by metal-exposed workers (a comparison of different neurotoxic tests of unexposed people was accepted); a study of musculoskeletal and social difficulties suffered by women entering nontraditional jobs (a study of musculoskeletal problems of men and women in traditional jobs was accepted). Thus, studies seemed to be funded in inverse proportion to their likelihood of supporting compensation or social change. In particular, no studies dealing with problems specific to women were funded during that time.

Other feminist researchers have had similar difficulty finding funds for their work. Although women are now almost half the workforce, research in women's occupational health is strikingly underfunded. In 1989, we were asked by the Health and Welfare and Labor ministries to prepare a critical review of women's occupational health studies in Canada,[16] and found that our federal granting agencies did not have much to offer. According to Health Canada, 64 projects on women's health were currently supported, of which only three addressed women's occupational health in any way. Only 3.1 percent of the small amount of money spent in that year on *women's* health went for research on women's occupational health. Many projects supported by Health Canada that should have included the effects of women's jobs did not appear to do so: premenstrual syndrome, factors associated with outcomes of surgery, risks for development of hypertension during pregnancy, women and health in the middle years, and so on. The situation has not changed dramatically since then, although it is slowly improving under pressure from feminists.[17] In 1994 the Medical Research Council of Canada admitted that only about 5 percent of Canadian health research funding is spent on women's health issues.[18]

How does this work? How can supposedly objective committees act with such unanimity to keep research on women's occupational health from being funded? In order to show how this can happen, I will describe the process in detail.

Part of the answer lies in the secret nature of the peer-review process. Grant applications are sent for review to experts who know the name of the applicant but whose names are concealed from both applicants and other committee members. These reports are then examined by committees composed of established scientists, who make the final decisions on funding. This peer-review process takes

place almost entirely in the dark. Judgments are irreversible; refusals of grants can never be appealed, even when the grounds for
refusal contravene the granting agencies' own published rules for
funding.[19] Discussion in committee is confidential; participants are
asked to disclose nothing of what is said. In some agencies, committee members vote by secret ballot so that no individual member will
know the final rating of a project.

The "peers" in peer review are chosen through various processes,
but most involve some degree of "incest," since peer-review members
are asked to suggest names for their replacements when their term ex-
pires. Recently, a medical researcher described the operation of an "old
boys' network" at the Medical Research Council of Canada, suggesting that the network acts to discourage projects conducted by outsiders.[20] It has been said that projects are approved almost automatically when the name of the researcher is well known to the committee,
while those from unknowns are examined more critically.

Similar problems have been described in the United States. Two
researchers examined the qualifications of peers who reviewed their
applications to the Tobacco Related Disease Research Program and
to the Agency for Health Care Policy and Research and concluded
that they were not true peers, in that they had few or no publications in the relevant areas. The researchers charged that the grants
were refused because the committee did not want to support policy
examination, despite the agencies' own guidelines.[21]

Funding agencies also request opinions on grant proposals from
outside experts in the specific field of the applicant. Scientists know
those working in their field and are usually familiar with the work
they are asked to evaluate. In the main, at least in Canada, "outside"
evaluations have a tendency to be positive, since evaluators often
refuse to evaluate an application when they do not like the applicant
or the work being proposed. (More rarely, evaluators seize the opportunity to block funding for a rival or for someone who belongs to another school of thought.) The committee often discounts outside evaluations and relies on its own judgment. I have been on committees
where almost all the evaluations of certain applications were positive,
but the committee unanimously rejected the applications anyway.

Thus, a great deal of power is in the hands of the committee. Often
members are assigned to review 20 or more 20- to 150-page applications, usually from outside their immediate area of expertise.[22]
On what basis do they choose among these projects? One basis for

evaluation has been simply to see whether the applicants have followed the rules and canons accepted for research in their field. Someone in our research group recently had an unhappy but enlightening experience when she sat on a government agency peer-review committee that judged environmental and occupational health projects. She was the only biologist and the only person with any experience in toxicology or any contact with workers. The 10 other participants were all from medical faculties: six members with training in epidemiology and biostatistics and four physicians in clinical practice. She was struck by the inability of this group to understand important parameters involved in environmental health research. In particular, any mention of pre- or nonpathological phenomena was met with disdain. Committee members wanted a clearly defined, well-diagnosed medical condition to relate to well-isolated, single factors in the work environment. They did not seem to realize that few sick people stay in the workplace. The committee members, not all of whom were actually involved in research and none of whom had done research in a workplace, wanted a perfection of study design that was unattainable in most studies of real phenomena.

Often, in addition to judging the proposal, committee members will try to get a feeling for the reputation of the researcher and the chance that the proposed work will succeed. This process is somewhat circular. Scientists of higher prestige will be more likely to be funded, but prestige is also a result of funding. A recent article in the *Journal of the American Medical Association* observed: "Institutional prestige was determined according to the monetary value of research and training grants and contracts funded by the National Institutes of Health."[23]

Because committees have been criticized for giving too much importance to the reputations of applicants and their institutions, a lot of emphasis has been placed recently on making the process "more objective" by the use of citation studies and "impact factors" to decide on the quality of research. Particularly energetic committee members may check in available databases to see whether the applicant's work has been cited by others, and how many times. The journals in which the applicant has published are also rated: their "impact factor" is calculated as the average number of times any article in the given journal is cited by anyone during the current year. A good journal is one that is cited often, and a good applicant is one who publishes in good journals and is cited often. Despite the apparent objectivity of this method, a case can be made that impact factors and citation studies reflect less the quality of science than the efficiency of scientists in making their work known, in making contacts with important journals, and in working in popular, well-traveled areas. Thus, these "objective" techniques may be just another way of determining whether the applicants are hooked into an "old boys' network" and whether they follow the crowd in their methods and interests.

What Happens at Scientific Meetings

Scientists meet each other and share their findings in scientific meetings. These are gatherings lasting two to five days where researchers present papers for discussion by others. In biomedical fields, major employers and chemical, pharmaceutical, and insurance companies are well represented, while unions are almost absent. Part of the reason for this is the cost: registration usually runs in the hundreds of dollars, and the meetings take place in expensive hotels.

In my opinion it is in these meetings more than anywhere that reputations are made. Scientists rise through the ranks by first having a paper accepted for presentation, then by being nominated to moderate a discussion or preside over a workshop, and finally by being an invited speaker. The road opens to being a member of a peer-review committee and eventually the editor of a learned journal. It is very hard for a committee to refuse funding to a scientist who has reached this level.

Meetings can be difficult for women, since men are usually in a numerical majority and always in an overwhelming majority among those in power.[24] I remember a meeting of the Environmental Mutagenesis Society where I was one of two or three women (among hundreds of people) in charge of my own university research program. The other women were students (the majority), employees of private enterprise, or subordinates to a male laboratory head. It is not surprising that I did not feel the male scientists took women seriously. A very few women successfully navigated between the hazards of being seen as young, cute, and subject to sexual harassment and those of being businesslike or old and therefore uninteresting, but most could not avoid both Scylla and Charybdis and were ignored.

The American Public Health Association and a few other professional organizations have formed women's caucuses and other support structures that are very useful to women scientists. They greatly increase women's sense of comfort at scientific meetings. However, many women scientists are reluctant to participate in structures that will label them as women for fear that their work will be taken less seriously.

How Papers Get Published

When researchers feel that they have a contribution to make to scientific knowledge, they write an article and submit it for publication in a learned journal. The editors of the journal then send the paper for "peer review" to other scientists in the same area of expertise, who write an opinion on the quality of the work and on whether it is sufficiently interesting to be published. The editors decide whether or not to publish after consulting the reviewers' opinions.

In the natural sciences, the paper states the intended contribution, the data that have been gathered together with the methods used to collect them, and the interpretation. In theory, the paper must contain sufficient information so that any other qualified scientist could reproduce the research and come to the same conclusions. In practice, peer reviewers almost never repeat the research. Instead, they judge the methods from their own knowledge of the field, look for flaws and omissions in the data-gathering process, and decide whether the interpretations given are justified by the data.

This practice is meant to guarantee that published information corresponds to the truth about the phenomenon the scientist has been studying. However, several factors can make the judgment of scientific quality less than objective. First, any process in which human beings judge each other's work is subject to bias. Having several reviewers comment on each paper is meant to prevent individual bias from being too important, but this would be effective only if the same biases were not common to many reviewers. Also, not all papers are in fact reviewed by several people.

I have participated in the process as reviewer and reviewee, and often only one reviewer's opinion was effectively available. Scientists are busy, and will often dismiss or accept a paper with one or two sentences or will neglect to review the paper. In practice, a thoughtful, well-presented opinion by one reviewer will suffice even if the others have not done their job or have expressed contrary opinions without much explanation. As pressures mount in the academic world and scientists have less time for unpaid work that never appears on a CV, this source of inaccuracy will become more and more important.

Moreover, the review process is not usually "blind." That is, the reviewers are almost always told the names and institutions of those whose papers they are reviewing, and they have a tendency to favor people from high-prestige institutions.[25]

The dominance of males may affect the judgment of women's work. That is, males "inside the establishment" of medical researchers can block women's access by judging their work more negatively. In a sample year, the *Journal of the American Medical Association* used eight male (five full-time) and five female (two full-time) editors, with 2,452 male and 930 female reviewers. It received papers from 1,767 male and 561 female authors. A detailed analysis showed that male reviewers recommended rejecting a disproportionate number of articles from female authors, while there was a tendency for female reviewers to reject more articles from males. The excess of male reviewers therefore affected women's success rate.[26]

Conclusion

My argument here is not that scientists are more closed-minded or biased than anyone else. In most cases the review process is an important stage of quality control in scientific funding and publishing. It can also be a form of censorship from within the profession. As I show later in this book, a process that is intended to keep errors of fact and judgment from being published is not well suited to preventing omissions, or questioning unwritten or written rules of the game, or encouraging input from new groups.

Heads of research laboratories are usually white, middle-class men. We have seen that several mechanisms operate to maintain this composition of the institutions involved in biomedical science; at the level of hiring, funding, and presentation of research results. Although men and women who have succeeded in becoming scientists share a common culture, that culture may be influenced by the fact that most scientists are men.

The culture is not only male but also far from familiar with the experience and environment of the working class. Financial and cultural barriers limit access to the ranks of scientists, and the demands of scientific research restrict social contacts and community involvement. Thus, scientists involved in generating biomedical knowledge have few contacts outside their social class.

We do not know the distribution of publishing occupational health scientists according to sex,[27] class, and race, but we can suppose that the attributes of occupational health scientists are those of health scientists in general. Although several of the pioneers in occupational health in North America were women (Alice Hamilton, Harriet Hardy, and Jeanne Stellman come to mind), at this writing (1997) the scientific council of the Québec Institute for Research in Occupational Health and Safety is entirely male, and the U.S. National Institute for Occupational Safety and Health has only two women on its 11-member Board of Scientific Counselors.

The class composition of occupational health science is important because scientists are asked to produce data that, in the last analysis, will support workers in their demands for prevention of, or compensation for employment-related injury. In North America, research and practice in occupational health have been conditioned by the workers' compensation system. Accidents and illnesses covered by workers' compensation are not subject to other recourse.[28] The compensation system is an insurance-like set-up paid into by employers. Employers' payments, like other insurance premiums, are affected by their workers' rates of compensation, as well as by the overall level of compensation paid. Thus, employers have a collective and individual interest in limiting the number of compensable conditions, and the workers have an interest in rapid identification of hazards.[29]

We must ask whether the skewed composition of the population of scientists influences the culture of scientific institutions and, eventually, the health of workers. When occupational health science deals with issues of life and death to women workers, are there practices that reflect bias and that keep their problems from being recognized?

5

"Rigor": The Scientific Basis for Funding

■ ■ ■

In this chapter and the next, I present some rules for the conduct of occupational health research, drawn from textbooks and comments on grant requests or submissions to learned journals.[1] These rules are quite important in the decision to accept or deny compensation to women workers because they are used to decide whether to perform studies relevant to their case and whether to reject or accept scientific evidence during hearings. Even cold, clear rules for statistical significance can conceal class- or sex-biased assumptions that can put workers at a disadvantage. Seemingly arcane debates on control groups and dependent variables are important in decisions to deny compensation to victims of occupational hazards. What passes for scientific rigor among researchers may in fact be as much a symptom of racism, sexism, or class bias as a burnt cross or a thrown stone, and may do as much psychological and physical harm.

This is not to deny that scientific rigor is important. Scientists have evolved techniques to weigh evidence and design studies. Usually these techniques help build the knowledge base on which decisions can be made. Sometimes, especially when there is a political agenda, a strong interest group, or fear of conflict, these techniques can be used to delay information gathering. Thus, as others have pointed out, rigor in research should not be guaranteed by the observance of rules, but rather considered as a global judgment on the whole process of research.[2]

Following a hypothetical research project through the peer-review process will allow us to see how the rules are applied. Since there has not yet been a study specifically on the occupational health of waitresses, one of the top 10 professions of U.S. and Canadian women, let us suppose that we want to know whether waitresses are especially likely to have sore feet, swollen legs, or other symptoms of discomfort in their lower limbs. Note that discomfort is not disease, and that many symptoms are necessarily experienced only subjectively.

Let us further suppose that we have been asked to identify conditions causing discomfort by a union representing waitresses at a particular restaurant chain. The union would like to know whether the limit on the number of hours worked without a rest break should be changed, and whether it should negotiate specific conditions for the rest break, or a limit to the number of tables for which each waitress is responsible during busy periods, or both. Since waitresses are paid partly by tips, they are reluctant to limit the number of tables they serve. Union representatives are also curious about some design modifications introduced by a new architect. The union would like us to administer a questionnaire to all 500 waitresses at the 50 restaurants in the chain.

Accepting the Research Topic

AGENCY ACCEPTANCE AND RELEVANCE

We first submit our application to a granting organization that will decide whether it is admissible. In Canada, a proposal about the health of waitresses could be submitted to a federal or provincial granting agency in the field of medical research or a specialized provincial agency working on occupational health. In my province, the specialized agency might immediately reject the waitress proposal without sending it for peer review, since waitresses are not in the priority groups defined by the Occupational Health and Safety Commission, and presence in the priority groups is one of the explicit criteria used for determining acceptance of research proposals. In fact, women make up only 15 percent of those in the priority groups, which are composed of miners, construction workers, chemical factory workers, and others who have a high rate of compensated occupational injury. Although some groups outside the priority groups have been studied in the past, there is an increasing tendency to study only those groups that are often compensated. Since waitresses are rarely unionized, they make few claims for compensation.

Health problems not leading to claims for compensation are not a priority either. Research is concentrated on injuries and illnesses that cause a worker in a legitimate, paid occupation to lose time and have a clearly defined cause, such as accidents among construction workers and miners. Health problems like lower limb discomfort, which makes workers uncomfortable or unhappy but does not lead to lost time from paid employment, will not appear in the occupational health statistics. The effects of women's unpaid work are not considered to be occupational health problems,[3] and occupational AIDS research in North America has concentrated on health care workers rather than on the much more heavily exposed sex workers.

Even severe menstrual pain related to workplace conditions does not lead to claims for compensation, since compensation is not set up to fund noncontinuous absences (a day or so a month because of pain rather than an absence of several weeks following a fall). There- fore, of nine research topics we submitted to the provincial health and safety funding agency, only the one on menstrual problems was excluded from review on the grounds of insufficient relevance.

The lack of compensated accidents and illnesses in women's jobs probably accounts for the fact that 73 percent of the projects funded by the Québec Institute for Research in Occupational Health and Safety during its first six years involved no women workers.[4] In a neighboring province, Ontario, the head of the Industrial Disease Standards Panel found that there had been only one investigation into a female-dominated workplace during the panel's ten-year life.[5]

In fact, few women's jobs have been studied by any researchers in occupational health. Women's health, women's work, and the occu- pational health of male workers are all extensively studied, but oc- cupational health has not usually been analyzed by gender. The 1995 issue of the Canadian government publication *Women in Canada* contains 177 pages of statistical tables on women, covering family status, income, occupation, health status, and more. There is, however, no information on occupational accidents or illnesses.

The *Atlas of Health and Working Conditions by Occupation* com- piled by Dutch researchers contains data on 129 men's occupations and only 19 women's occupations. When the scientists responsible suggested to other scientists that their atlas could be used to identify dangerous conditions, they gave no reason for the discrepancy. They added, "The method will be demonstrated by presenting an occupational ranking list of 129 occupations with male employees on the item 'back ache complaints.'" Again, no reason was given for excluding women, many of whose occupations cause back problems.[6]

Greenberg and Dement[7] reviewed the literature and found a large excess of studies of occupational disease involving only males. A well-documented example is the field of occupational cancer. Zahm found that of 1,233 cancer studies published in 1971–1990 in the eight major occupational health journals, only 14 percent presented analyses of data on white women and only 10 percent on nonwhite women.[8] Almost all of the studies on gastric cancer reviewed by Stock[9] excluded women (although one found an increase in female mortality among jewelers). The choice of jobs for study helps explain the exclusion: miners, refinery workers, and foundry workers are almost always men.

Women are sometimes eliminated to make samples uniform, in order to "simplify" the analysis. In 1988, Block and her colleagues published a study of cancer among phosphate-exposed workers in a fertilizer plant.[10] Among 3,400 workers, 173 women were eliminated with the sole comment that "females accounted for only about 5% of the study population, and were not included in these analyses." However, the 38 male workers in the drying and shipping department were not considered too small a population for study: a significant rise in their death rate was noted.

Women may be eliminated because data on them are lacking. For example, a Canadian study of the effects of exposures to agricultural chemicals was forced to eliminate women, since only the husband of a farm family was identified as a farmer in most provincial records.[11] Also, many death certificates contain no information on a woman's profession, in part because once a woman has retired she may be considered to be a housewife.

Another reason that occupational health research underestimates the problems in women's jobs is that a major and growing problem, stress-related mental illness, is not easily recognized as having an occupational origin. Because of its low rate of compensation among men and women,[12] work-related mental illness has received little attention; only 3 percent of the 1985–1989 budget of the Québec granting agency went for studies including mental health. This is a circular problem, since government agencies may not want to fund research that could lead to compensation. In addition, women's claims for compensation for problems caused by stress are refused in the United States[13] and Canada[14] much more often than men's, so occupational stress problems in women's jobs would probably be understudied even if studies on mental health problems were initiated.

MEDICINE, PATHOLOGY, AND WOMEN'S JOBS

The proposal on waitresses would probably be accepted for review by one of the purely medical research agencies. It would then be sent to a peer-review committee. These committees are responsible for deciding on whether research on a particular subject will be funded.

Naturally enough, medical research committees decide on the relevance of research topics on medical grounds. They have often limited their interest to *pathologies*, that is, to defined and diagnosed disease entities. The pathologies may be studied in humans or animals, but they must be diseases with clear diagnoses. For example, because only symptoms were considered, a recent, careful study of determinants of hand and wrist pain among grocery cashiers performing repetitive movements was dismissed with the comment: "It is highly unlikely that the superficial survey question[identifying a high level of pain] truly identifies carpal tunnel syndrome."[15] Lower limb discomfort would probably meet a similar fate. Sore feet may be painful, but they do not constitute pathology. Even swollen legs, an indicator of a circulatory problem, are not a disease.

In our experience, studies of indicators, signs, or symptoms of deterioration in physical or mental states are usually rejected. The reasoning may be that the presence of pathology guarantees that the problem examined is worthy of serious consideration. The process of diagnosis itself increases the probability that a condition will be carefully defined. However, a requirement for diagnosed pathology may be premature when studying women's occupational health. Since the aggressors present in women's traditional work have been understudied, and the effects on women workers of even well-established conditions are often unknown, identification of occupational disease in women's work is embryonic. For example, bank tellers told us of unusual-looking and painful red streaks on their hands, which they attribute to handling money. A literature search revealed one article on nickel allergy among cashiers,[16] but no other reference to skin disease among those handling money. It may be years before sufficient research enables us to decide whether to define the bank tellers' problems as an industrial disease.

The requirement for pathology has a further consequence. It forces the researcher to consider events that are rare among populations still at work. If waitresses suffer twice as often from pathology related to the circulatory system, perhaps there will be 10 cases of heart disease among the 500 actively working waitresses, compared with 5 in 500 among women of comparable age. This difference will probably not be picked up in our proposed study, given that not all the 500 waitresses will participate, and most of them will have worked for under a year, too short a time to develop detectable pathology.[17] In addition, those with heart disease may no longer be working or may have changed to less demanding jobs. We will have trouble seeing a statistical difference between waitresses and other women because there will only be a few cases of heart disease in each group. This requirement for pathology is a particular obstacle to identifying women's occupational health problems because women work in smaller workplaces.[18]

The waitresses would also like to know whether they should slow down during pregnancy. Very little research has been done on problems of working women (as opposed to problems of fetuses) during pregnancy (see Chapter 10.) A French colleague, not subject to North American research standards, was able to find funds to study hypertension during pregnancy as an indicator of difficult working conditions. She found that women were more likely to become hypertensive if they did heavy, noisy work, but her findings were rejected by North American journals on the grounds that hypertension during pregnancy might be a temporary problem and not pathology. Her work was finally published in French in a European journal, where it is inaccessible to most researchers.

Many more waitresses will have lower limb discomfort than will have heart disease, so lower limb discomfort could be compared between occupational groups. In our study, we will probably be required by the granting agency to find diagnosed pathologies at the origin of the lower limb discomfort, increasing the cost of the study and decreasing the number of cases that will be found.

Pathology must be assessed by a physician. A colleague's request for money to study warts, a common problem of poultry slaughterhouse workers, was initially refused because she proposed to ask the workers to count their warts. The committee replied that the workers were not competent to count them and that this should be done by a medical practitioner, even though workers, with up to a hundred warts on their hands, were quite familiar with the appearance of warts. (Warts are now, in part because of her efforts, recognized as an industrial disease of poultry workers.)

The requirement for pathology is sometimes extremely stringent. My colleagues and I have proposed many studies using biological indicators of prepathological conditions. For example, we have measured the number of changes ("mutations") in a metabolic gene in white blood cells as an indicator of exposure to radiation or chemicals. We examined cells of 58 nuclear power plant workers and found that they had from 54 to 533 genetically changed ("mutant") cells per 10 million white blood cells, depending on their radiation exposure.[19] True, mutations in white blood cells cannot affect offspring—the genes important for future generations are the ones in egg and sperm cells. And mutations in metabolic genes do not cause cancer, so these mutations cannot cause cancer. Therefore the test does not detect pathology. What such tests can do is detect biological effects of workplace agents before harm is done.[20] They have, however, been harshly criticized by peer-review committees because their relationship with pathology is indirect.

Our proposal for studying waitresses will probably be rejected because sore feet and discomfort in the lower limbs are not pathologies. Despite this, we will continue with our example in order to look at some other problems involved in funding research in women's occupational health.

"SUFFICIENT EVIDENCE TO JUSTIFY A STUDY"

We might have to be able to show that waitresses have a problem with lower limb discomfort even before doing the study. A very important criterion for funding a study is, paradoxically, a demonstration that there is sufficient evidence to show that a given exposure–effect link exists. This tendency is particularly pronounced in Canada, where many researchers expect scientific questions to be generated first in the United States. Our applications for grants to study the effects of manganese and styrene on chromosomes were refused on the grounds that insufficient evidence linked these substances with these effects; the same teams were given large amounts of money to study neurotoxic effects of the same substances in the same workers, since some evidence existed for these effects. Informal comments from grant reviewers mentioned that the men involved had almost all finished their families and that nothing could be gained from upsetting them without sufficient evidence that there was a problem. Grants were given to the same teams for studying the exhaustively well-known effects of ionizing radiation on chromosomes, on the basis that well-characterized biological systems provided a better opportunity for studying genetic effects.

Women have been eliminated from studies on the ground that their problems have not been demonstrated. One million-dollar government-supported study related cancers to a huge number of occupational exposures. When we asked the researcher why his study excluded women, he replied, "It's a cost–benefit analysis; women don't get many occupational cancers." He did not react when we suggested that his argument was circular, nor when we pointed out that for women taxpayers, the cost–benefit ratio of a study excluding them was infinitely high. The resulting papers, published in peer-reviewed journals, made no attempt to justify the exclusion of women.[21] Recently, under pressure from women's health advocates, a number of occupational risk factors for cancer have been demonstrated—for chemists, workers in drug companies, beauticians, and cosmetologists, among others.[22]

A cost–benefit argument was also used to reject a study proposing to examine difficulties of women in nontraditional jobs using tools and equipment designed for larger people. These acceptances and refusals may also be motivated by the fact that government and employers do not lose money by re-establishing a known causal link, since they will not be asked to spend extra money on prevention and compensation. In the rather puzzling phrase of a member of the scientific council of a granting agency: "We don't want to spend our money preventing problems that haven't even happened yet!"

IS THIS HEALTH PROBLEM REAL?

The "reality" of health problems is an especially important issue in occupational health because decisions about whether to fund a study and eventually to compensate work-related diseases or to improve working conditions are often based on a cost analysis. If a problem will lead to so many compensated cases that it is cheaper to eliminate it, then working conditions may be improved. Thus, a ventilation system was installed in one plant after 27 years, not when the company was made aware that its dust was radioactive, but when workers became sensitized to the results of exposure to the dust.[23] With women workers, it is possible to delay recognition of a health hazard by using sexist denials of women's problems. Complaints of workers, especially women or minority workers, about their own health may be ignored or treated as the individual's psychological problem.

So the waitress study may be rejected because the waitresses' complaints of sore legs and feet are not illnesses and because waitresses' reports may not be credible to the peer-review committee.

Should Waitresses Be Studied?

Would the waitresses otherwise be considered an interesting group to study? Perhaps, but it is then hard to explain why a search of the Medline database did not turn up a specific study of waitresses' health.[24] This may be because there is high turnover among waitresses. As mentioned above, it is hard to associate pathologies with short-term employment, so scientists may be understandably reluctant to study the pathologies of waitresses. The neglect of this group may also be due to their social distance from occupational health scientists. How else can we explain the fact that nurses and hospital workers are the most often studied women workers?[25]

Many scientists are reluctant to study any human beings because of the technical difficulties involved and the inability to control the behavior of the experimental subjects. When we proposed a study of mutations in the cells of radiology technicians, we were criticized for proposing the use of the tests with cells from workers. Several of our colleagues made remarks like, "Why not do it with Chinese hamster ovary cells instead?" In fact, Chinese hamster ovary cells are much easier to work with than workers' cells. And testing the effects of chemicals on isolated animal cells is much more likely to yield clear, unequivocal results, because the effects are not complicated by the organs and organ systems of a complete organism. But Chinese hamster ovary cells are unlikely to furnish the answers to all our questions about the effects of working conditions on workers, or yield results useful for judging compensation claims.

Finding an "Unexposed" Control Group

Suppose half the waitresses have lower limb discomfort. Is this a large proportion? Compared with whom? Epidemiology textbooks suggest two types of comparisons.[26] The "case-control" study divides people into well and not-well, and looks at the proportions of workers exposed and not-exposed to a risk factor. We would have to examine the people with lower limb discomfort in the population and see whether an especially large number are waitresses. The "cohort" study divides workers into those exposed and not-exposed to a risk factor (such as being a waitress), and looks at the proportions of well and not-well among them. In this type of study we see whether waitresses are more likely than some control group to have lower limb discomfort. The relevant other variables are "adjusted for" (are the waitresses and controls the same age, is one group more likely to wear comfortable shoes?). If the associations between the exposure and the health effect are statistically significant after adjustment, a relationship is established.

Our proposal is a cohort study, so we must compare waitresses with another group. In order to divide workers into exposed and unexposed, most peer-review systems will insist on "reference" populations, controls who differ from workers only by not being exposed to the agent under study. They wish to be sure that the waitresses "really" are especially likely to have lower limb discomfort, compared with an "unexposed" group.

The apparently simple requirement for a comparable unexposed population poses the question of what is comparable and what is unexposed. Thus, we must find a group of 500 or more women who are not waitresses but are comparable in other respects. We could compare the prevalence of lower limb discomfort among waitresses with that among saleswomen or supermarket cashiers, because they have similar incomes and educational levels. The fact that they also may have lower limb discomfort does not mean that waitresses' problems are not due to their working conditions. Waitresses, saleswomen, and cashiers have similar working conditions and also spend long hours on their feet. To satisfy the reviewers, we would have to think of a low-paid service job with easy physical requirements. Does such a group exist?

Our own inclination would be to compare our waitresses with each other in order to study the effects of specific working conditions. That is, we would compare waitresses who work different numbers of hours or different days in the week. We would categorize restaurants according to the size of the clientele, the number of tables per waitress, and the possibility of sitting down while on break. However, many reviewers object to using an "internal" control group. For example, we presented a study in which 720 poultry processing workers reported in detail their work schedules and their menstrual cycles.[27] We found that those (about half) who had variable schedules had more irregular cycles than those who went to work and left at the same time every day. Workers' menstrual cycles also were affected by the cold temperatures and fast workspeed in this industry. Reviewers criticized the study because we did not compare poultry processing workers with workers in some other industry: "Menstrual cycle abnormalities were studied retrospectively . . . in 726 women working in poultry slaughterhouses or canning factories. The most serious problem with this study is that a control population was not studied." Seven years before, a paper written by my CINBIOSE colleagues Donna Mergler and Nicole Vézina on determinants of menstrual pain had been rejected out of hand for the same reason. They were persistent and courageous enough to win a fight with the editor and have the paper published. In our case, we were lucky enough to have an intelligent editor who published the study without a fight; others have not always been so persistent or so lucky.

Such criticisms represent reviewers' belief that some factory environments involve no relevant risk factors. They wanted us to find a group of women working in a factory in the same region who were never exposed to irregular schedules, cold, or a fast workspeed. In fact women factory workers are always exposed to some toxic factors, and the reviewers' demands are evidence that they have little notion of what most factory jobs are like. It is hard for us to imagine the control group these referees are asking for. If we compare waitresses with others who work on their feet, we minimize the differences due to working on one's feet. Since there are no similar jobs where waitresses work sitting down, what is the appropriate comparison?

Determination of Exposure

Determination of exposure is a key element in occupational health studies. If we want to know why waitresses have health problems, we need to know what their jobs involve. In particular, in view of our hypothesis about hours spent on their feet, we need to know how many hours they spend standing and walking.

JOB TITLE

The exposure measurement most commonly used in occupational health studies is job title. The reason for this is the need for large populations. It would be very expensive to send scientists to study the details of working conditions for large groups of people, but job title can be easily recorded.

Information on women's job titles is notoriously inaccurate. Studies of mortality by profession are hampered because, as noted above, many death certificates do not contain information on the woman's profession. In addition, women's job titles appear to be less precise descriptors than those of men. The fact that 52 percent of women, but only 32 percent of men, are in the 18 top jobs for their respective sex can be interpreted in two ways. Usually researchers say that women's choice of jobs is more restricted. As the numbers of men and women in the workforce approach equality, this interpretation may be superseded by another. It may be that more attention has been given to job content in men's than in women's jobs. If secretaries and stenographers are lumped together, why not carpenters and construction workers? Why not farmers and farm workers? Why not motor vehicle mechanics and industrial mechanics? Or, to put it another way, why lump secretaries who work in pools with private secretaries of top executives? Why not separate secretaries in factories, exposed to fumes and dusts, from those in hospitals, exposed to infectious diseases?

The fact that women and men are treated differently in the workplace makes it inappropriate to assume that women and men with the same job title have the same working conditions. Using job title as a proxy for exposure may introduce inaccuracy and bias according to the gender of the worker. Hsairi and colleagues[28] used expert estimates derived from job titles to classify workers in 13,568 jobs as exposed or not exposed to dust. Workers' reports of their own exposure and self-reports of symptoms of dust exposure (e.g., difficulty breathing, asthma) were correlated with experts' ratings. Self-reports of symptoms were better correlated with self-reports of exposure than with experts' estimates of exposure. Expert estimates were significantly closer to men's self-reports than women's. The authors interpret these results as implying a "better perception" of exposure by the men, but it is also possible that experts' estimates of exposure according to job title are based on experience with male job-holders. Females in these jobs may be assigned to different tasks.

Similarly, workers are often divided into groups according to the department they work in, but these divisions may or may not correspond to actual work content. In her study of poultry slaughterhouse workers, Vézina points out that cold exposure is variable within a department, depending on drafts, on whether the hands are in water, and on how much the worker moves around.[29]

In the case of our waitresses, we cannot use job title as an indicator of exposure, since all our waitresses have the same job title. We need to know their exposure to the risk factors of time on their feet, number of breaks, and so on. An obstacle to finding this out is cost: it would be very expensive for the research team to observe the work of 500 waitresses at a variety of times of day, days of the week, and seasons of the year.

OTHER MEASURES OF EXPOSURE

Research instruments derived with all-male populations are sometimes used without further validation on female populations, a clear source of bias. Examples include the well-known Karasek questionnaire on job demands[30] and biomechanical testing done with instruments validated on male populations.[31]

In order to measure social class, researchers often use a husband's occupational prestige scales or social class scale to ascribe a score to the wife.[32] This causes problems when data on occupational health are adjusted for social class, as is often done.[33]

One way to ascertain exposure has been to ask the workers. Several studies suggest that worker reports are a good source of information on exposure[34] as well as health status.[35] This is a possible solution to the problem mentioned above: the length of time a team of ergonomists would require to unearth all the potential risk factors for lower limb discomfort. We could save some of this time by asking the waitresses via a questionnaire or interviews. However, this source of information has been criticized as leading to bias. Scientists have suggested that workers may have an ax to grind, and some researchers think that people with a given disease or condition will overreport exposure to whatever they think may have caused it. This tendency is known as "recall bias"[36] and is invoked whenever interview or questionnaire data are used. Although scientists are not sure that recall bias exists, [37] worker reports of exposure are not usually accepted as a good source of information.

Several researchers have compared information from scientists with that given by workers.[38] Wiktorin and colleagues found that workers' evaluations of some parameters were close to scientists'. In particular, information on heavy weights and complicated movements agreed more than information on light weights and simple movements.[39] Saurel-Cubizolles and her colleagues compared information furnished by workers and occupational health physicians on environmental conditions in poultry processing. The level of agreement varied, but was fairly good.[40]

I know of only one study dealing with the quality of information furnished by employers, another potential source. Behrens and colleagues compared health information in employer reports to the U.S. government and that obtained in interviews with workers. They concluded that the employers underestimated the prevalence of back pain, hand discomfort, and dermatitis.[41]

For our study of waitresses, we will maximize our chances of getting grants if we assess exposure status by job title, compare the waitresses with some other group, and assess pathologies by medical examination. However, our precision would be better, in my opinion, if we compared waitresses with each other, using their perceptions of time spent on their feet. Even better, we could ask them to identify "average" workdays and train them to use pedometers to measure the number of steps taken on that workday. We could assess health problems by consulting waitresses through their union, compiling a list of health problems with a representative group of waitresses and then asking the whole pool of waitresses to use the list to report their problems. These methods would probably not be considered to be rigorous.

"A Funny Atmosphere"

Union involvement[42] would be key to the success of our study. We need the union because it is the best source of information on workers' health problems. Union representatives have an overview of health conditions, since they are in constant contact with workers and have no interest in minimizing or concealing problems. We want to consult the union at the beginning of a study when we are seeking a group of representative waitresses in order to gain a global understanding of the job. For example, in our study of bank tellers, the union assembled for us a group of bank tellers assorted as to family situation as well as such bank branch characteristics as size, number of bank robberies, and the age, ethnicity, and financial situation of the clientele. Bank management would probably have used different criteria, since they would not necessarily be aware of their importance in determining workload. Managers might have used criteria that had more to do with the financial performance of bank branches or the age of the buildings. They certainly were not aware of the importance of the number of bank robberies for tellers.

Finally, we need the union to help distribute the questionnaire and follow up its completion. Unions have structures that permit rapid contact with all members. We have used these structures, not only to distribute questionnaires, but to give explanations to large numbers of workers in widely spread out regions. Contrary to what many people believe, this practice may minimize certain kinds of bias. Most unions have no interest in exaggerating the health problems of their workers, since they have enough battles to fight. They readily collaborate in giving explanations such as: "Everyone should fill out the questionnaire because if only people with health problems fill it out, then we will overestimate the problems. We might waste time solving problems that never existed when we could be working on problems that affect everyone." Unions have expertise in explaining this kind of subtle scientific point in accessible language.

If we cite union collaboration as a strong point of our approach, we may never be funded. Probably the most frequent question we hear from scientists is about our relationship with unions.[43] Whenever workers are involved in efforts to improve their working conditions, this is thought to be evidence that they will fake symptoms to gain their point. Our work has been criticized on these grounds even when elaborate study designs are used to take these factors into account, and even when the patterns of physiological change are so specific to the toxic effect that the worker would have to be a specialist in order to produce them. We have often heard rumors that discussion of our grant applications is fraught with references to our close relationship with trade unions. The fact that our studies are often initiated by workers is thought to lead to bias.

In several cases that we know about, this was a reason for refusing our grant requests. A colleague who had been part of a committee that refused a grant request from a member of CINBIOSE explained the decision to me as follows: "She works for [sic] unions, doesn't she? Of course this didn't influence our decision, but it made a funny atmosphere around the table." Another colleague told me after a grant request had been refused that I should not have mentioned unions "all over" my curriculum vitae. I looked, and there was exactly one reference to a joint union-university publication in a 20-page vita.

Many published studies were initiated or inspired by employers, and the major granting agencies have put forward programs for university–industry collaborative research. Bias does not seem to be as much of a problem for these programs. In fact, the capacity to attract corporate funds gives prestige to university researchers.

The treatment of absenteeism in the occupational health literature exemplifies the field's support for the employers' perspectives. In the scientific literature, absenteeism is much more often considered as a problem behavior than as a result of an occupational health and safety problem or poor working conditions.[44] A government researcher illustrated a published discussion of absenteeism with a picture of two workers stretched out on the grass in the sun![45]

How do we explain the pro-employer bias in scientific research, even that sponsored by governments? Does it occur because scientists feel far removed in sex, social class, or both from seamstresses, hairdressers, and factory workers?

New Tendencies

Readers may think at this point that they are getting a double message. I describe many obstacles that slow the production of knowledge about women's occupational health, yet many of my counterexamples are taken from funded CINBIOSE studies and the published literature. If it is so hard to get a study funded that will produce information useful to women workers (or indeed any workers), how is it that we and some others are able to do such studies? Why is there a growing scientific literature on the value of consulting workers, the causes of women's health problems, and the importance of good exposure assessment? The answer to this question is that feminists, workers, and worker-friendly scientists have been able to find some holes in the system and develop ways to finance and publish alternative research. Some of these are described later in this book.

In general, it is still difficult to fund a study on women workers' health problems. The fact that few studies exist creates an image of women's work as safe, which in turn militates against funding to study it.

6

Constructing Scientific Knowledge

■ ■ ■

Interpreting scientific results is a social process that depends on the point of view of the researcher. If researchers found that waitresses are more likely than waiters to experience lower limb discomfort, they could interpret that result in the light of biological characteristics (stronger, more resistant waiters), psychological differences (complaining waitresses), or contrasting working conditions (waitresses in restaurants with higher customer-to-server ratio). Scientists may ascribe different importance to analyzing the three types of determinants. The three interpretations have very different implications for addressing the problem. If we think waitresses have lower limb discomfort because they are weak or "whiny," a solution might be to hire men instead. If we think waitresses have lower limb discomfort when they work too fast, a solution might be to hire more waitresses. Scientific interpretations are dependent on the type of analysis that is done, but they also come from the scientists' ways of looking at the data.

Scientists, like other humans, bring to their jobs their own point of view. This may lead to different approaches to a problems like waitresses' lower limb discomfort. Because of their experience or upbringing, they may know food servers as friends or only as instruments for providing food. They may harbor beliefs about women's likelihood to complain. Endocrinologists may think in terms of hormones, whereas chromosomal predispositions may come to a geneticist's mind. Although certain procedures are used to promote objectivity in data analysis, and the scientist may be acting in perfectly good faith, no procedure can wipe out all experience and ideology from anyone's approach.

Analysis

Several procedures routinely used in data analysis lead to the underestimation of women's working conditions as determinants of their health.

ADJUSTING FOR CONFOUNDING
FACTORS; OR, SEX AS A VARIABLE

"Adjusting" for a variable while analyzing data means using a mathematical procedure to eliminate its effect. It is reasonable, for example, to adjust for smoking when examining the relationship of dust exposure to lung damage, because smoking is often an independent determinant of lung damage and might confuse the issue if those exposed to dust smoke more or less than those not exposed. We may need to add a correction factor to the lung performance of smokers before testing the relationship between dust exposure and lung damage. This procedure allows us to determine the effect of dust on the lungs while taking into account the well-established deleterious effects of smoking. Almost all epidemiological studies of occupation and health adjust for nonoccupational characteristics such as smoking, previous illness, and age.

"Overadjusting" is an error scientists make if they "adjust" for a variable that is a synonym for the exposure. This would happen if those more exposed to dust belonged to a particular ethnic group, perhaps because blacks or Hispanics were assigned more often to cleaning or maintenance. We would add a correction factor to the lung performance of the ethnic group if we thought ethnicity was the cause of their poorer lung performance. If their lungs had been damaged by a more intense exposure to dust, adjusting the data would conceal the effect of exposure. Adjusting for ethnicity would diminish the possibility of finding the true effect of the dust exposure on lung cancer.

Descriptors representing the place of people in society (gender, race, class) pose a special problem for adjustment during data analysis. They may represent higher probabilities of some biological characteristics (hormonal status, blood groups, nutritional status), but they also represent probabilities of different occupational exposures. Waitresses usually have higher levels of circulating estrogens than waiters, but they also may work in different kinds of restaurants and have different workloads. Their relaxation time after work may also be different. Adjusting for sex may be an error, if sex is a synonym for a work exposure.

Studies that examine the health of workers often find that women workers report more symptoms of poor health or psychological distress than their male counterparts. Since women and men have different exposures because of their different task assignments, it is appropriate to analyze exposure data for women and men separately before deciding whether they can be pooled. However, very many researchers adjust for gender without previous examination of the data and without considering whether gender is a surrogate for some exposure parameter such as amount of repetitive work. For example, all the studies examined in a recent review of the relationship between jobs and carpal tunnel syndrome adjusted for gender.[1] In adjusting, the authors attribute to hormonal or other woman-specific factors the fact that women have carpal tunnel syndrome more often than men. Adjusting for sex will make it less probable that an effect of women's occupations on carpal tunnel syndrome will be found.

Adjusting or treating gender as an independent variable would be appropriate only if gender were an independent determinant of poor health reports—for example, if women were weaker or complained more than men, or if the health effects had an important independent and constant contribution from sex hormones or other biological differences. Even then, it would be important to separate out the contributions of gender and working conditions, which is often not done. For example, our research at CINBIOSE has shown that if we pool data on men and women we get entirely different results than if we analyze data on the two sexes separately. By treating male and female poultry slaughterhouse workers separately, we were able to link their very different working conditions to different health effects (health-related sickness absences).[2]

CONSEQUENCES OF PROBLEMS IN
EXPOSURE ASSESSMENT AND STUDY DESIGN

At the beginning of Chapter 5, I asserted that some scientific practices were actually dangerous for workers. One of these is the blurring of exposure categories, either by improper choice of compar-

TABLE 12: Hypothetical Data on Sore Feet among Waitresses and Saleswomen

Group	Number in group	Number (%) with lower limb symptoms
Waitresses (incl. hostesses)	500	145(29%)
New restaurants	100	60 (60%)
Old restaurants	300	75 (25%)
Hostesses with chairs	100	10 (10%)
Saleswomen	500	116 (23%)
Chair	60	6(10%)
No Chair	440	110 (25%)

ison populations or by inaccurate exposure assessment. When categories are blurred, this means that the difference between "exposed" and "not exposed" groups is minimized. For example, let us suppose that waitresses who work in newer restaurants are on their feet more than those in other restaurants because the design of the newer restaurants encourages the customers to congregate at tables farther from the kitchen. If we are correct in thinking that leg problems among waitresses are caused by being on their feet, many more waitresses in new restaurants than old will report problems (see Table 12). Furthermore, let us suppose that some women called "waitresses" are in fact hostesses and cash register operators and have access to chairs. If our hypothesis is correct, few of them will have sore feet. Finally, we will also suppose that working conditions differ within our comparison group of saleswomen. A minority have chairs and rarely have sore feet.

If the comparison is made simply between waitresses and saleswomen without any further information on working conditions, no significant difference will be seen (23 percent is too close to 29 percent). The results will be reported as negative, and waitresses will not be identified as a group with lower limb problems. We will not have learned anything about the health of waitresses. If detailed information permits a comparison of the 160 people who have access to chairs with the 840 who do not, the results are highly significant; those without chairs are about three times as likely to have discomfort in the lower limbs. If the detailed information on access to chairs and restaurant design is used, we will have a much better idea of how lower limb problems are caused, including the very useful information that the new design may be responsible for more than doubling the prevalence of lower limb symptoms. So researchers' knowledge of working conditions makes all the difference to whether a study gives an accurate picture of risks to women's health.

It is fair to say that techniques used by many occupational health researchers would not permit them to identify the risks inherent in the new restaurant design. Because of the large populations used in most studies, detailed exposure information is not available. Comparisons are made by job title, a very rough exposure measurement. Thus, waitresses would be compared with saleswomen. Sometimes, as with chemical or radiation exposures, more detailed information is available. Even then, for statistical reasons, workers are categorized as "exposed" or "not exposed" to dangerous conditions. This would be all right only if researchers were familiar enough with working conditions to know that use of chairs was important. Even closer familiarity with working conditions would successfully identify those workers who had seats available but were not able to use them because of the pace of work or the design of their work station.

STATISTICS; OR, WHAT IS SIGNIFICANT

Many of the constraints preventing early recognition of industrial disease have to do with the need to obtain statistically significant results. It is the requirement for statistical significance that results in the requirement for large sample size and for simplifying data on exposure.

There is usually a rather long interval between the first doubts about particular working conditions and the final word on the exact level of risk. Initial studies may show a weak relationship between an exposure and an effect, so that scientists have had to set a standard for accepting that a relationship exists. Scientists hesitate to conclude that there is a relationship if they may be wrong. Standard scientific practice is to acknowledge that there is a risk if there is less than one chance in 20 that the observed association was due to happenstance. In other words, in order for scientists to accept that the new restaurant design causes problems for waitresses, a study must establish the hurtful effects "at the 5 percent level." This means that even if the researchers would have only two chances in 20 of being wrong if they concluded that there was a risk, the study is considered to be "negative"—that is, no risk has been demonstrated.

The risk of being wrong in concluding that there is a risk is called "alpha," and, as mentioned, it is almost always set at less than 5 percent. Thus, scientists would not consider themselves justified in asking an employer to change a workplace if there is more than a 5 percent chance they could be wrong. Furthermore, for scientists to be really sure of their conclusions, more than one study must show the same relationship. Given the small number of workers in most women's workplaces, the variations in conditions between workplaces, and the large numbers of potential hazards, it is no wonder that very few dangers have been established.[3] I still remember my surprise when a colleague, presenting the results of a million-dollar study in a meeting, rejected his only statistically significant conclusion (stating a relationship between sawdust exposure and nasal cancer), saying it needed to be confirmed. In a province where the pulp and paper industry is a major employer, it seemed to me that it was time to alert the industry to a need for prevention; for my colleague, rigorous methods required a confirmation before taking action.

This extreme prudence has been useful in epidemiology, ensuring that panic is not induced prematurely and that science advances on a sound basis. But to exposed populations, it may seem dangerous to wait until scientists are convinced. For example, people in the gay community complained that scientists waited too long before warning them of the dangers of the AIDS virus.[4]

What about the complementary risk—that of the worker being exposed to a danger that the scientist fails to identify? That risk is called "beta," and it is sometimes used to calculate the number of workers who should be involved in a study. The more people in a study, the more likely it is that a risk can be demonstrated. We may doubt that a risk of one in 10 has doubled if we find one extra cancer in a group of 10 workers, but we will certainly be entitled to suspect that something is wrong if we find 100 extra cancers among 1,000 workers.

Some scientists do not bother to calculate beta, and not all journals insist on it, although an increasing number do.[5] When beta *is* calculated, the risk of wrongly exposing workers is almost always set at 20 percent. Recall that alpha is always set at 5 percent. Thus, the burden of proof in these statistical tests is put on the side of minimizing the costs of improvements in hygiene rather than on minimizing questionable exposures. This is a political decision, but in the scientific literature it is presented as a scientific decision about "the standard level of statistical significance," and is never justified or explained.

Before a drug, cosmetic, or food product can be marketed in North America, it must undergo extensive testing on animals. Although these tests do not guarantee that these substances are safe for humans (or even for animals in their natural environment), they do show a concern for human consumers. Contrary to the situation with regard to drugs and cosmetics, no law requires employers to be sure that a new worksite condition is safe before exposing workers to it. For example, tens of thousands of women worked with video display terminals (VDTs) before the first study of VDT effects on pregnancy. Even now, no one is absolutely sure that VDTs do not pose a danger for pregnant women. Most pregnant women have not stopped working with VDTs while waiting for the evidence to come in. In this and many other cases, a decision has been made to place the burden of proof on the worker rather than on the employer. That is, an agent or condition must be proved dangerous before being removed from the workplace or the environment.[6]

Interpretation of Results

At the end of a scientific article, researchers are allowed to speculate on the meaning of their results. This very important section of the paper often reveals bias concerning women and workers.

One very common problem is that women are rarely considered as workers. As mentioned earlier, the exclusion of women from scientific studies has created a circular situation where there is evidence of health problems only among men, leading to a reluctance to study women because of an impression that not many women get occupational disease (Figure 1).

Reflecting this attitude is the suggestion that the male–female ratio in heart disease be used to identify occupational hazards.[7] This ratio was high (50 percent more men than women with heart disease) in higher social classes, leading the authors to propose: "That wives of men in social classes I and II are not at as high a risk as their husbands suggests that it is *what happens at work* that produces a risk." (emphasis added) In lower social classes, the ratio was low (three men with heart disease for every four women). Surprisingly, the authors did not conclude that the work of women in the lower social classes was more dangerous. Their interpretation then be-

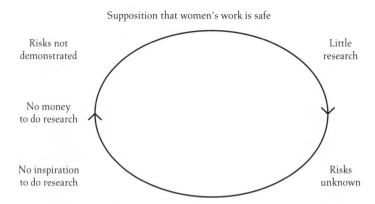

FIGURE 1: The Vicious Cycle in Research on Women and Occupational Health

came: "There may be particular risks for women married to men in unskilled jobs—*perhaps related to lifestyle*" (emphasis added). This article does not accept the possibility that women of lower social class may have occupational exposures that make it likely for them to get heart disease. The assumption is that women do not work, or at least that they do not work at dangerous jobs.[8]

Prejudice concerning gender roles is not the only one that passes peer review. Strong pro-employer bias appears in very respected journals.[9] In a study of 2,342 workers who had been compensated in 1981 for a spinal injury, records for the following three years were examined in order to see whether the worker was compensated for any subsequent spinal injury. This paper shares many of the flaws mentioned above: it adjusted for sex and age without any information on working conditions, and without justifying these choices; no exposure information at all was presented; we have no idea what job the worker was doing during the three years of follow-up.

The authors found that the recurrence was less likely when the initial absence was shorter. Their discussion mentioned other research showing that 70 percent of those going back to work still feel pain, and inferred that symptoms are not a major factor in determining when an injured worker returns to the job. Their interpretation: "A longer duration of the initial episode [of absence from work] *resulted in* more absence from work in the three year [follow-up] period, both in terms of total cumulative duration of [subsequent] absence and risk of recurrence"(emphasis added). The authors suggest that physicians should return injured workers rapidly to the workplace in order to lower the likelihood of recurrence.

Another interpretation would be that workers who return quickly are less severely injured, are less likely to relapse, and have jobs that are less dangerous and likely to lead to a relapse.[10] We would attribute the fact that 70 percent of workers feel pain but return to work anyway to the difficulties of dealing with the compensation system (no information was sought on the reason for return to work) or even perhaps to machismo (sex differences were not presented, they were "adjusted for," so we cannot test this hypothesis).

This image of workers as lazy malingerers coddled by their colluding physicians was published in the clinical literature, where it can be cited in order to block compensation to injured workers who stay out "too long." Although it is possible, even probable, that it is better for injured workers to go back to a safe and appropriate job as quickly as they can, rushing workers back to the jobs where they were originally injured is not a safe practice. Thus, the likelihood of human suffering can be increased by a class-biased analysis of data on workers.

Consequences for Workers

Several of the rules presented here make it hard for workers, particularly women workers, to use research results to improve their working conditions. For example, occupational health scientists' preference for studying pathology diagnosed by a physician rather than symptoms reported by workers seems like a justifiable requirement for rigor. The problem is that pathologies are rare among populations still at work. Ill people often leave the workplace. They can still be studied, but finding them is hard, and relating their illnesses to their prior working conditions requires a great deal of extrapolation.

Studying workers who are still able to work can be a valuable tool for identifying more precisely the workplace causes of health problems. It also offers better possibilities for prevention, since symptoms may precede diagnosed pathology and offer early warning signals. Even when symptoms are not precursors of pathology, they often involve suffering that should be prevented for its own sake.

The requirements for pathology and the 5 percent significance level force researchers to study working populations of very large size in order to find a few cases of illness. Studies become extremely expensive and are restricted to the largest workplaces, the best recognized scientists, and the most clearly defined risks. Subgroups of workers are too small to allow statistical significance, and variations in exposure cannot be examined. Thus, funds to work on women's occupational health problems are scarce, since women work in smaller workplaces and their problems have not interested the best-known scientists.

The focus on statistical significance at the 5 percent level has other consequences. It also indirectly keeps scientists from getting the maximum amount of information about the relationship between exposures and health problems, since it induces them to use statistical tests rather than descriptions. The fact that most data collection involves a very few exposure levels (not exposed/low exposure/high exposure) and only two health statuses (ill/well) impoverishes analysis.

Waiting for pathology to occur causes human suffering. Prevention strategies are most successful before pathology occurs. Symptoms of pain and distress may indicate that musculoskeletal disease is just around the corner. Women with irregular menstrual cycles caused by variable schedules or men with pesticide-associated low sperm counts may someday have fertility problems. Waiting for the disease to happen is a delaying tactic; it gets in the way of improving working conditions that could have been related to physiological or psychological effects. Insurance companies refused to insure asbestos miners in 1918, but scientists were still debating whether asbestos caused harm 60 years later.[11]

Unnecessary exposure to chemicals may result from ignorance of problems women experience. A consequence of gender-blind studies of toxicology is that workers are approached as if they were all men. Recently, the U.S. National Institutes of Health established the Women's Health Initiative to make sure that male–female physiological differences are taken into account when testing drugs, so that drugs will be safe and effective for both sexes. No analogous procedure yet exists for testing responses to toxic chemicals. Many biological differences between women and men can affect their responses to chemicals,[12] but standard-setting has usually been based on tests carried out on "normal" males.

CONSEQUENCES FOR SCIENTISTS

Scientists are among the groups of workers who are directly "supervised" by the largest number of people. Their work is openly examined and criticized by departmental colleagues, university committees, granting committees, and journal reviewers. It is held up to scrutiny in scientific meetings, university seminars, and, occasionally, the media. The worst thing that can happen to scientists is to lose their credibility and their reputation for objectivity. They will no longer be able to get research grants or publish articles.

Any appearance of partisan behavior can affect scientists' credibility, particularly if doubt is cast on the accuracy of their results. Occupational health scientists who testify before juries, compensation hearings, and human rights commissions are under tremendous pressure. This is true particularly if they testify for workers, since the opposing side usually has much more money to hire lawyers and the best-known scientists to produce counterevidence.

Herbert Needleman presented results on lead poisoning among children at a scientific meeting. He describes his experience: "This was no scholarly debate on the toxicology and epidemiology of lead; this was war . . . . Arrayed against each other were a small and defensive group of environmentalists and health scientists on one side, and on the other the representatives of the gasoline companies . . . . Any paper suggesting that lead was toxic at lower doses immediately faced a vocal and well-prepared troop."[13] Needleman was formally accused of misconduct and had to defend his results before a panel of scientists in 1992. He was exonerated, but few researchers are prepared to face the kind of opposition he confronted, involving threats not only to his job but to his employability.

I learned about the relative strengths of the opposing forces the first time I testified for a worker. A pregnant radiologist had asked for paid leave during her pregnancy, available under the terms of her contract to pregnant workers exposed to dangerous conditions. She had stayed on the job during a previous pregnancy and blamed radiation exposure for her child's malformations. The union asked me to testify for her. I was a new professor and had done no research on pregnancy and radiation, so I based my testimony on a review of the literature. The worker had no lawyer and was represented by a union counselor.

The employer, a large hospital, hired a well-known specialist in radiation effects on humans who had published over 200 articles. The employer's lawyer made quick work of my testimony, and the union counselor was unable to counter his attacks or to question the specialist effectively. The union tried to hire an equally well known specialist who had published books and articles on the dangers of radiation, but was unable to attract him with the money available. The worker lost her case.

I felt demolished. Even though I was sure that what I said was correct, the speed and flexibility of the lawyer's attacks left me breathless and confused, since my scientific training had not prepared me for the confrontational style of the hearing. The union counselor was easily outmaneuvered. The misinterpretations of scientific statements in the judge's final decision made me feel that my explanations had been incompetent. I felt it was my fault that the worker had lost her case. And my credibility was damaged by comparison with a much older and more respected scientist. It would be a long time before I would put myself in a similar position.

Scientists, particularly young scientists, who take on employers can find life very difficult. In the United States, they may find it hard to get and keep a job.[14] Their students and collaborators suffer when their work is not supported, and the psychological burden of public criticism is very heavy. Occupational health scientists who are perceived as being too close to workers must be very careful. Every statement must be checked and rechecked before publication for fear of nitpickers and even lawsuits.

Conclusion

The way that scientific principles are set up militates against recognition of job hazards, particularly those in women's jobs. When forced to choose between scientific certainty and the ability to detect hazards, most scientists in occupational health have insisted on certainty. They insist on pathology rather than symptoms, large rather than small samples, alpha rather than beta. This means that most questions of interest to women workers cannot be studied rapidly in most of their workplaces.

It also means that political decisions have often been made in the absence of what scientists would consider to be conclusive evidence. For example, judges cannot wait until all the scientific evidence is in before deciding on compensation. Since it is relatively easy to pick holes in any scientific study on methodological grounds, the cards in these hearings are stacked against the workers.[15]

The jobs scientists have studied have usually been traditional men's jobs, such as those in mining, construction and manufacturing. Concepts developed in relation to those jobs have in some cases delayed our understanding of problems of women and their jobs. This is certainly not due to an absence of women occupational health scientists. Although women researchers are relatively few, the field was pioneered in North America by Alice Hamilton, and Harriet Hardy and Jeanne Stellman are recognized authorities in occupational health. At a recent meeting of the International Congress on Occupational Health, about one-third of the thousand or so people who presented papers were women. Many of the examples of institutionalized sexism given in this book come from laboratories headed by women. It is not the individuals but the social institutions of science that are responsible for gender bias.

7

Musculoskeletal Problems

■ ■ ■

I have chosen to examine work-related musculoskeletal disorders (MSDs) as my first case study of sexism in occupational health research for two reasons. First, MSDs are an important problem for women, *the* most common women's health problem, so it is important to prevent this suffering. Second, MSDs make up the majority of cases of occupational disease,[1] so they have been well studied by scientists. They occur among women and men, and it is interesting to see how gender is handled in research into and compensation for work-related MSDs. We can see that scientists have not always been fair to women. As a result, although both women and men encounter obstacles when trying to use scientific studies to support their compensation claims, women encounter difficulties not usually seen by men.

MSDs include inflammations of muscles and tendons such as tendinitis and bursitis, some cases of osteoarthritis, various types of back problems, and nerve compression syndromes such as carpal tunnel syndrome.[2] They may be associated with a single, well-defined event, but they usually build up over many years from repeated injury to the same tendon, muscle, or nerve. In the scientific and popular press, subcategories of these disorders are called repetitive strain injury (RSI), cumulative trauma disorders (CTDs), and soft tissue disorders. In this chapter I shall concentrate on disorders associated with repetitive strain, since this is a common problem in women's work.

Unlike some other research areas in occupational health, research in MSDs often includes women and women's jobs. This has enabled some researchers to uncover different patterns among women and men. In Québec, 55 percent of women's work accidents, but only 42 percent of men's, involve such MSDs as sprains, backache, and tendinitis.[3] Women report more musculoskeletal symptoms, and have symptoms in different parts of the body. Men have more musculoskeletal injuries when they are young, whereas women's appear with age.[4] Men and women hospital workers who lift patients have injuries in different parts of their bodies, corresponding to their different work methods. Men lifted patients vertically and hurt their backs, while women tried to push or pull them horizontally and hurt their shoulders and arms.[5]

In the United States, back pain among 30,074 workers who responded to an interview survey was analyzed by sex. Women had relatively more pain in the upper back and men in the lower back. Men had slightly more back pain overall, and the men peaked at ages 35–44, while the women peaked at 45–54. Men were much more likely than women to associate their pain with activities at work. The jobs where back pain was common differed for women and men: the top category for affected women comprised nursing aides, orderlies, and attendants. For men, construction laborers topped the list.[6] Cleaners, hairdressers, supermarket checkout clerks, various classes of health care providers, waitresses, cooks, sewing machine operators, teachers, and cashiers had more work-related back pain than other women workers.

Women often acquire tendinitis and carpel tunnel syndrome (common MSDs) while doing repetitive work in factories and offices. In many jobs assigned to women (as well as some assigned to men), the work cycle is under 10 seconds long, and the same movements are repeated many thousands of times in a day.[7] (The work cycle is the interval between repetitions of a single operation. For a university professor, it would be the time between beginnings of successive introductory lectures to the same course [months]; for an otorhinolaryngologist, it could be the time between beginnings of successive tonsillectomies [hours or days]; for a sewing machine operator, it is the time between successive pant legs [6–10 seconds]; for a data entry operator, it is the time between characters entered [as little as 0.2 seconds].) These movements may individually make trivial demands on the human body, but the enormous degree of repetition makes tiny details of the setup extremely important. A chair the wrong height or a counter the wrong width may cause constant overuse of the same tendons or joints, even though the problem may be imperceptible to someone observing the work.

Among those doing repetitive work, garment and other factory workers,[8] cleaners, hairdressers, and secretaries/keyboard operators[9] have been found to have excesses of neck, shoulder, arm, wrist, and/or hand disorders. Brisson and her collaborators found that sewing machine operators were seven times more likely than other women workers to suffer from disability due to MSDs.[10] Although men also do repetitive work, they are quickly promoted out of it. In a large French study of poultry processors, the proportion of men doing repetitive work fell very significantly with age, while the proportion of women was unrelated to age.[11]

We can see that MSDs are an important occupational health problem for women workers. We would like to understand the male–female differences in site, distribution, and age at onset for these disorders. However, research on MSDs is full of contradictions and controversy that bear on gender differences. These relate to two major points: (1) linking specific exposures to specific disorders; (2) the role played by psychological factors.

To understand how scientific treatment of women and men differs, let us examine these controversies and their implications for the study of women's and men's MSDs.

Linking Movements and Postures to MSDs

IDENTIFYING THE DISEASE

Establishing an association by epidemiological methods requires a disease to be consistently associated with a risk factor or factors. In research projects, diseases have been considered separately (epicondylitis, shoulder tendinitis, carpal tunnel syndrome, etc.) or grouped according to the body region involved.[12] Both approaches have their advantages and their problems. Grouping several diseases together may make it easier to detect early effects of working conditions by increasing the number of cases of disease that can be analyzed, but it will then be more difficult to find the precise cause of each. Considering each disease separately may result in too few cases to analyze, although the quality of information will be improved.

Physical injury is quite difficult to demonstrate for many types of MSDs. Muscle and tendon damage does not show up on X-rays, and many injuries cannot be detected by any diagnostic test. Workers often say they feel pain, and then face a credibility gap because there is no "objective" evidence that they have a problem. Researchers use widely varying criteria for including cases in their analyses.[13] Some researchers justify accepting workers' descriptions of their symptoms as reliable evidence of disease: "In epidemiologic studies, self-reporting of disease is usually considered a less accurate measurement and is sometimes referred to as a weakness of the study. However, back pain is a self-reported condition often without any objective clinical findings, and no medical test can really refute the existence of back pain."[14]

Workers describe great difficulty in getting their employers, physicians, co-workers, and even families to believe them when they have MSDs.[15] Co-workers told us about a woman who worked for 20 years in a cake factory before making a claim. She was proud that she had never been late or absent. However, when the repetitive motions involved in wrapping small cakes finally caused shoulder pain that made her unable to work, the company contested her compensation case with scientific testimony that she was not ill. Her friends described her distress: how could the company for which she had done honest work for so long call her a liar?

Scientists also have a problem when studying MSDs. They need a well-identified phenomenon to study, but they are faced with a choice. If they choose to include only clinically defined MSDs in their study, they will seriously underestimate the problem and will have trouble showing statistically significant relationships. If they include all workers with symptoms, they may dilute the effect they are looking for and, again, not find statistically significant relationships. They will almost certainly be criticized by other researchers for using such "soft" criteria. With some diseases, symptoms are the most reliable method for selecting cases; with others, there are appropriate tests.

IDENTIFYING THE CAUSES

Is it harder to define MSDs when the injured worker is a woman? It is certainly easier to identify an injury when it occurs as a result of a well-defined event.[16] If a worker lifts a heavy weight and wrenches his back, resulting in acute pain and possible torn ligaments, the case is clearer than when a worker feels more and more chronic pain until it becomes unbearable. Given the different tasks of men and women, the first situation is more likely to occur with men's jobs and the second with women's. In this sense, it is easy to see why one-third of women's compensated injuries (but only about 6 percent of women workers) are in the health care sector: apart from the fact that health care workers are unionized and sensitive to health issues, it is primarily in that sector that women lift heavy weights all at once. Therefore, compensation may be more accessible for those workers.

Unlike infectious diseases, where a single causal agent (germ) can sometimes be isolated, movements and postures are not easy to analyze. Job title has often been used as the exposure measure, but some studies have examined movements at work by questionnaire[17] or observation.[18] Physical risk factors considered in relation to repetitive strain injury have usually included number of repetitions, cycle length, position of limbs during repetition, forces involved, rest periods, and years of exposure.[19] For example, the classic study of Silverstein and her colleagues compared factory workers whose cycle length was less than 30 seconds with those whose work was less repetitive, and those who exerted more than six kilograms of force during the repetitions with those whose work required less force. They found that the combination of high force and high repetition was especially apt to produce the wrist disorder known as carpal tunnel syndrome. Repetition was more important than force.[20]

The role of repetition is hard to isolate, and repetitive movements are hard to define. As a union representative assigned to defending occupational health claims said: "What is a repetitive movement? I . . . ask everyone and even the doctors can't tell us. I say to people in my union, You'll see, you'll ask your doctor, he doesn't want you to do repetitive movements. How many times are you allowed to do that movement? The doctor doesn't want to answer that one."

Drawing that line is difficult for everyone. In some jobs the degree of repetition is obvious. A sewing machine operator who sews the same seam in the same pant leg hundreds of times in an hour is generally considered to do repetitive work. In other jobs, it is harder to demonstrate repetition. Employers have asserted that a supermarket checkout clerk does not do repetitive work because she both punches in prices and bags groceries, even though she alternates the two operations all day.

CINBIOSE researchers observed a worker who apparently did a varied series of tasks—mixing paint, conveying materials, and packing lightbulbs.[21] In fact, these tasks required many of the same movements. Fifty-three valves were turned against resistance as part of this job, and one valve requiring a particularly difficult movement was turned 20 times in one day. Every day, she did at least 61 different operations that put her at risk for epicondylitis (inflammation of the muscle-tendon unit at the elbow), some of which were performed repeatedly. So a worker can do repetitive work without ever doing exactly the same task twice, if she uses the same muscles and tendons.

MAKING CAUSE-EFFECT ASSOCIATIONS

Contrast the rather fuzzy definitions of diseases and possible causes with easily recognized accidents. When a construction worker falls off a scaffolding and breaks his leg, there is not much doubt that there is an injury, or that the injury is related to something that happened on the job. It is harder to link repetitive movements and MSDs. Personal contributory factors muddy the waters, and "logical" associations are not always found. For example, repeated wrist movements are not always associated with wrist disorders, part-time workers do not always have fewer problems than full-time, risk of a disorder does not always increase with years of exposure.[22] Quite often, doctors have testified that an injury could not be related to working conditions. Several female post office workers were refused compensation in Québec because, although they manipulated thousands of pounds of mail each day with a work cycle of less than 10 seconds, they did not exert a large force each time.

Several reasons can explain the failure to find the logical associations. As mentioned before, job titles may not reflect uniform exposure categories. In my university department, most secretaries do a lot of typing, while the secretary attached to CINBIOSE does almost no typing but corrects texts, writes and sends faxes, makes phone calls, and probably supplies more aid, comfort, and humor. Other university secretaries may spend a great deal of time photocopying. Exposure to repetitive movement varies widely among the secretaries, despite their common job title. So, even though many secretaries may have arm and wrist pain, proving that being a secretary at my university is risky for the wrist and arm might be difficult.

It would seem logical that, if work is related to MSDs, part-time workers should have fewer MSDs than their full-time colleagues. But part-timers may not do the same tasks as full-timers with the same job title. For example, our study of bank tellers found high levels of back and leg and foot pain, which we had reason to associate with prolonged standing, as well as neck and shoulder pain associated with reaching. We found no difference in pain reporting between full-time and part-time tellers. We understood why: during our observations we had noticed that full-time workers spent proportionately less time in direct customer service than part-time workers. In fact, part-timers were brought in to cover peak hours when there were more customers. Also, part-timers were less involved in the bank procedures, so they were not assigned to certain tasks that were done sitting down, such as entering transactions in the bank's account or controlling currency reserves.[23] We would not have been able to interpret this contradiction had we not spent hours observing the tellers at work. We know researchers who have never been inside the factories whose data they analyze, and interpretation of data can be a problem for them.

Musculoskeletal problems also depend on the interaction of the workers' specific dimensions with those of the worksite. The study of the poultry processing industry in France found that women reported much more often than men that their worksite was ill-adjusted to their size.[24] A similar result was found by a pan-European survey of over 12,000 workers: women were more apt to report that equipment was inappropriate and that they worked in uncomfortable positions.[25] A desk or counter the right width for a tall worker is too wide for a shorter worker to reach across.[26] Shorter bank tellers have more trouble with the height of their working surface, related to the level of symptoms in the neck and upper limbs.[27] Thus, even two workers doing exactly the same job may perform very different movements. Silverstein and collaborators advanced this hypothesis to explain why men and women in her study did not have the same rates of injury.[28]

Workers develop ways to avoid pain. This too makes it harder to find a relationship between MSDs and specific movements. Unlike "silent" diseases such as cancer and heart disease, musculoskeletal problems cause immediate pain and lead to changes in behavior that can obscure the relationship between exposure and disease. The relevant job title or hours of work may not be current but past, because workers with pain may ask for a transfer or leave the workplace. It would be useful to have biological indicators that can be used to show impairment before the workers are disabled. For example, Japanese researchers were able to show that VDT operators who spend six hours a day or more making repetitive keystrokes had below-normal rates of nerve conduction between the wrist and the finger segments.[29]

Even when workers cannot afford to leave their jobs, workers with pain adjust the way they operate. A person with pain in her arm may try to avoid the movement that gave rise to the injury. She may find a way to accomplish the same task in another way that hurts less (such as using her other arm), or she may arrange to cooperate with another worker so as to reduce her share of certain movements and increase others. The scientists who observe her work may be unable to understand why the pain is in the arm she hardly uses, while her other arm seems to be overused. Even if they ask her, she may no longer remember that she has changed her work method because of pain.

These complexities mean that epidemiologists may have difficulty relating current movements to current illnesses. They often result in great difficulty for the worker who wants a change in her work station or is claiming compensation. Four of these complicating factors are found more often in women's jobs: women are more likely to be found in broad, catch-all job definitions, to work part time, and to have work stations poorly adapted to their size. They are less likely to be promoted out of repetitive work, and therefore more likely to have to develop strategies to work while feeling pain. Courville and collaborators have movingly described poultry processors who live with pain while doing their jobs.[30]

POLITICS AND SCIENCE

Controversy has grown around the relationship between repetitive work and injuries.[31] The fact that tendinitis and other MSDs can be multicausal has led some scientists to insist on personal factors like diabetes and pregnancy as causes to the exclusion of occupation. Some scientists maintain that there is no such thing as repetitive strain injury and that it is a "neurosis."[32] A review of over 750 repetitive injury claims in California found that insurers were more likely to delay or deny claims for repetitive strain injuries than any other injury or illness.[33] According to some, "Compared with . . . individual characteristics, job-related factors such as specific occupation, duration of employment and occupational hand use, have contributed relatively little to abnormal median nerve conduction [carpal tunnel syndrome]."[34] Or even: "We find here the same mass neurosis as in Australia characterized by a mutual interactive influence among workers as well as personal physicians, favoring the propagation of ideas, concepts and dogmas which are only hypothetical and not proven and which on the contrary glorify victimization and are thus detrimental to society and the worker."[35]

Scientific articles on the definition and causation of MSDs, particularly in connection with repetitive motion, cannot be separated from this political controversy around compensation. Articles are cited for and against compensation, scientists testify on both sides of a case. Some insist on personal factors; others emphasize occupational causes of injury. Gender issues are hard to untie from all this. Is it coincidence that many scientists who have been pioneers in relating repetitive movement to injuries are women? Would doctors and judges be as skeptical about repetitive strain injuries at low force if most workers exposed to these conditions were not women?

Psychological Distress and Musculoskeletal Problems

Several studies show a relationship between psychological factors and the occurrence of musculoskeletal problems.[36] Interpretation of this relationship is varied, extending from physiological explanations relating stress to muscle tension through psychological explanations that pain is depressing and stress increases pain perception to accusations of malingering, "neurosis" or "hysteria." Again, the political positions of the investigators are quite varied and hard to untangle from the research results.

One set of studies examines MSDs to find acts of conscious or unconscious malingering. "Few if any medical interventions proved their effectiveness at shortening the period of working disability, which duration might be more related to the aggressivity of the clinician to promote early return to work and to the motivation of the worker to return."[37] These investigations, usually involving back pain, are aimed fairly explicitly at lowering the "societal" (usually employer) costs of disability. The often mention the fact that a small proportion of back pain sufferers account for almost all of the costs.[38] One study has gained international celebrity by suggesting that doctors return back patients quickly to work (irrespective of working conditions) in order to improve the cure rates.[39] According to its author, "The best treatment for low back pain without radiation or objective clinical signs is work."[40] Some researchers who think the speed of rehabilitation is determined by psychological factors attempt to understand and predict back or other pain using psychometric tests, often with the idea of doing pre-employment screening. They also may test the relationship between pain and the fact that a worker has or has not claimed compensation, a positive association implying that workers claiming compensation will consciously or unconsciously exaggerate their pain.[41]

Another set of studies also considers pain as having a psychological origin *as opposed to* a physiological cause. For example, one study tested workers on "fear-avoidance beliefs," the tendency to avoid situations thought to cause pain.[42] The authors suggest that "patients' perception of physical activity and its relation to pain and also their perception of their physical capabilities are often quite erroneous" and that patients may underestimate their ability to work if they fear pain. Using a scale with items like, "My work might harm my back" and "My work is too heavy for me," the researchers gave "fear-avoidance" scores to 184 back pain patients, 81 of whom were women. They found that the time absent from work over the previous year was related to the scores for "fear-avoidance beliefs about work." The more the patients felt that their work might be harmful, the more time they took before going back to work. The researchers interpreted this to mean that "fear of pain and what we do about pain may be more disabling than pain itself"—that is, that it was fear and not pain that made the patients miss work. Work content was ignored in this and other such studies. No information about the work done was sought in order to find out whether the fear was justified by a strong likelihood or actual experience that the work could hurt the patients' backs. A similar study that found that "Type A" behavior was related to musculoskeletal problems also ignored work content.[43] The "Type A" behavior could have been required by the job.

Another study looked at medical secretaries, over 60 percent of whom said they had neck or shoulder pain, or both. They filled out a questionnaire on physical discomfort and on the psychological work environment. Those with a "poor" psychological work environment had more pain than others, so the researchers inferred that the pain reports were related to psychosocial stress. No information was gathered on the physical work environment, so we do not learn whether those in a poor psychological environment also had a poor physical environment.[44] A similar study of neck, shoulder, and back pain concluded that pain was greater when the environment was perceived as unmanageable, but did not consider whether this might be because of uncomfortable environments that the worker was unable to modify.[45]

All the research in the above two categories implicitly or explicitly treats the pain of workers as "unreal"—that is, unrelated to a physical cause. A third set of studies examines the relationship between work organization and musculoskeletal problems, postulating that stress and tension in the muscles may arise from organizational problems and contribute to pain. Thus, the pain is considered to be "real," and the psychological factors are contributory. Often, these studies use the tests developed by Karasek and colleagues to measure job control and job demands.[46] (See Chapter 9.) For example, newspaper employees were found to have musculoskeletal pain related to work environment and posture as rated by observers. There was more pain among those subjected to poor work organization, such as low control over their job content. The two kinds of circumstances interacted: workers with better scores on work organization reacted less to uncomfortable keyboard positions or seat back heights.[47] These and other such studies conclude that MSDs are related to both physical and psychological factors.

These relationships may not hold for women. One group of researchers who (unlike most) separated their analysis by gender found differing relationships between pain and psychological symptoms. MSDs were more common among male factory workers with depression and stress symptoms than among men with no such symptoms. The researchers mentioned that the finding did not hold for women factory workers, but did not try to explain this discrepancy.[48]

Women who do repetitive, boring tasks are more likely to have MSDs than other workers. How can we tell whether the MSDs are due to the repetition (physical) or the boredom (psychological) or a combination of both? The question may appear trivial, since the pain is caused by the job in any case, but it has practical implications: it is infinitely harder to gain compensation for boredom-induced injury than for physical injury.

Gender and MSDs

In April 1994 CINBIOSE researchers met with union representatives responsible for defending workers with compensation claims. Asked what was difficult to defend in the case of women workers, representatives mentioned the nature of women's work ("I've never seen a worker compensated for work on a VDT keyboard") and their personal situations ("If she has four children, then that must be the cause").

The nature of the work done by women is often confused with the nature of women because of the widespread tendency to adjust for gender rather than analyzing the results separately by gender. Since women are often found in repetitive work, gender reflects the degree of exposure, and adjusting for gender tends systematically to underestimate risks in highly repetitive jobs primarily held by women. Almost all the studies of carpal tunnel syndrome cited in a major review article[49] adjusted for gender, even though it has been shown that gender is not related to carpal tunnel syndrome if anthropometric measurements related to wrist anatomy and physiology are taken into account.[50] Adjusting would be appropriate only if gender were an independent determinant of carpal tunnel syndrome for hormonal reasons, (for example), rather than a determinant of job content or of inadequate job engineering.

Silverstein's study distinguished between gender and type of movement in determining wrist disease. In the factory she studied, women were more likely to do highly repetitive, low-force jobs, and men were more often found in less repetitive, high-force jobs. Women and men were found together in only about half the jobs. In "mixed" jobs, women and men were about equally likely to suffer from wrist disease. Although Silverstein's study has been important in the process of gaining recognition for the industrial causes of MSDs, the design did not permit a full description of the very highly repetitive conditions common to women workers. Jobs with cycle lengths of less than 30 seconds were grouped together, whereas cycle lengths in women's jobs we have studied (sewing machine operators, postal workers) were often less than 10 seconds.

Hormones and MSDs

The fact that aging women tend to have more musculoskeletal problems has not escaped the notice of those who look at menopausal women as disease-prone. At the 1994 meeting of the International

Ergonomics Association, a doctor harangued a plenary session for several minutes, asserting that it had been scientifically proved that *all* carpal tunnel symptoms among older women were due to the menopause. At a meeting of union health and safety representatives, one described personal conditions that could be spoken of as causes of MSD and used to block compensation: arthroses (joint diseases—actually sometimes due to work), age, and menopause. "A woman developed a tenosynovitis [inflammation of the tendon sheath] and we lost at the appeal board. [They said] she hadn't done enough repetitive movements, that wasn't the cause, and the company doctor came to tell us that it was because she was close to menopause and it was due to that. She packs 25,000 boxes a day" (a cycle time of less than two seconds).

However, the problems of younger women can also be attributed to hormones. "If you're a young woman and you were pregnant during the year or the year before and you have problems with carpal tunnel, they will often say it's because you have had pregnancies. And they will often bring in a doctor who will say that a woman who has had a child this year or the year before, it's common, it's normal that that would be the cause of her carpal tunnel."

Several studies have in fact examined the reproductive status of women in relation to musculoskeletal problems, with quite variable results. In one investigation by Dieck and collaborators, carpal tunnel syndrome was found more frequently among women who were older at menopause or who used estrogen replacement therapy.[51] This implies that the syndrome is more common among women with lots of estrogen. Some scientists have hypothesized that pregnancy or estrogens cause swelling that compresses a nerve in the wrist.[52] However, the Dieck study found no relation between carpal tunnel syndrome and ever having been pregnant, number of pregnancies, or age at first live birth. Nor did they find a link to having had the uterus or ovaries removed or to menopausal symptoms.

Another group of Dutch investigators found results quite different from the Dieck study. They found that carpal tunnel syndrome was more common among women who had had a hysterectomy without removal of ovaries or had recently undergone menopause, but noted no relationship with age at menopause or with ovary removal.[53] Yet another study found a relationship with hysterectomy with removal of ovaries but not with hysterectomy if the ovaries were not removed; it found no effect of taking estrogens.[54] So there is certainly no clear evidence that taking estrogens causes carpal tunnel syndrome, from these or any other study we found when doing a computer search of the medical literature (*carpal tunnel syndrome* crossed with *hormones* or *menopause*). The different results may be due to differences among the three populations or to the fact that only the Dutch study included occupational factors. Or it may be that, since this syndrome appears after years of exposure, it occurs often in older women. Since the factors mentioned, such as menopause, are common among older women, they may be associated with the syndrome by chance.

Other MSDs have been investigated for their relation to hormones. A study of Finns with chronic neck pain found that each additional child added about 10 percent to the probability that a woman would suffer neck pain.[55] "At this time," the authors affirmed, "there is no good biologic or social explanation for this association." We might suggest that pregnancy alters the shape of the body and thus the interaction with the worksite.[56] Although occupational factors were examined in this study, interaction between pregnancy and occupation was not considered.

Three physicians reported having found de Quervain's tendinitis of the wrist among a total of six pregnant patients, leading them to consider a hormonal basis.[57] However, two of them, a librarian and a nurse, both mentioned that their symptoms were aggravated by work activities. There seems to have been no attempt to consider occupation among the other four patients, since we are not told whether they were employed. Physicians who read anecdotal case reports such as this one are left with the impression that pregnancy alone may cause tendinitis.

According to workers, menopause and pregnancy are often brought up in compensation hearings as the "true" cause of injuries. Since most older women are menopausal and very many younger women have recent pregnancies, it seems to be rather easy to attribute women's MSDs to personal rather than occupational factors.

Conclusion

Examining the research on musculoskeletal problems is a good way to understand some of the reason for delay in identifying and compensating women's occupational health problems. Of course, it is not easy for men to be compensated for MSDs, either, and those intervening in compensation cases often interpret scientific evidence whatever way will make their points. But women are still at a disadvantage in the research and in the judicial system. Some of the disadvantage comes from outright sexism, such as we can see in relation to menopause. Much more of it comes from the nature of jobs usually assigned to women, in which dramatic, easily identified dangers are rare. In a context of employer–worker opposition, where each side will jump on weaknesses in the case made by the other, women and women's jobs make an easier target.

To what extent are scientists responsible for the rejection of women's MSD compensation claims? First, they are no more responsible than any of the other actors in the process: unions, employers, physicians, and lawyers. It is only because they are sometimes thought to be nonpartisan observers, even when they testify for one side or the other, that they are expected to be objective. Second, scientists are part of scientific institutions that have their own imperatives and procedures. If scientists have been slow to demonstrate that women's MSDs cause disabilities, it is because the support for such studies has been lacking and some of the rules for doing them may be inappropriate.

8

Office Work and Health

■ ■ ■

Examining the health effects of office work provides us with another opportunity to see how scientists treat women, since more women work in offices than in any other situation. Among the top women's professions (see Chapter 1), we find secretaries, office clerks, receptionists, accountants, auditors, data entry operators, and bookkeepers. Secretaries and typists alone account for one woman worker in 14 in Canada. Stellman and Henifin calculated that two-thirds of American women workers were in offices.[1] In Canada in 1993, 28 percent of women workers (compared with 6 percent of men) were classed as office workers; to these we must add many women who work in offices as administrators and managers, as well as those who work from offices at various sales and service occupations.[2] It is therefore relevant to examine how scientists and occupational health professionals respond to the problems reported by office workers.

People did not usually think of office work as dangerous until a 1983 book alerted workers to many kinds of risks: musculoskeletal problems, injuries, fires, chemical exposures, noise, and poor climatic and lighting conditions.[3] Since then, a growing literature and increasing union activities have dealt with three types of risks for office workers: MSDs, pregnancy problems associated with work on VDTs, and indoor air pollution. This chapter touches briefly on the first two problems and then concentrates on the scientific treatment of indoor air pollution as another example of how women's problems are treated in the health and safety literature.

MSDs and Office Work

Whereas typists had to move the roller bar, change paper, and unstick keys, VDT operators can work for hours without varying their posture. Since operators are able to type faster at a keyboard than at a typewriter, movements are repeated more often. Data entry can mean keying in 20,000 characters in an hour.[4] Shoulder, arm, wrist, and hand problems can result. In fact, several studies of MSDs among those who work with keyboards show that operators of VDTs are likely to have such disorders.[5] Correcting texts with a mouse may be especially likely to lead to upper limb problems.[6]

As mentioned in the last chapter, it is hard for office workers to gain recognition for MSDs. In fact, office workers are frequently used as a "control group" when examining MSD problems: levels of MSDs among other workers are compared with those of office workers as a baseline because the office workers are thought to have very low levels of work-related problems. For example, three studies of carpal tunnel syndrome in a recent review used office workers or clerical workers as a reference group.[7] As more and more office workers get carpal tunnel syndrome, this appears to be a poor idea.

VDTs and Pregnancy

VDTs were introduced massively in many offices in the 1970s without health and safety testing (for example, for radiation emissions or ergonomic problems). These machines have become so common that a recent study of randomly selected working women found that more than half used them.[8] Unions expressed concern about visual damage and musculoskeletal problems, and then were alerted to the possibility of reproductive hazards by questions from women workers.

In the late 1970s and early 1980s, pregnant women working with VDTs in some offices experienced "clusters" of miscarriages or malformed children.[9] They suspected that exposure to radiation from VDT screens might affect fetuses. Some machines were tested, and a very few were in fact found to give off detectable levels of potentially dangerous "ionizing" radiation (similar to X-rays). These results were publicized, and many pregnant women refused to work with

VDTs. Some people were surprised to hear that a danger had been identified in a "woman's" job. Some unions requested leave or transfer for pregnant women working with VDTs, while others suggested that they wear lead aprons. However, pregnant women complained that lead aprons were too heavy for them to wear comfortably while working. Meanwhile, consensus built among scientists and workers that ionizing radiation was not usually a problem with VDTs.

However, the evidence was less clear on other types of radiation released by VDTs, and the controversy persists. Some researchers link work with VDTs to problem pregnancies; others find no relationship. Even when there are more miscarriages, the cause is not clear. Another kind of radiation, extra low frequency electromagnetic radiation (ELF), is emitted by some older VDTs and may be dangerous for fetuses.[10] Rigid postures may also be a problem. Environments where screens, keyboards, and chairs force operators into cramped positions are not good for blood circulation and may affect maternal and fetal health.

One reason for the persistent controversy is that the effects of VDTs on pregnancy were not studied before the machines were introduced in offices on a large scale. Consumer protection regulations require that new foods and drugs be carefully tested before being introduced into the marketplace, but no such protections exist for the workplace. An employer can introduce an untested procedure at any time, after which a standard-setting process begins that may take years. Unlike consumers, workers continue to be exposed to unregulated agents while committees weigh the scientific evidence on toxicity. Even when a standard finally emerges, reproductive toxicity has often not been considered during the regulatory process (see Chapter 10).

Although no striking effects of VDTs on pregnancy have been shown, research results are still equivocal. Women remain very suspicious of VDTs. When asked to identify health risks in their jobs, Canadian women gave first place to "proximity to VDT screens."[11] This may be understandable, given the large number of women who work with VDTs, but it is a strange choice in view of the other risks to which many women are exposed. Negligibly few women mentioned MSDs, for example.

Employers have been relatively willing to accommodate these fears. In Québec, pregnant telephone operators can be transferred away from VDT screens on request, although compensation for musculoskeletal problems is contested. David and LeBorgne have suggested that women find it easier to struggle against VDT radiation than many other occupational health and safety risks because it may be easier to gain recognition for risks to the fetus than for women's own discomfort. Also, women are heard more readily when they complain about "real" radiation than about MSDs from repetitive work or stress.[12]

The third area of risk for office workers is poor air quality, mentioned by 20 percent of women workers as an important health risk.[13] When people talk about indoor air, they can be concerned about physical properties such as humidity and temperature, chemical problems such as smoking residues, or microorganisms contaminating the filters in the ventilation system. The rest of this chapter examines how gender is treated in studies of indoor air pollution.

Scientific Treatment of Indoor Air Pollution

Office workers in North America very often work in buildings whose principal source of air is a ventilation system. Some buildings may cause workers to suffer from symptoms like headaches, fatigue, eye problems, and nose and throat irritations. In the early 1980s, workers accused a number of sealed buildings of giving them "sick building syndrome" (SBS). SBS has been defined by the World Health Organization as a "set of general, mucosal and skin symptoms perceived by inhabitants of buildings with indoor climate problems."[14] If an illness is diagnosed, it may be known as "building-related illness."

Scientists have tested a number of components in office buildings, but have often been unable to explain why the inhabitants complain. We searched the CISILO database on the occupational health literature and found 13 studies relating health symptoms to air quality (not necessarily the only existing studies).[15] It is hard to draw a unified conclusion from the 13 papers, each of which relates discomfort to a different set of conditions. The same conditions are not examined in all the studies. One study, for example, could be interpreted to mean that indoor pollution was not a problem.[16] About half of the workers in four buildings suffered from symptoms of eye, nose, or throat discomfort or from headaches or excessive fatigue. The researchers compared symptoms among workers in the four buildings while varying the proportion of outside air in the ventilation system. The levels of one chemical pollutant, used as an indicator of pollution levels, reflected the proportion of outside air. (The more outside air, the less pollutant.) Even when the levels of pollutant dropped, symptoms persisted at the same level. However, the authors themselves suggested that they had not taken into account all the conditions that could have caused the symptoms—for example, humidity levels and contamination of the ventilating system by microorganisms were not monitored. A different article reports that levels of bacteria and fungi were related to symptoms in 15 buildings and that dust levels were not related, but it does not examine the same chemical components.[17] Yet another study accents dryness, odors, ventilation, and noise as more important than chemical contaminants, but could not look at microbes because their concentrations were too low.[18]

It is understandable that all possible determinants were not considered important in all the studies. Decisions on what to include were probably made on the basis of the researchers' best guess, on the types of complaints from the building inhabitants, and on the time, equipment, and resources available for the study. The variety of studies is included here in order to show that the science of studying indoor air pollution is still in its infancy and that the list of potential contaminants is not complete.

Women by and large suffered two to four times more symptoms than men. As we have seen earlier, at least part of this difference could be due to differences in working conditions by sex. Women in offices probably do more photocopying (exposure to ozone, toners, and electrostatic effects) than men and share offices more often (exposure to second-hand smoke). Only three articles even discussed this difference in symptoms,[19] and only one of them took into account the gendered division of labor in such a way as to allow us to understand why women had more symptoms. Three studies ignored gender entirely, treating all workers as undifferentiated. One of these noted that nurses had more symptoms than hospital administrators but did not report the gender distribution or exposure specificities of either group.[20]

Other studies adjusted the analysis for gender without reporting any details on symptoms or exposure by gender. The authors of one of them concluded their article by insisting on the necessity to control for gender.[21] Seven others reported gender as if it were a separate cause of difference in symptom levels. For example, one reported without any other discussion that women were 2.6 times as likely as men to suffer central nervous system symptoms.[22] Another laconically reported "female" as one of a list of associations with symptoms that also included "handling carbonless paper," "hay fever," and "clerk." The reader cannot judge whether a difference in some other exposures partly or completely explained the gender differences in symptoms.

Many studies found that self-reported "hyperreactivity" was related to symptoms. This may be due to a circular definition of hyperreactivity: those who react are called hyperreactive. But some populations may be particularly susceptible. It is possible that women, for hormonal or other reasons, could be more susceptible than men to certain pollutants, as suggested by the only group of researchers who seriously examined the sex difference in symptoms. The bases for this susceptibility, if it exists, are not clear. They could be hormonal or have to do with the length of the workday or with psychosocial factors.

"Multiple chemical sensitivity," a condition that may be related to SBS, is attracting more research. People with multiple chemical sensitivity suffer from respiratory, digestive, and other symptoms when exposed to chemicals present in the everyday environment. The syndrome is thought to be triggered by prior exposure to organic solvents or other chemicals, including "sick buildings."[23] Multiple chemical sensitivity is much more common among women than men.[24]

As with other conditions primarily affecting women, many scientists are skeptical about the "reality" of multiple chemical sensitivity. In response to a questionnaire, only 9 percent of occupational physicians reported believing that the syndrome results from predominantly physical roots.[25] A number of researchers have attempted to demonstrate that the syndrome is psychiatric in origin, due to hypochondria or stress.[26] Some of the debate recalls the controversy about repetitive strain, in that again the "reality" of a syndrome more common among women workers is questioned.

Skepticism about Women's Chemical Exposures

Reactions to indoor air take several forms, extending from cold-type symptoms to headaches to more severe infections and intoxications. As we have seen, the science of indoor air analysis is still in its infancy. It is often difficult to identify the agent or agents responsible for the health problems, and results are often hard to interpret. In the workplace, these scientific difficulties often translate into hard times for women workers. In the absence of clear scientific evidence and established procedures, health professionals' response to women's complaints may reflect their own prejudices.

Our own experience echoes stories that I am constantly hearing from women workers. A few years ago, CINBIOSE was located in the science building at the university, sharing a ventilation system with chemistry and biology laboratories. Many of us had headaches and felt unduly tired at the end of the day. Two people noticed that their vision had deteriorated. Those whose presence was not strictly monitored (mainly professors) worked at home as much as we could and noticed that our symptoms disappeared at home.

We called the local community health service (part of the Québec public health care system), which sent over an inspector. The inspector tested for standard indoor air contaminants, and the report came back negative. There was some carbon monoxide, but not enough to surpass the permitted levels; some carbon dioxide but not enough; some nitrogen oxides but not enough. We kept having symptoms and making complaints. Finally a ventilation specialist found that because of a quirk in the system, the effluent from the chemistry laboratories was vented directly into our offices. No single component was ever high enough to exceed the prescribed levels, but we were sure that the combination of different pollutants accounted for our symptoms. The university refused to re-engineer the system, since we could not demonstrate that any level was too high, but, in view of our persistence, they offered to move us into another building. A group of male scientists took our place, saying that they were not afraid of the air. (One of them told me some months later that he regretted the decision because he felt tired all the time since the move.)

In the new building, our headaches and vision problems disappeared, but we still felt tired toward the end of the day. We felt that the ventilation system did not supply enough fresh air. In fact, it was all but shut down after five and on weekends. Our office staff (all women) engaged in battle with the building supervisor and the university services (almost all men). The tone of these exchanges is conveyed by the last words of a male university representative: "With all your complaints of victimization, you sound like a bunch of battered women." A compromise was finally reached in which the university tried to limit the emissions from the underground garage and also enforced cleaning of the filters in the ventilation system, which were black with accumulated contaminants. The problem, while not solved, has been alleviated.

If we, scientists with a recognized specialty in toxicology and confidence in our interpretations of the problems, have had trouble getting our complaints heard and dealt with, how much harder is it for those without such advantages? Our colleagues elsewhere have not been so lucky. Two psychology professors at the Ontario Institute for Studies in Education resigned, saying that they could no longer work in the building. Their complaints and those of other professors were met with skepticism, since no one was able to identify specific pollutants in the air. Many women work at home in order to escape these problems, with consequent risks of isolation and loss of union protection. In the absence of a matured scientific approach to this problem, prejudices about building occupants seem to prevail.

As an editorial on sick building syndrome in the *American Journal of Public Health* puts it, "In the absence of an explanation in the traditional industrial hygiene conceptual framework, many investigators ascribed the complaints to mass psychogenic illness."[27] The occurrence of the symptoms in workplaces dominated by women was not cited in the editorial as a reason for skepticism. But the widespread use, without explanation, of gender as a possible explanatory variable gives scientists and health professionals the impression that women complain about indoor air because of their sex.

Two studies have specifically examined the hypothesis that, in the presence of the same symptoms, women complain more than men. Stenberg and Wall say that the results obtained while validating their questionnaire on sick building symptoms with male and female respondents "conflict with the common opinion . . . presuming an overestimation of the symptom prevalences among females."[28] In another study, Macintyre examined women and men with the common cold and found that men tended to overreport symptoms more than women.[29]

Skepticism regarding women's symptoms is nevertheless extremely common. In examining the literature on chemical intoxications in the workplace, we found that the term "mass hysteria" or "mass psychogenic illness" was often associated with women's

TABLE 13: Episodes Designated as Mass Hysteria
in the Medical Literature

Employment sector	Number of episodes [Type of industry]	Women/Cases
Food and agriculture	2 [food-processing]	61/65
	3 [growing]	60/60
Textile	5 [production]	189/200
	1 [storage]	53/72
Service	3 [telecommunications]	100/103
	1[data processing]	35/35
	1[hospital]	102/102
Industry/manufacturing	5 [electronics]	263/265
	4 [mechanical parts]	95/95
	5 [assembly]	314/406

Source: Compiled from Brabant, C., Mergler, D. and Messing, K. (1990) Va te faire soigner, ton usine est malade: La place de l'hysteria de masse dans la problématique de la santé des travailleuses. Santé mentale au Québec 15: 181–204.

symptoms.[30] We noted that, of 1,403 workers involved in 30 episodes described as "mass hysteria" in the literature, 1,272 were women (see Table 13).

Because of results like these, the proportion of women in a workplace has been put forward as a suggested diagnostic criterion for mass hysteria in a workplace with unexplained symptoms.[31] Some authors suggest in somewhat more subtle language that the proportion of women be used as a criterion for chemical versus psychogenic origin of SBS.[32] "Several epidemiologic features that might be used to help differentiate between building-associated illness caused by chemical exposure and that with a psychogenic origin. . . . (4) characteristic personality profiles and age/*sex* distribution among patients" (emphasis added).[33] The impression is given that, when SBS affects a female workforce, scientists need not bother looking too long for chemical exposures. If many women report suffering symptoms at the same time, the symptoms are more likely to be "psychogenic" or "hysterical" (not based on "real" chemical, physical, or biological exposures) than if those suffering from the effects are men.

A more likely explanation is that the diagnosis of mass hysteria is more readily offered when women are involved.

Conclusion

Reading about mass hysteria as an explanation for women's complaints about indoor air reminds us of the accusations that repetitive strain injury is a neurosis. In both cases, an aspect of women's work presents a problem for scientists and health care workers because the causes and the effects are multifarious and hard to untangle. Office air pollution is not like the fumes in the refineries or the dust in the mines where men work. Thanks to decades of union and medical intervention, contamination in refineries and mines is a known danger. There are standards, although perhaps too high, for contaminant levels, and there are ventilation and filtering systems, albeit inadequate, to reduce them. Workers are provided with personal protection devices that may not suffice for the task, but that at least symbolize the importance given to the workers' health.

In offices, symptoms are due to a combination of a very large number of factors whose individual levels are usually too low to be qualified as dangerous. Because scientists have not succeeded in finding a clear relationship, they suspect that the symptoms are "unreal" or not related to working conditions. This may happen more often with women because they are less likely to be exposed to obvious dangers and clear, single-cause, single-effect situations, or because women are more vigilant about health risks, but it also seems to be much easier to doubt women's word than men's. It becomes that much harder for women to get recognition for problematic conditions. While protection is often provided for risky areas in traditional factories, few offices have provided extra ventilation around photocopiers or in offices where people smoke.

Several researchers think that debates about the "reality" of women's musculoskeletal or other symptoms are misplaced and result from an artificial separation between physical and psychological working conditions. The workplace should be regarded as a whole, they suggest. Yassi examined telephone operators who said they suffered from electric shocks in their workplace. After an exhaustive study of the working environment, she was unable to find any cause for the shocks. She suggested that the shocks were related to a collective stress reaction due to pressures from management.[34] Similarly, Ong and colleagues reviewed the literature on MSDs among VDT operators and concluded that health and safety experts should attack monotony and repetition at the same time as the physical work environment.[35] Stenberg and Wall come to an analogous conclusion regarding SBS, suggesting that psychosocial work stress should be considered.[36]

It is only sensible to take a multidisciplinary approach to complex problems. But there is a real danger that women workers will be refused compensation if they admit psychological explanations for their physical problems.

Women, aware of these prejudices, have usually concentrated their struggles on the more palpable dangers from chemicals and radiation. As mentioned above, the health hazard from VDT radiation is probably far inferior to that from cramped postures, repetitive movements, and too-fast workspeed. Nevertheless, many women have found it too difficult to get changes in their work organization and fall back on radiation, perhaps because they can more easily make a case that it is dangerous. Indoor air pollution is at least composed of "real" chemical and biological factors that are more easily admitted to be risky than "stress" or "overwork," although these may be more important complaints.

The next chapter considers how occupational health scientists deal with stress felt by working women.

9

Emotional Stressors in Women's Occupations

■ ■ ■

Many workers in North America are troubled by stress, especially in the current context of job insecurity and downsizing. Women appear to be especially affected. Analysis of data from the 1992–93 Québec Health Survey[1] showed that 31 percent of women workers and 22 percent of male workers suffered from psychological distress (Ilfeld Scale),[2] up from 18 percent and 9 percent on the same test in 1987.[3] Women in traditional jobs such as service and office work were particularly likely to experience stress by this criterion.[4] A study of women data entry clerks showed that they were more stressed if they were assigned work from several different people.[5] Our own studies have identified particularly high levels of stress among bank tellers undergoing job reorganization, who report stress over twice as often as other Québec women workers.[6]

American studies have also revealed effects of stress among women workers. Secretaries have been identified by the National Institute of Occupational Safety and Health as a group particularly affected.[7] In Britain, women workers in industry report being more tense and feeling more worn-out than men.[8] In a recent international conference entitled "Women, Health and Work," about one presentation in five was on stress.[9] The title of a recent book, *Women, Work and Health: Stress and Opportunities,* also expresses the extent to which stress is identified as *the* women's occupational health problem.[10]

We must ask whether women are "really" more stressed than

men. To some extent, the emphasis on women's stress may come from the problems in identifying women's health problems mentioned in previous chapters. Such problems may be erroneously attributed, by both women and physicians, to psychic causes to the exclusion of physical ones. Since women's physical health problems are not well studied, they may not be identified as such by physicians. A diagnosis of mental health problems may then be given in the absence of other explanations for the women's symptoms. This may explain why 9 percent of women's visits (at ages 45–69) are attributed by physicians to "anxiety states and other neuroses," whereas fewer than 1 percent of the visits are initiated by women complaining of these problems.[11] Women themselves may be led to believe that their problems are "all in their minds."

Whether or not women's mental health problems have been overestimated, women workers certainly feel considerable psychological distress. A few years ago, I toured a poultry processing plant in France where we were doing a study. The temperature was close to freezing, so that people had to wear many layers of clothing. The room was damp and drafty. It was impossible to talk in the plant because of the tremendous noise. Workers wielded sharp knives very rapidly, and I knew that there were many accidents. The union worked to prevent MSDs due to repetitive movements, an important problem according to our questionnaire results. After the tour, we met with the union representative for health and safety. I asked her to identify the most important problem in the plant. I expected to hear about musculoskeletal problems, and I was astonished by her answer: She tapped her forehead and said, "Between the ears, the worst is between the ears." I protested, "Not cuts, not noise, not pain?" "No," she answered. "Stress." She explained that workers felt that they were not listened to or respected and were often in conflict with their immediate supervisors. This, she felt, was much more troubling than physical discomfort. However, her union, and the scientists working with them, were exclusively concerned with the physical problems.

Occupational health scientists have developed few approaches to identify and combat causes of collective stress in the workplace. In some professions such as nursing, teaching, and social work, a lot of union activity centers on stress reduction. However, stress reduction has not been easy to accomplish. Scientists and workers are often ill-at-ease with what seems to be a soft, fuzzy problem.

Some Definitions

The expression "stress at work" can cover many phenomena, from problems with fellow workers to sexual harassment to difficulty reconciling family and professional responsibilities. Workers' reactions as well as the distressing circumstances are both called "stress." We talk about stress when mental health is involved, but also when there are physical health alterations (ulcers, heart attacks) in response to psychic stimuli.

For the purpose of this discussion, I would like to define some terms.[12] Technically, *stressors* are agents that induce a stress response in humans. The *stress response* is a complex set of reactions mediated by the brain and by hormonal secretions that change the functioning of the circulatory, digestive, and respiratory systems, among others. It is important to emphasize that the same stress response is evoked by many situations. Being threatened by a patient or client, working in a noisy office, or demanding work schedules may all induce the stress response.

The stress reactions have been given the shorthand designation "fight or flight" to express the way the body coordinates its responses to a perceived threat. It is as if the body suppressed every physiological function not immediately relevant to dealing with the threat, and mobilized only those systems useful to its defense. Initiation of these changes comes about through the secretion of hormones, known as catecholamines (epinephrine, for example), which activate the organ systems concerned. Thus, those functions that deliver immediate energy to muscles go into high gear, while "housekeeping" functions that maintain the body are temporarily downgraded. Digestion and waste elimination are neglected at the expense of oxygen and energy delivery via the circulatory system. When we experience acute stress, we breathe more often and our hearts beat more quickly, but we usually do not feel like eating. Other physiological changes come about through the action of another group of hormones called corticosteroids, which act on the immune system. These stress responses are accompanied by conscious and unconscious reactions and emotions.

Stressor-induced changes have immediate and long-term effects on the body. A coordinated response works to make the worker able to defend herself in the here and now, but repeatedly mobilizing these defenses at the expense of maintenance may result in damage over the long term. Exposure to stressors may result in digestive disorders through disturbance of eating and waste elimination, high blood pressure through constant calls on the circulation, MSDs due to constant tension, or lowered resistance to infection due to altered immune responses.

Stressors also produce psychological effects experienced by the worker as discomfort or distress. Because of this, workers aware of stressful situations take evasive action, which may itself have psychological and physiological effects. Some workers will suppress anger; some may engage in physical or verbal battles; some may become long-distance joggers; others may smoke, drink, or take drugs. Some will unite with fellow workers, others will bear the burden alone, still others will mobilize their families and friends. Behavior in response to stress depends not only on the stressor but also on the state of the stressed worker. Bank tellers explained to us that their reactions to a bank robbery were not necessary related to the type of robbery (gun, knife) nor to whether they themselves had been personally threatened. In fact, sometimes they would be more upset by other events than by an actual robbery: "Sometimes there's an accumulation, they wore me out—little things—a guy who came in wrapped up for the cold weather [giving the impression of a mask], he stamped to get the snow off. I started screaming and ran away." Another teller explained: "Sometimes you react, it depends on your life, too, because if you're in a vulnerable period, there's that too." The branch managers found it hard to understand why the tellers did not react the way they would have predicted: severe reactions to armed robbers and less reaction to more routine experiences.

The variety of individual and collective coping strategies and the interrelations of their effects make studying stress responses a very difficult task. Workers, union health and safety representatives, and health care providers realize that it is impossible to separate out stressors in the home and work situations. Yet it is important to identify stressors in the workplace in order to develop strategies to make work less stressful.

Studying Stress

Conditions inducing a stress response can act primarily through the body or the mind. In general, agents that threaten the body will induce a stress response in addition to their other effects. Wounds, loud noise, and even chemical intoxications can induce a stress response. When we think of stress, however, we usually think of the conditions that are primarily mediated through the mind, so-called psychosocial job characteristics like work organization, threats of violence, or hierarchical relations. The worker perceives a threat to her job, her body, her self-respect, or her ability to meet her family's needs, and the stress response is induced.

It is useful if a bit simplistic to divide immediate stress responses into four categories, as presented in the examples in Table 14.

Scientists use various techniques to study the effects of workplace stressors. Stress responses can be detected physiologically by monitoring heart rate, blood pressure, levels of circulating catecholamines or corticosteroids, muscle tension, or the state of immune defenses. Awareness of stressors and of people's responses can be detected using questionnaires and interviews.

The short-term responses can develop into more lasting conditions, which can be schematized in a similar way (see Table 15).

This framework may be useful when we examine the results of scientific studies of stress among women workers. It is oversimplified, since few experiences or stressors can be easily characterized as only physical or only mental. Ascribing the stress response to one category or the other may also be difficult.

Some questionnaires used to assess psychological stressors may measure physical stressors as well. Studying factory work, Johansson and Nonas found a very strong association between "psychological work load" and musculoskeletal symptoms of the back. They concluded that "symptoms in the back were associated with both psychosocial factors and physical stressors." The questionnaire items used to establish "psychosocial" workload, however, did not clearly separate physical and mental stressors and effects. Terms used to characterize psychological workload included the ambiguous "work load," "extent of feeling tired and exhausted after work," "opportunity for relaxation and having a break," as well as the more clearly psychological items such as "mental strain" and "stress at work."[13]

Separating physical from mental and emotional factors and responses may be a problem for many researchers in occupational health. After reviewing many papers on psychosocial factors at work, Bongers and her colleagues concluded that "monotonous work, high perceived work load and time pressure are related to

TABLE 14: Causes and Effects of Workers' Stress Reactions

	Stress-Inducing Agent	
Worker's Response	*Physical*	*Psychological*
Physical	Heart rate increase in response to noise	Heart rate increase in response to supervisor's remarks
Emotional	Psychological distress experienced in response to noise	Psychological distress experienced in response to supervisor's remarks

TABLE 15: Long-term Effects of Stress on Workers

	Stress-Inducing Agent	
Effect on the worker	*Physical*	*Psychological*
Categorized as physical	Heart disease in response to noisy environment	Heart disease in response to conflicts at work
Categorized as emotional	Mental disease or disorder associated with long-term exposure to taxing physical environment or physical suffering	Mental disease or disorder associated with conflict at work

musculoskeletal symptoms."[14] Expressed in this way, the three potential determinants sound like elements of work organization and would be expected to act on the mind. But the same determinants could be expressed as "repetitive work, heavy musculoskeletal demands, and rapid movements," whereupon they would be expected to act directly on the body. The same confusion can be found with "job satisfaction," an indicator commonly used in studies of stress. Dissatisfaction with one's job is thought of as a psychological stressor, which it is, but it may also be physical and environmental conditions that cause the worker to be dissatisfied.

To avoid confusion, I confine the discussion of stress in this chapter to the right-hand columns of Tables 14 and 15: conditions that act on the mind, whether they produce psychological or physical effects.

Stressful Conditions in Women's Jobs

Since few have directly studied the physiological reactions of people while they are exposed to workplace stressors in real-life situations, we do not know much about which workplace factors produce the stress reaction. The following list of psychosocial stressors is necessarily somewhat hypothetical. Still, some issues in work organization and organizational policies have emerged as potential stressors from the scientific literature and during our discussions with workers.

Some of these stressful conditions are shared by women and men. Both sexes react when the supervisor gives conflicting instructions, when the workload is too heavy, or when clients are disagreeable. Women are also exposed to specific psychological stressors because of the type of work they do, because of the ways they have been trained to respond, because of discrimination, and because of their situation outside paid work.

PSYCHOSOCIAL REQUIREMENTS IN THE SERVICE SECTOR

Work with people has its own specific demands. Physical risks in the service professions where many women work have been reviewed by Sprout and Yassi, and include postural constraints, risk of infection, and exposure to the risk of violence.[15] The emotional demands of these jobs, harder to describe, can be very heavy. Service workers such as waitresses, bank tellers, sales clerks, and receptionists must respond to clients' needs, emotions, and behavioral variations while remaining calm and smiling.

In most service jobs where there is contact with people, the worker is paid not only for giving a service, which could possibly be done by a machine, but also for producing pleasant emotions in the client. Arlie Hochschild calls this kind of work "emotional labor," defined as "management of [the worker's own] feeling to create a publicly observable facial and bodily display; emotional labor is sold for a wage."[16] Emotional labor has its own requirements and skills. Cashiers and tellers, for example, must keep customers moving quickly while remaining polite, friendly, and helpful. They must defuse difficult situations while keeping their self-respect and making the customer happy.[17] A bank teller told us about her day at work after an upsetting fight with her husband: "It's hard to smile at the forty-second customer who says, 'What's wrong, you're not looking so well?'" I asked her how she coped, and she answered, "When it gets too bad, I faint."

Women are often assigned to jobs where they keep potentially annoyed, angry, or violent people calm and well-disposed toward their employer: patients, social welfare clients, or customers. Although men are more often the target of violent physical attacks, women who work in service professions are often prey to verbal or physical violence.[18] Those in professions where robberies or clashes with clients are frequent may feel apprehensive. In our study, bank tellers reporting excessive psychological distress were more common among those who had experienced a robbery within the previous two years.[19]

Emotional requirements may go beyond being cool and pleasant under pressure. A subgroup of service jobs requires the workers to care about their clients, even to love them. For day care workers, primary school teachers, health care workers, and social workers, love and caring are essential to their tasks, whether or not the clients/children are lovable. A teacher told us: "I had a parent who stuck his face right in front of my nose the other night. My husband said, why don't you just slam the door on him? But it's for the child, and not just her, she's the oldest of three. If I can make the father understand, three children will be better off."

Many jobs in the service sector also have an intense cognitive component. Women in office work often say they are overwhelmed with overlapping tasks. This is the sequence followed by a bank teller during the course of a morning (Table 16.) When the ergonomists started to observe her, the branch manager had just asked her to pay the bank's outstanding utility and other bills. She alternated this task (column 1) with serving clients until the manager asked her to order paper for the branch. She continued alternating the second task (column 2) with serving clients and giving advice to colleagues until the manager came and asked her to do some photocopying (column 3). She alternated the second and third tasks with serving clients and helping colleagues even after the manager added a fourth task (column 4).

There was also overlap in client service. The teller usually finished the paperwork from a transaction with one client while initiating service with the second. When asked to identify stressful parts of their job, the tellers listed the need to keep too many things in their minds at once. This type of job has been characterized by psychologists as "high demand."[20]

TABLE 16: Task Alternation in the Work of a Bank Teller

		Task	
1 Pays bills	2 Orders paper	3 Photocopies	4 Cashes bond
9:37–9:42 1 client interrupts 9:45–9:50 3 clients interrupt 9:59–??			
	Observers break 30 min. 10:30–10:35 2 clients interrupt 10:38–10:44 1 client interrupts 10:46–10:48 1 colleague, assistant manager interrupt		
		10:50–10:53 1 client interrupts 10:57–11:00 1 client, 1 colleague interrupt	
	11:03–11:05	11:06–11:09	
			11:09–11:10 1 colleague interrupts 11:11–? Observers break 45 min.
		12:00–12:01 1 client, 1 colleague interrupt 12:03–12:04	
12:07–12:08			12:05–12:07
			12:08–12:09
		12:10–12:13 1 client interrupts 12:15–12:17 9 clients, 4 colleagues interrupt	

Emotional or mental labor is not *intrinsically* stressful, although some tasks may be overly demanding. Women in the helping professions find that caring is an important part of their job, making it more rewarding.[21] Only when the workers feel unable to take adequate care of those for whom they feel responsible do they run a risk of burnout, "a syndrome of emotional exhaustion, depersonalization and reduced personal accomplishment that can occur among individuals who do 'people work.' "[22]

As for assessing the mental workload, some ergonomists point out that it is hard to quantify even a physical workload using only external criteria. That is, a load too heavy for one worker may be perfectly acceptable to another. A weight handled with ease in the morning is not so light in the late afternoon, when the worker is tired. Picking up a weight in a twisted position is much harder than picking it up while standing straight. Lifting a squirming child is more difficult than lifting a box of the same weight. Ergonomists suggest that weighing physical loads gives the illusion of being able to measure a workload but that the number of pounds or kilograms does not correspond to the effort exerted and perceived by every worker. Scientists have worked for years to develop labor standards for a stressful physical load—so many kilograms lifted so many times over so long a period. Nevertheless, most physical workloads are too complicated to be assessed in this way, and the guidelines are recognized as being approximate.

We do not have even the illusion of being able to measure mental workloads. Ergonomists believe that information overload can exist, but that the threshold cannot be accurately described, since it is related to the individual's capacity to treat information in the given environment.[23] Similarly, the emotional requirements of a task may be acceptable to some workers at some times but unbearable in other circumstances. Are four tasks at once too many for a bank teller? How long should a waitress be required to smile?[24]

RESPECT

Workers often mention lack of respect as a stressor on their jobs. Both male and female cleaners dislike the way they are treated and bring it up as a particularly hard part of their jobs. "We're the hospital trash," said the cleaners. Blue-collar workers in general resent being treated as inferiors. Lack of respect can be felt when workers are left out of important consultations, when their physical environment is inadequate, when their problems are not listened to, or when they must ask for permission to go to the bathroom.

In the case of women, the sense of lack of respect can arise from discriminatory practices. The most obvious such practice is low pay, a consequence of the lack of recognition of women's skills and competence.[25] In North America, the woman worker takes home about 70 percent of the hourly pay of the average man. Differentials for women of color are even greater.

Women also experience discriminatory treatment in task allocation. As described in Chapter 3, women cleaners are usually assigned to "light cleaning" and men to "heavy cleaning." Many cleaners and supervisors of both sexes think "light" cleaning is harder because of the faster pace and more taxing postures. Yet women cleaners told us that they had to take a test to enter "heavy cleaning," which the men did not have to take to enter "light cleaning."[26] They felt that calling their work "light" expressed an underestimation of its difficulty. As pointed out earlier, this type of division of labor is common in factories and services. Women find it difficult to be promoted and hard to get recognition for their contributions.[27] This lack of recognition may affect women's general state of mind and gnaw away at their self-image.[28]

Sexual harassment, one form of discrimination, has recently been recognized as a source of stress, and women in several provinces in Canada have been compensated under workers' compensation for psychological damage. [29] However, women's claims for psychological disability have been refused on the ground that sexual harassment is a normal working condition for women in some jobs, such as prison guard.[30] (However, a man *accused* of sexual harassment was compensated by the same tribunal, who found that the accusation put him in an unusually stressful situation, not to be expected at his job.)

BALANCING WORK AND FAMILY

Probably the largest group of studies of women workers relates mental health symptoms to the problems of balancing work and family. Mothers of young children are particularly absorbed by the competing demands of workplace and family. Some studies emphasize feelings engendered by "role conflict," a psychological problem in reconciling contradictory expectations, while others suggest that stress comes from the time pressure and schedule adjustments required of working mothers.[31]

Cries of distress are regularly heard from organized women workers. In Québec, the women's committee of the largest trade union launched a campaign to find solutions for work–family problems and encountered a very enthusiastic response. Their booklet on these problems sold out twice, and their office received many calls for information on the subject. In response to the demand, they made a video that was extremely popular. The union campaign was successful, I believe, because it named and described the workplace origin of factors contributing to work-family conflict. Instead of blaming the women workers for not being well organized, it explained why it is impossible for an individual worker to be the perfect mother and the perfect worker in the conditions provided by many companies.

We studied a group of workers who were very unhappy because of work schedules incompatible with family life.[32] Telephone operators are now scheduled according to just-in-time principles: that is, no more operators should be present at any time than the minimum needed to handle incoming calls. To accomplish this, a clerk responsible for scheduling collects information for the following week about holidays, weather predictions, popular television programs or sports events during which few phone calls would be made, and historical data on call density for the same week in previous years. She enters these data into a computer program along with operators' requested hours and days off, in order of seniority. Every Thursday, the program produces the time sheet for the following work week. The workers then learn what their schedule will be.

Operators enter at 15-minute intervals and work for eight hours. The beginning time can vary as much as 10 hours from one day to the next and back again the following day. A worker can start at 6 AM on Monday, 4 PM on Tuesday, 8 AM on Wednesday, and so forth. Somewhat less severe but similar principles are now being used to adjust supply and demand for supermarket cashiers, airline reservation clerks, hospital workers, and bank tellers.

These schedules create problems for operators with young children, especially since their salaries are too low to allow them to pay for day care. Couples have tried to adjust their hours so that one would always be home and they would not have to get babysitters. One operator with a newborn took the night shift (midnight to eight) because she could be sure of having an invariable schedule (there was little competition for this shift) and her husband, who worked days, could "babysit" while sleeping. She snatched her sleep during the day in the intervals between feeding the baby and household tasks. Couples using this kind of arrangement rarely spent time together, particularly if the husband was forced to work overtime. One operator told us she had not seen her husband awake in six days.

When schedules conflicted, the company had at least 10 different systems whereby hours could be exchanged. The most common was exchanging hours with another operator. We saw an operator glance at the time sheet and instantly activate her mental computer. Less than a minute after looking at the schedule, she explained: "I want Marie's hours but she won't like mine. She does like Jacqueline's. Jacqueline won't like mine either but she'll take Annie's and Annie will take mine. So I will trade with Annie to get hours I can trade with Jacqueline to be able to trade for Marie's." The company responded to this practice by limiting the number of people involved in these exchanges to four, but the operators studied continued to screen the time sheet for exchange possibilities. The 30 examined the time sheet to check their hours or someone else's 314 times during the 10 working days of the study.

Operators could also request unpaid time off or accumulate time to be traded in for future time off. However, all changes had to be approved by the company, usually by reaching the right person over the telephone. Astonishingly, operators at work could not use the telephone, a key tool for keeping in touch with the family, being reassured about family safety, and checking on babysitting arrangements. None of the procedures undertaken to trade or change hours could be done during worktime. Fellow employees could not be contacted because workers had staggered breaks and mealtimes. Breaks, lunchtime, and family time were taken up by the 156 procedures used to change hours during the 10 working days. To this should be added the 212 other procedures they used to rearrange existing day care arrangements in order to meet new schedules.

This type of work–family conflict occupies a great deal of women's time and creativity. Even in families where men share the actual housework and child care (or elder care), women say they still have major responsibility for planning and assuring that these tasks are done.

Linking Stressors to Health Effects

Scientists have demonstrated some physical effects of stress, such as heart disease and possible impacts on the immune system. Their results are not as conclusive as they might be because studies have been gender-insensitive or even frankly sexist. Effects on the psyche have been even harder to establish. It is not easy to demonstrate associations between psychological stressors and health effects in such a way as to satisfy compensation boards or orient changes in the workplace.

The cause and effect link is even more difficult to establish than for cases involving physical disability. After 20 years as an asbestos miner, a worker can develop a fairly limited number of asbestos-related diseases: mesothelioma, asbestosis, and other lung diseases. A single cause—asbestos fibers—can be linked with a defined series of effects. Even with such a very specifically asbestos-linked disease as mesothelioma, it took time for scientists to identify the cause of the disease, and it was exceedingly hard for workers to gain compensation. With less-defined diseases, such as musculoskeletal problems, the battle is harder. With stress-related problems, establishing links with the workplace is still more difficult because both the causes and the effects are hard to identify and establish. Stressful events or conditions at home may amplify the effects of stressors in the workplace, with no single stressor emerging as overwhelmingly responsible for a symptom. Symptoms themselves are varied and hard to link with the stressors. Since the stress reaction involves many physiological systems, stress-related diseases and disorders can range from unhappiness to digestive problems to psychiatric illness to heart disease. The scientist or health and safety activist wishing to establish a cause for workplace stress reactions has trouble identifying the relevant symptoms, picking out which conditions to look at, and making the links.

It is therefore no wonder that many scientists have chosen to study stress in the workplace by examining "real," objectively defined phenomena such as heart disease rather than psychological symptoms. If the causes remain undefined, at least the effect is relatively easy to document.

WORKING CONDITIONS AND HEART DISEASE

The physical effect that has been most often studied in relation to workplace stressors acting on the mind is cardiovascular disease. Most scientists who have studied heart disease by occupation have restricted their samples to men.[33] Although coronary artery disease is the most common cause of death among women,[34] and as many women as men report hypertension, heart disease is still thought of as a man's problem.[35] For example, in discussing a 1996 article relating heart disease to psychosocial working conditions among 12,517 men, the editor of a scientific journal spoke of the results as though they related to all heart disease. Without reference to the gender limitation, he praised the authors because they "further expand our understanding of the possible causal contribution to . . . coronary artery disease, of occupational and nonoccupational psychological demands, control of the work process by employees and social support at work."[36] It is impossible to tell from the editorial whether the relationships mentioned apply to women, and some evidence suggests they not.[37]

This attitude reminds us of the recently revealed biases in the *treatment* of coronary artery disease. Women do not manifest heart disease in exactly the same way as men. Since physicians think that women are less likely to have serious coronary artery disease, they may not recognize this disease among women. They intervene later and do fewer procedures on women than on men, even when the women have more serious symptoms.[38] Women with diagnosed coronary artery disease admitted to hospital are therefore more likely to die.[39] Delay in recognizing that women get heart disease may have unfortunate consequences for women workers as well. We do not know whether the working conditions associated with heart disease in women are the same as those most important for men, or whether new determinants ought to be looked for.

Even when women are included in studies of heart disease, scientific practices such as adjusting for gender and gender-insensitive analysis also keep us from understanding specific factors that may be related to cardiovascular diseases of women. Using data from a large health survey, Leigh studied blood pressure by job title in an attempt to relate working conditions to effects on the cardiovascular system.[40] Several job titles commonly held by women were found among the 10 professions with the highest diastolic blood pressure:[41] laundry and dry cleaning operatives, food service workers, private child care workers, and telephone operators. This study adjusted for gender rather than examining job title and blood pressure separately for women and men. The latter procedure would have been more appropriate, since men's and women's blood pressure varies differently with age, and since men and women with the same job title do not necessarily do the same work. Because of these sources of inaccuracy, the study may underestimate links between job strain and signs of heart disease for all workers.

A review of studies on the relation between the nonchemical work environment and cardiovascular disease yields no evidence that the re-viewer considered gender important either in identifying working conditions or in influencing the physiology of the circulatory sys-tem.[42] The author reviews the effects on the heart of working in the heat and in the cold, but, despite well-known sex differences in ther-mal regulation,[43] does not consider effects separately by sex. In fact, I could not tell from the review whether any women at all were included in the studies reviewed, aside from a mention that studies were con-sidered to be better if they adjusted for sex. This gender-insensitivity is particularly surprising since the author is known for having care-fully investigated women's and men's working conditions in indus-try.[44] Probably his insistence, based on scientific rules, on giving pri-ority to studies that adjusted for sex prevented him from considering the influence of gender on workplace-induced cardiovascular disease.

Because of the importance of this health problem, it is important to examine women's working conditions in relation to cardiovascular disease. Before the late 1980s, on those occasions when women were included in studies to determine the causes of heart disease, their working conditions were rarely mentioned. At best, their general em-ployment status (employed versus unemployed or housewife) was considered. The exclusion of women's working conditions could be ex-treme, as when Moser and colleagues examined the effects of unem-ployment on the coronary health of unemployed men *and their wives,* but did not include unemployed women or their husbands.[45]

The studies of heart disease that have reported results concerning the employment status of women found no difference in actual car-diovascular disease between employed women and housewives.[46] However, hypertension and other risk factors for such disease were found more often among housewives. This difference may be re-lated to the fact that people with health problems tend to leave the workplace (the "healthy worker effect"). We are unable to evaluate this source of bias, since information on the employment history of the housewives was not included in these investigations.[47]

Recently, researchers have started to include women when exam-ining the cardiovascular effects of stressful working conditions.

Women working on shifts,[48] women with clerical or sales jobs,[49] and women reporting that their work is both hectic and monotonous have a higher incidence of coronary heart disease.[50] Blood pressure of women (and men) in unskilled work is higher than that of managers, and blood pressure of those who are exposed to noise or work on an assembly line is higher than that of people not exposed to these conditions.[51] Noise exposure has also been associated with higher blood pressure among pregnant women.[52]

Although many of the above stressors act on the mind, factors like shift work, hectic work, and noise may produce effects on the circulatory system through other mechanisms as well. Researchers have therefore tried to develop instruments specifically to measure psychosocial and organizational factors associated with heart disease. The best-known of these was developed by the psychologist Robert Karasek and the cardiologist Töres Theorell, who use a questionnaire to measure "job strain," a combination of heavy demands and little control over how the job is done.[53] This questionnaire has been used by over 100 research groups. Initially studying male subjects, Karasek and colleagues found that high job strain predicts the occurrence of heart disease. Using the Karasek-Theorell approach, Hall found that jobs assigned to women were characterized by a low level of job control and were more likely to be stressful.[54] However, of 36 studies relating job strain to cardiovascular disease symptoms or risk factors, reviewed by Schnall in 1994, 22 concerned only men, 12 both men and women, and two only women. The average all-male study involved an average 2,533 subjects and was therefore fairly large, expensive, and definitive; the two all-female studies involved a total of 576 subjects.[55]

Studies concluded that both sexes had more cardiovascular disease if exposed to more job strain. However, women and men in four professions studied by Theorell did not have the same psychosocial work environment. Because of differences in job content, co-workers of one sex could have more or fewer risk factors for cardiovascular disease than opposite-sex workers in the same profession.[56]

When research teams sought to build on the job-strain theory by examining whether the level of social support available to the worker was an additional determinant of heart disease, results were inconclusive. Very recently, researchers have discovered a reason for the confusion: women and men with the same job title react differently to their social networks.[57] Researchers are now wondering whether the difference lies in the workers' reactions or in their environment. As we have seen, women and men with the same job title do not face the same expectations.

Research on another aspect of physiology, hormone metabolism, leads us to believe that the average woman and man may deal differently with the same stressors. Marianne Frankenhaeuser and her colleagues initiated a series of laboratory tests in order to examine the effects of the normal work day on male and female managers and clerical workers at the Volvo plant in Sweden. Within these job categories, women and men reported different working conditions and different levels of work–family conflict. The resting levels of stress-related hormones did not differ between women and men, but reactions to psychological stressors in the laboratory did vary by sex.[58]

OTHER PHYSICAL EFFECTS

Studies on other physical effects of stress are in their infancy. Learning about the effect of psychological stress on the immune system may help understand the processes leading to occupational cancer and to infectious disease. Effects of stressors in the workplace on the immune system have been examined by very few investigators, and none has considered gender. A group of Norwegian researchers led by Vaernes are among the few to have done several studies of stress and the immune response. They have studied the effects of perceived work stress on the immune system of military aviators and some other occupational groups, such as divers and nurses. Using a questionnaire, they found that aviators' reports of time pressure on the job were associated with raised or lowered levels of certain proteins involved in immune defense. The results were not clearly comparable with the authors' earlier studies of immune responses of stressed workers,[59] and no consistent relationship between stressors and immune responses has yet been demonstrated.

This study was not gender-sensitive: it neglected to report the sex of the workers, although the way the authors report their results makes it probable that all pilots and offshore divers were male. The authors qualify offshore divers as a "high stress group," in contrast to nurses and primary school teachers with what are called "more ordinary jobs."[60] No explanation is given for calling conditions of nurses and teachers "more ordinary" than those of divers. In fact, the same article reports that measurements of stress level related to the work environment were similar for the nurses and the divers. In another article, signed by two of the same authors, teachers are described as having "intense work periods and subjective stress levels."[61] In the absence of another explanation for the discrepancies, we must suspect the authors of prejudice regarding women's work.

Research on hormones and immune receptors is of critical importance to women workers. Given the difficulties women confront when trying to demonstrate health effects of their work, being able to show "objective," "real" biological effects of workplace conditions is of particular value to them. Demonstrating psychological effects is harder and does not, at least not yet, have the same credibility. It may not be rational for decision-makers to ascribe more importance to physical than to psychic effects of jobs, but it is a common practice. It is therefore unimportant that these psycho-physiological studies demonstrate awareness of the stressors in women's jobs and at home.

HOW OCCUPATIONAL HEALTH SPECIALISTS LOOK AT PSYCHOLOGICAL EFFECTS

Although occupational stress is recognized by psychologists as an important problem for women and men, few occupational health specialists have explored mental health problems related to work. This may be a cause or a result of the fact that compensation for mental health problems is extremely difficult to obtain. "Most medical experts [called in compensation cases] seem uncomfortable with the inevitable uncertainty involved in all claims for psychological disability, and find comforting the idea that all claims should be refused."[62] It is particularly hard for women to be compensated.[63]

One scientific procedure that has been used with some success is to analyze psychic states or disorders by job title. For example, Gervais found that women cleaners had much higher levels of all mental problems (depression, anxiety, distress, etc.) than other workers. The cleaners may suffer at their jobs, or those with social problems may have chosen this profession because it is possible to do one's job with relatively little human contact.

According to Gervais, waitresses and saleswomen also experienced more psychological distress than other women workers.[64] She notes that women are at risk because of the kinds of jobs they do and not their sex, since women make up the majority of workers in those jobs where men have the most mental health problems.[65] Again, interpretation is not simple: the psychic requirements of these jobs may be too heavy for the average man, or men with mental health problems may choose nontraditional jobs.

Suicide should be a good indicator of psychological distress, even for women, who are seven times less likely than men to commit suicide. There are relatively few studies of suicide among women workers. One review of the literature suggests that, among women workers, health professionals, psychologists, chemists, social workers, draftswomen, unskilled workers, schoolteachers, secretaries, and cashiers have high suicide rates.[66]

Diagnosed psychiatric illness has also been used as an indicator of psychological effects of work. Shift work was found to be associated with psychiatric illness diagnosed during an annual medical examination of female hospital workers.[67] A recent issue of the journal *Work and Stress* was devoted to the problem of shift work and stress among nurses and other women.[68] Night shifts, long shifts, shifts that start early in the morning, and rotating shifts each appeared to cause problems, affecting the worker's mood and job satisfaction and spilling over into other aspects of life. These shifts are a problem because of disruption of physiological rhythms and also because workers find some shifts particularly hard to reconcile with family life.

The job-strain model developed by Karasek and Theorell has been used to look at psychological as well as cardiovascular effects and has served to standardize studies of stress in the workplace. Karasek has found a relationship between job strain and symptoms of depression, exhaustion, and psychological distress. Because these studies controlled for sex, we have no idea whether women and men react the same way.[69]

HOW PSYCHOLOGISTS LOOK AT EFFECTS OF WORK

The traditional agencies responsible for occupational health and safety research have allocated few resources to studying psychological distress.[70] The variables examined in relation to psychological distress of working women have usually been different from those used in standard occupational health research. Because the field is driven by mental health specialists, they less often include careful descriptions of workplace conditions and more often concentrate on characteristics of the worker. This makes it difficult to identify specific working conditions that cause psychological problems. It is hard for health and safety representatives to know which factors to change, and it is hard for workers to get compensation.

To investigate industrial psychologists' approaches to psychological problems produced by stressors in the workplace, I went to the American Psychological Association's 1995 conference on Work, Health and Stress, held in Washington, D.C. My hope that I would encounter a large sample of current work in industrial psychology was justified. About 400 scientists proposed explanations for the interactions of different factors that produce psychological distress. Not surprisingly, I was in for a culture shock: the orientation of these presentations was quite different from that found in occupational health meetings. It was no longer taboo to talk about feelings, sex was always included in the list of variables, qualitative research was allowed. One session treated problems of women, and several spoke of work and family. A panel dealt explicitly with gender differences in mental health in the workplace. The authors suggested that women and men in the workplace were exposed to different stressors and reacted differently to them. They mentioned power relationships, emotional labor, and work–family conflicts as well as differences in coping.[71]

However, scientific biases identified elsewhere in this book and in occupational health research in general were also present at the APA meeting. Men and women were sometimes lumped together without reference to the possibility that, because of their social situations, the mechanisms regulating their psychological states might not be the same. Controlling for sex was often done without any consideration of whether this was an appropriate procedure. In addition, gender insensitivity seemed to be hidden in some of the instruments used to measure psychological states. These instruments, like the Karasek job content questionnaire, were sometimes validated for men only and then applied to women, leaving out variables important for women.

Some assumptions about women's innate characteristics have created biased instruments. For example, a recent study of workplace determinants of depression scored women as depressed at a score of 23 and men at 17 on the same test.[72] Thus, the fact that women had more symptoms of depression was "normalized" and could not be related to working conditions in this study. That this attitude may be unjustified was shown by another study. U.S. Army researchers showed that when civilian and military army employees and their spouses reported sexual harassment and gender discrimination, they were very likely to suffer from depression. Although women scored higher on depression than men, the difference disappeared when sexual harassment and gender discrimination were accounted for.[73]

When psychologists study work and stress, they examine different variables from occupational health scientists. Understandably, they often emphasize identifying successful individuals' coping strategies or personal characteristics rather than pinpointing workplace determinants of stress. They have done extensive research on the effects of paid and unpaid work on psychological health, often expressed as "role conflict." For technical reasons, it may be easier to find statistically significant associations between health symptoms and difficult conditions in family situations than in paid work. Family and work may be equally complex, but researchers can easily find out whether a woman is married, if she has children, and the ages of the children. Researchers are usually familiar with family relationships, and many are also acquainted with the domestic workload, so that they can ask relevant questions.

Precise information about the widely varying conditions of paid work is hard to come by. As mentioned in earlier chapters, job titles are relatively uninformative, and other sources of information on exposures are hard to access. In addition, the most difficult working conditions are often unfamiliar to researchers, who have jobs with very different requirements. Not many researchers worked on assembly lines or in banks. Production workers are usually excluded from the family-friendly policies designed by human resources specialists.[74] It is hard for most university researchers to get access to the paid workplace or to find out what questions to ask of workers in order to identify relevant psychosocial variables. They are often reduced to asking general questions about job satisfaction or relations with supervisors or to using standard job content questionnaires that may miss essential elements in a given workplace.

For example, not much information is available on how company policies relevant to work–family conflict influence psychological distress in the work force. I have seen no studies relating psychological problems to policies on absence for family reasons, on access to telephones, on penalties for being late, or on length of maternity leave. Close scrutiny of life at work is necessary in order to identify the ways some management practices affect work/family conflict. For example, in a clothing factory studied by Nicole Vézina of CINBIOSE, women had problems when quality circles were introduced.[75] A job that had been done on an assembly line by workers, each assigned to a separate operation, was reorganized. It was reassigned to a quality circle, a group of workers who shared responsibility for the job as a whole. Theoretically, quality circles are just what workers need: they are supposed to increase job satisfaction and lower the incidence of MSDs by decreasing repetition and increasing autonomy. In this factory, however, a change from the piecework system (workers paid per item produced) to a group quota system (workers in a group paid according to the group's production) was a nightmare for the women involved. Among other problems, they cited their inability to take time off for family reasons. Before, only they themselves lost pay if a child was sick and they took the day off. With the new system, the group's production was lowered when they were replaced by less experienced workers. They felt guilty for depriving the others of their pay, other workers were resentful, and relations with colleagues, formerly a source of pleasure, became painful and even ugly.

Prevention

Although studies of the health effects of stressors abound, not very many are of use to women workers wanting to identify and remove sources of distress on the job. The studies give insufficient detail about working conditions and often concentrate on worker characteristics. Most are more useful to managers seeking to identify workers who will suffer from psychological problems.

Health and safety inspectors and union representatives have developed ways of examining physical risks in factories and offices. If workers are feeling dizzy, the air is checked for chemicals. If they find excessive levels of chemicals, they can suggest changes in ventilation or in procedures. If workers have tendinitis, repetitive work may be pinpointed for attention. The methods may not always produce satisfactory results, but at least there are procedures to follow that make some sense.

With psychological distress, it is harder to get a grip on the problem. A stressful situation is often composed of many small details rather than a single stressor. They may involve and affect aspects of family life that are rarely mentioned in the workplace. In addition, the problem may involve such "untouchable" or taboo aspects of working life as the supervisor's personality, ability to call home from the workplace, relationships with co-workers, or inability to cope with problem clients. Perhaps for this reason, employer-based and many union-based stress interventions emphasize the development of coping skills rather than elimination of stressful working conditions.[76]

Recent years have seen a proliferation of stress-reduction programs directed at redesigning the worker. The programs may locate the source of stress in the home or in personal problems and tell the workers that they should learn how to handle it. Teachers, social workers and others in the helping professions are encouraged to set limits on their involvement. "Health promotion approaches, which have constituted the overwhelming majority of worksite stress reduction efforts, include educating employees about the causes and consequences of stress, teaching strategies for solving problems or thinking differently about problems, and providing resources for reducing the symptoms associated with elevated levels of perceived stress (e.g., fitness centers, quiet relaxation areas, biofeedback equipment)."[77]

In fact, attacking stressors in the workplace may require a different approach, one more oriented toward a different kind of worker involvement in transforming the way work is conceived, allocated, and accomplished.

Stressors in a workplace can be diverse and they can affect multiple targets.[78] Therefore a single-factor, single-effect model is not appropriate for stress investigations. Changing relationships between different job parameters and worker strain has led several researchers to propose a more global approach to occupational stress.[79] In the Netherlands, a law requires employers to do an annual survey to report on the collective mental and physical health of their employees, encouraging employers to intervene in work organization as well as the work environment. Similar initiatives are beginning in Scandinavia.

"Work psychodynamics," a psychoanalytically inspired approach that proposes to "cure" sick workplaces, has been developed in France.[80] The "therapist" meets with workers in a given workplace who describe the sources of pleasure and pain in their work. They describe their coping mechanisms and thus reveal "collective defense strategies" that are pointed out by the psychologist. In some cases, the psychologists have collaborated with unions in order to press for changes that would reduce the suffering of workers.[81] The reports of projects in work psychodynamics are original in that they use workers' own words to convey their experience of workplace constraints. The secret defenses of workers confronted with impossible situations are respected, but are used as a basis for suggesting changes in work organization. For example, (male) workers in one very dangerous job were forced by management to initial reports saying that they had observed safety procedures that were in fact impossible to follow. According to Dejours (personal communication), they responded to this confrontation with a risk to their lives by denying their fears and the risk itself. Their denial led them to perform feats of derring-do that actually increased the danger. The psychologist recommended instituting realistic safety procedures in consultation with the workers.

This approach is still in its infancy. Dejours has worked primarily with all-male groups exposed to physical danger: pilots, nuclear power plant workers, soldiers, construction workers. Little attention has been given to gender, although several collaborators have done studies of telephone operators, nurses, and teachers. The feminist sociologists Hirata and Kergoat have suggested that gender relations be considered in developing concepts in work psychodynamics as well as women's specific relationship to paid work.[82] A student of Dejours, Marie-Claire Carpentier-Roy, discusses in psychoanalytic terms how nurses deal with the stress of caring for patients with AIDS.[83] She sees the employer as exploiting feminine fantasies of mothering (l'imaginaire féminin),[84] and suggests several measures to increase nurses' self-esteem and power through recognition of their work, giving them more autonomy and discretion over task content.

Although I agree with her conclusions, I am a bit ill at ease with the analysis behind Carpentier-Roy's work. I have trouble with an essentialist approach[85] that presumes that women share fantasies of mothering and men do not. This approach, rooted in psychoanalysis, seems to me to have some of the problems for women that others have identified in Freudian analysis. I am also uneasy with the technique where the expert in psychodynamics is responsible for interpreting workers' behavior.

I prefer the approach of Catherine Teiger, a French psychologist who teaches workers to analyze their own work activity and accompanies them as they become aware of its risks[86] and change their working conditions. Several groups now employ the same approach: participatory training, recognition of worker knowledge, a global approach to the workplace, questioning the role of experts.[87] So far, these approaches have concentrated on traditional physical risks like chemicals and physical strain. But it seems to me that they would also apply to the improvement of mental health, and we (and others such as Dorothy Wigmore at NIOSH) are experimenting with this.

Conclusion

Stressful conditions are common in traditionally female jobs. To these are added the stressors involved in ensuring that family needs are met. Many, probably most, women workers would nevertheless say that they love their jobs and their families. They would not want either to leave work and become full-time housewives or to abandon their family ties. Most service workers would not even want to become less involved with the recipients of their services. All groups we have studied say that the relationship with other people is the best part of their jobs. These advantages, however, do not protect the workers from experiencing health effects from the various stressors.

It is therefore especially hard to prevent workplace stress for women, since the very aspects of their jobs that they find pleasurable can become the most important stressors. The caring and loving they do on the job are thought even by researchers to be natural aspects of their feminine characters rather than job demands that should be examined and, perhaps, re-engineered.

10

Reproductive Hazards

■ ■ ■

The analyses in Chapters 7 to 9 concerned gender insensitivity among occupational health scientists. We found that although musculoskeletal problems, indoor air pollution, and stress are not specific to women, scientists who study them often fail to take into account the context of most women's work and lives. With reproduction, the situation is different. It is hard to be unaware of the importance of gender because women and men have different reproductive systems. One would think, therefore, that scientists who study reproduction would be gender-sensitive.

At the crudest level this is true, but women workers' needs have not been fully met by the studies of reproductive hazards in the workplace. In fact, paradoxically, women have been *excluded* from most studies of risks for pregnancy, and other reproductive problems important to women have been neglected.

Work and Pregnancy

The reproductive system of working women "belongs" to society in a way that men's does not. If they wish, men may have many children without their colleagues and superiors being aware of it, but pregnancy is visible. In addition, while sperm are generally considered to belong to the male worker alone, pregnancy concerns not only the woman but also the fetus, which may sometimes be considered to be a member of the general population (for example, in regulations regarding radiation exposure).

It is therefore not surprising that, unlike the occupational risks mentioned previously, reproductive hazards in the workplace have been most studied in relation to women, particularly pregnant women. Injuries to male and female fertility, sexual and reproductive functioning, and the ability to nurse babies take second place to concerns about pregnancy. The preface to a 1985 textbook with the rather general title *Occupational Hazards and Reproduction* justifies the interest in reproduction by citing the presence of women in the workplace. It begins: "The percentage of women among the labor force has increased markedly during the past decades. With improvements in the equality of employment, women have entered jobs where exposure to harmful chemical agents may occur."[1] In its first lines, the 1993 feminist guide *Reproductive Hazards in the Workplace* declares: "Work is as much a part of a woman's life today as is marriage, pregnancy and motherhood."[2] The initial paragraph of the 1994 "Occupational Health: State-of-the-art Review" explains its focus on reproductive hazards, after mentioning the large numbers of chemicals in the workplace, by noting the growing numbers of women in the workplace and in nontraditional jobs in particular.[3] It is clear from these and other books and articles that pregnant women have been the starting point for studies of reproductive hazards.

Initial research concentrated on chemical hazards: lead, arsenic, mercury, benzene. During pregnancy, a woman's respiration and metabolism are more active, increasing her exposure to chemicals. This remains a popular research area, and evidence has accumulated on teratogenic effects of occupational exposures to pesticides, solvents, pharmaceuticals, metals, and dyes (teratogenic agents are those that harm fetuses if a pregnant woman is exposed). The 1995 edition of Shepard's catalog of teratogenic agents lists 2,571 chemicals with effects on the fetus.[4]

Some physical agents have also attracted attention. The effects of ionizing radiation such as X-rays have been extensively studied because developing cells are preferentially attacked by radiation. Children exposed before birth may develop malformations or cancer.[5] More recently, scientists have shown that operators of some sewing machines with dense electromagnetic fields risk fetal damage.[6] Possible risks to the fetus from the mother's work with VDTs have also excited scientific interest (see Chapter 8). Noise has been shown to affect the developing fetal ear as well as lowering birth weight and shortening the pregnancy.[7]

Other effects on pregnancy are beginning to be documented. The pregnant woman changes in size and shape, and her interaction with the work station changes. Increased demands on or interference with her circulatory system may affect the blood supply to the fetus. Ergonomic hazards such as prolonged sitting or standing or exertion of physical effort have been associated with increased risks of miscarriage,[8] low birthweight, and prematurity.[9] Shift work has also been found to affect pregnancy outcome.[10] Psychosocial stress is thought to affect rates of spontaneous abortion and possibly prematurity and low birthweight.[11]

The vast majority of these studies concern effects of working conditions on the fetus: miscarriage, low birthweight, prematurity. This is surprising, since most conditions that affect fetuses also affect pregnant women. In 1987, Cherry remarked that "there appear to have been few systematic studies that have focused on the health of the [pregnant] woman herself rather than on the threat to the infant."[12] Since then, a few researchers have studied such phenomena as back pain or hypertension among pregnant workers,[13] but concern about health effects on the woman is still rare in the occupational health literature. This is why I say at the beginning of the chapter that women have been excluded from studies of pregnancy.[14]

Women themselves may have trouble asking for changes in the workplace to benefit themselves, and may find it easier to ask for help for their fetuses. Consider this advice given to pregnant women by a feminist- and union-sponsored organization: "If you experience severe physical fatigue [during pregnancy], this could mean that the fetus is not getting enough nutrition from your blood for extended periods of time. Take rest breaks that are long enough and often enough to allow your heart rate and breathing to return to normal."[15] As if severe physical fatigue is not reason enough to take sufficient rest, rest has to be justified by potential damage to the fetus.

With all the fuss about possible effects of electromagnetic radiation from VDTs on fetuses, it is especially striking that no one has studied whether working with VDTs induces breast cancer in office workers. Male breast cancer, occurring at less than 3 percent of the female rate, has been studied and related to electromagnetic radiation among electrical workers, exposed to cumulative levels of radiation that are not all that different.[16]

We could interpret the lack of interest in the effects of working conditions on women as sexism or androcentrism, but we find it also among those with a feminist perspective. The American scientific journal *Occupational Medicine* publishes "state-of-the-art reviews" on questions of interest. In 1993 it published a 215-page issue entitled *Women Workers,* edited by feminist physicians and containing articles primarily written by those with a similar outlook. I consulted it to answer a question from a health care workers' union about the effects of work on lower back pain during pregnancy. The chapter on "Occupational Reproductive Health Risks" is wholly about fetuses and contains no information on effects on pregnant women. I also tried the section "Women and Ergonomics," which discussed only issues surrounding the integration of women into nontraditional factory jobs; there was no mention of pregnancy.[17] The 196-page "state-of-the-art review" on reproductive hazards (1994) contains no mention of back pain or any other women's health problem except as such problems affect the ability to become pregnant or to carry a healthy baby to term.

To understand why feminist scientists would ignore women's needs in this way, we have to look at the preface to *Women Workers,* which sets the context with the question, "How do we protect fetuses while at the same time providing women with equal employment opportunities?" The chapter on reproductive risks begins with the same preoccupation: "Today's obstetrician practices in a climate of increasing litigation for adverse pregnancy outcomes or birth defects. It is no wonder that many take a conservative view toward women and work."[18] The "state-of-the-art review" on reproductive health contains a whole chapter on discrimination against pregnant women.[19]

Women in North America have had to fight for their right to work. In the past, women in the workplace were regarded as aberrations. It has only recently become illegal to fire women who married or became pregnant. It is not surprising that the female reproductive system has been treated as if it rendered women unfit to work. The U.S. Supreme Court found in the case of *United Auto Workers* v. *Johnson Controls, Inc.* that women's reproductive specificity should not be treated as abnormal. In 1992, Johnson Controls excluded fertile women but not fertile men from working in its battery-production department, with the argument that exposure to lead in the department could damage a fetus. Although lead also damages sperm, only the women's reproductive damage was a concern for Johnson Controls management. The resulting suit by the union was refused by the U.S. District Court but accepted by the Supreme Court.[20]

Although these rights have been won, they are still fragile. Women are still paid much less than men and have less secure jobs. Employers are still impatient with any trouble caused by childbearing or child care, and will not hesitate to punish the worker whose pregnancy appears to pose a problem.[21] Brazilian chemical workers told me that pregnant women were frequently given the heaviest jobs in order to induce them to leave before they would be eligible for maternity leave. From 1990 to 1995, 67 percent of complaints brought before the Québec Labour Standards Commission involved the firing of pregnant women.[22] In the United States, several thousand cases per year are filed under the Pregnancy Discrimination Act.[23]

In this context many feel that the less fuss made about pregnancy, the better for women. It would be most convenient for equal rights activists if pregnant women could perform for nine months as though they were not pregnant, take a few days to give birth and recover, and return to work shortly with no ill effects on themselves or the fetus. And many women in many jobs can do just that. But women with poor health, unusual problems, or dangerous jobs need extra rest, more time off, or a change in working conditions. In a number of countries these are provided by legislation. But when it became clear that exposure to lead could cause damage to fetuses and possibly lead to multimillion-dollar claims against an employer, the response of many American employers was to bar fertile women from jobs where they could be exposed to lead. "Fetal protection" policies excluding women became common in workplaces where women could be easily replaced by men.[24]

Thus, scientific studies on the effects of working conditions on fetuses have resulted in problems for those concerned with equal rights in the workplace. These problems have been especially acute in North America, and especially in the United States. The United States, alone in the industrialized world, has no national maternity or parental leave policy and no general provisions for financial support for pregnant women. There is no universal medical care. These employment and health care policies may be responsible for some differences in research practices between the United States and other countries. France, for example, has universal paid maternity leave and extra leave for those exposed to difficult conditions. Several other provisions ease working conditions for pregnant women:

a shorter work day, time for prenatal visits to the doctor, and more comfortable work stations in some industries where adjustments appear necessary.[25] A research unit belonging to INSERM, the French equivalent of the National Institutes of Health in the United States, specializes in studies of women's health and has done research on work and pregnancy since the early 1980s.

It may not be surprising that most of the research on the effects of working conditions on the health of pregnant women themselves comes from Europe: Jeanette Paul of the Netherlands has studied the changes needed to make work stations more comfortable for pregnant women;[26] Marie-Josèphe Saurel-Cubizolles of France has examined the effects of working conditions on blood pressure;[27] a group in Italy has studied employment parameters that promote depression among women shortly after the birth of children.[28]

Québec is true to its position halfway between the United States and Europe. There is a maternal and parental leave policy, but financial support during maternity leave depends on eligibility for unemployment insurance and is available to most but not all working women. There is no general policy for changes in working conditions during pregnancy, but precautionary reassignment is legislated for women exposed to conditions that pose a danger for the pregnant woman, the fetus, or nursing babies.[29] The woman is reassigned without loss of pay or benefits or, failing suitable reassignment, given leave at 90 percent of net salary.[30] In this context, where pregnancy is recognized as legitimate, feminists feel safer in doing research on conditions that pose a risk for pregnant women. Nicola Cherry's article on working conditions for pregnant women came from Québec and that on back pain of pregnant women came from Canada, whose laws and practices are similar if somewhat less favorable.[31]

IGNORANCE: WHO BEARS THE CONSEQUENCES?

Pregnant women, like other workers, may be asked to bear the costs of scientific ignorance. Testimony has often been solicited from scientists in the United States during cases on fetal protection, and in Québec in order to decide when to allow precautionary reassignment. But despite the fact that researchers have been actively exploring risks for fetuses for about 30 years, information is incomplete. Over sixty thousand chemicals are used in North American workplaces, and relatively few have been tested for reproductive effects.[32] Testing is often done by firms that have an interest in finding the chemicals safe.[33] Even when threshold limit values have been determined, usually testing has not involved females. We do know that many of the chemical substances that enter the mother's bloodstream, or their toxic metabolites, pass into the fetus or breast milk. We know little about the levels at which exposures to such chemicals as organic solvents and lead affect intellectual and psychomotor development among fetuses and babies. Even less is known about the effects of most other conditions to which pregnant women are exposed: repetitive work, fast-paced work, cramped postures, static effort.

What happens if a worker is exposed to chemicals or other conditions whose effects are unknown? The scientific impetus varies according to the legislative context. In Québec, the consequences of reproductive hazards are shared between the worker and the Occupational Health and Safety Commission. The scientific evidence serves to determine whether the worker will be relocated or whether she will be allowed precautionary leave. Since 60 percent of these reassignments and leaves are given for "ergonomics,"[34] and there is very little information on the relationship between ergonomic constraint and fetal effects, battles rage over what physical working conditions constitute a "danger" in the sense of the legislation.[35] Decisions have been made and contested over the levels of exposure to untested chemicals that will justify precautionary reassignment. Because of the costs to it of scientific uncertainty, the Québec government supported a study costing millions of dollars in order to decide which conditions produced miscarriage, low birthweight, and premature birth.[36] Feminist scientists have endeavored to justifying precautionary reassignment by demonstrating dangerous working conditions.[37]

The social context in the United States is very different and governments, employers, and feminists act a bit differently. In the United States the costs of uncertainty are borne by the individual workers, because there is no paid precautionary reassignment or leave. Therefore those interested in women's rights are more interested in downplaying the effects of unknown hazards on pregnancy in order to protect women's right to work.[38] In 1985 the Office of Technology Assessment of the U.S. Congress published a review of "current knowledge of hazards and suspected hazards to the reproductive health of America's working men and women and to the health and well-being of their children."[39] The advisory board included representation from the American Civil Liberties Union, and the report included a 44-page chapter entitled "Sex Discrimination Issues." In the chapter, as in the "state-of-the-art review," scientists concentrated on demonstrating that the same conditions that are dangerous for pregnant women are dangerous for all workers.

I was struck by the difference in the U.S. and Canadian approaches when I testified in Québec for a pregnant X-ray technician to whom precautionary reassignment had been refused (see chapter 6). In collaboration with her union, I tried to demonstrate that there was a danger for her fetus, mainly due to the possibility of accidental exposure in what seemed to be a rather careless department. The fact that the usual exposures respected international limits was irrelevant, I maintained, if there was a possibility of overexposure. I also carefully pointed out indications in the scientific literature pointing to effects on pregnancy at very low radiation doses. Meanwhile, in the United States, I heard that other scientists were defending X-ray technicians who had been fired because their employers feared that they would be liable if a malformed child was born. Feminist scientists tried to show that there was no danger to the fetus as long as international radiation standards were respected. In Québec, scientists hired by the employer tried to show that there was no danger; those hired by U.S. employers tried to establish the danger.[40]

In the absence of sufficient information, scientists can lean one way or another, depending on their political positions, just like anyone else. Each tries to support her/his position with reference to the relevant scientific literature. In the above case, we were all able to defend our positions by reference to published scientific papers. Statistically, the fetus of a pregnant X-ray technician exposed to the usual levels of radiation for her profession probably runs very little risk of damage, probably not much, if at all, more than the fetus of a male technician whose sperm also risk exposure. But since the fetus of a female worker is in her workplace, it is exposed to whatever probability of accidental exposure exists as well. I thought that the worker should be protected just in case, even though we could not show a high level of danger.

The level of protection of pregnant women in Québec should not be exaggerated. Employers protest loudly and often against the cost of precautionary reassignment (4.4 percent of the annual costs of the Occupational Health and Safety Commission).[41] Periodically, union women's committees are forced to mobilize against plans to attack the system. Recently, the researcher in charge of the multimillion-dollar study of pregnancy has suggested that the cost in dollars and in the risk to women's employment may outweigh the benefits of the legis-lation.[42] However, she calculated the benefits only in terms of the ef-fects on fetuses. I myself was initially opposed to the leave on similar grounds, until I met with several hundred women workers in union educational sessions on reproductive hazards. I summarized the effects of chemicals on fetuses, explaining that leave usually started too late to prevent most damage, and that those chemicals harmful to fetuses usually damaged sperm. Thus, I suggested, cleaning up the workplace should take priority over getting leave.

The workers explained their situations carefully so I would un-derstand better. One group had called the inspectors many times to report unlawful levels of solvents, very dangerous to pregnant (and nonpregnant) workers. The employer shrugged and paid the tiny fine every time. In the short term workers saw no way to prevent exposure to chemicals without leaving the workplace. Only the most hardened theoretician could want them to wait until similar protection was available for all in their workplace.

Besides, chemicals were only a small part of the women's work-place exposures. They described working over benches that pressed their growing stomachs, standing all day at counters till they were dizzy and their legs swelled, getting ill from bad odors in food pro-cessing, slaving over ironing machines in hot laundries, lifting chil-dren in day-care centers. These were all conditions that oppressed them at the best of times, but became unbearable during pregnancy. Leave even late in the pregnancy would ease their load. The remark that has stayed with me was made by a food processing worker: "I put up with it all the rest of the time, but I'm damned if I'll stay there when I'm pregnant." In other words, the only time she felt able and entitled to protest effectively against her working condi-tions was when she was pregnant.

In this way, precautionary reassignment in Québec has caused light to be shed on dangerous conditions in women's jobs. The fact that many working conditions are ill-adapted for pregnant workers is demonstrated dramatically by the fact that one-third of pregnant women have been granted such leave, which requires demonstra-tion of danger for themselves, the fetus, or the nursing infant.[43] Studies have shown that the women who have had access to pre-cautionary reassignment are in fact those with the harshest work-ing conditions.[44] In an ideal world, discovery of dangers for a large group of workers would result in pressure to improve the working conditions. All workers could be insulated from chemicals, allowed to sit down, and protected from infection. But the discovery that dangers for pregnant and nursing women are common has not affected the widespread notion that women's working conditions are safe. Pregnant women are just considered to be exceptionally fragile. And women in Québec support this idea, since it is the only way that most can envisage any relief from their difficult conditions.

MALE REPRODUCTIVE HAZARDS

In 1989 a student and I made a presentation to doctors at the local fertility clinic on environmental causes of male infertility. We were greeted with astonishment: "We never think of the husband, we only treat the patient!" The "patient" was, of course, the woman in the infertile couple. This idea is changing. While most clinical infertility specialists still concentrate on the female partner, the idea of protecting sperm from workplace hazards is given more and more importance.

Recent discoveries that male fertility can be affected by the workplace show that exclusion of women does not suffice to protect reproduction. A California union was responsible for the first well-publicized study. Male workers in a pesticide plant noticed that they were having trouble conceiving children. Several studies confirmed that the problem was exposure to the pesticide dibromodichloropropane (DBCP).[45] Strikingly, DBCP was outlawed in the United States shortly afterward; I can think of no workplace chemical that has been outlawed because of its effects on pregnancy.

This and other demonstrations that male reproduction could be affected by the workplace made it appear more unjust to exclude fertile women from jobs. As a pioneer researcher in male reproduction put it in 1986, "While the major focus continues to be on women and the fetus, events in the 1970s triggered a new interest in potential reproductive effects on the male."[46] We have learned that various substances and conditions affect sperm and male fertility, among them pesticides, radiation, metals, and heat exposure.

Men exposed in one Québec factory are now allowed to withdraw from lead-exposed areas if they wish to conceive a child. A few months ago I got a call from an ambitious young researcher from a fertility center. "What's hot in reproductive damage?" he asked me. He wanted to know what chemicals he could use to test his new system for detecting genetic damage in sperm. Young researchers are now aware that male genetic damage is a good area for getting research funds.

However, I am not getting calls about "hot" areas for research on pain and discomfort among pregnant workers. In fact, women's problems in these areas receive the same lack of credence as those in other areas like musculoskeletal problems and stress. The situation with regard to risks for pregnant women is similar to the situation with regard to other risks for working women. Little attention is paid to their problems if a fetus is not involved. Any problems result in pressure to eliminate the woman rather than the difficult working conditions. In this context, many women feel pressure to behave as much like men as possible so that their presence in the workplace will not be questioned.

Menstruation

Nowhere are the effects of this pressure more obvious than with regard to menstruation. Women menstruate and men do not, so menstruation clearly characterizes women. Menstruation is considered by North Americans to be highly personal and shameful.[47] Over drinks at a scientific meeting, one woman remarked to the group, "We'll know we're free when we can openly carry a tampon through the office on the way to the bathroom." None of us felt able to do that. When I was doing my Ph.D., the male lab technician told me proudly that he could always tell when a woman was menstruating by the fact that she carried her purse to the bathroom at those times. I immediately stopped carrying a purse to the bathroom, and, for years afterward, would hide my tampons in my lab coat pocket instead.

The only time CINBIOSE researchers have been thrown out of a workplace by the workers was when we asked about menstruation. When my colleagues Donna Mergler and Nicole Vézina were studying food processing workers, some mentioned severe menstrual cramps, which they associated with cold conditions. Mergler and Vézina devised a questionnaire to study this and other effects of cold, and administered it in nine poultry processing plants. In the tenth, workers refused to answer the questionnaire, saying it was "too personal." When pressed, they pointed to the questions on menstrual cramps.

This study was, however, carried out in the other nine factories and led to the first report of dysmenorrhea related to cold exposure in the workplace.[48] This was an exceptional article: the scientific literature on menstruation has rarely concerned itself with the effects of workplace risk factors on menstrual cycle symptoms, and Western occupational health literature has almost never included menstrual symptoms among outcome variables. At the time, the authors did a literature search and found that almost all scientific papers on menstruation and work concerned whether women were *fit* to work at various stages in the menstrual cycle.

In 1995, I repeated the search in the Medline medical database for English-language articles, using as keyword "menstr-" associated with "work" or "environment" to identify articles dealing with menstruation and the occupational environment. The search yielded the results shown in Table 17.

The total literature (articles in medical journals found with "menstr-" as a keyword) went from 624 references in 1983 to 767 ten years later, a rise of 23 percent. Articles on menstruation and work rose by a slightly larger proportion, and the focus changed. In the first four years, papers dealt primarily with the effects of the cycle on fitness. During the next period, the research concentrated on the effects of sports or physical exercise on the menstrual cycle, with several papers on amenorrhea among athletes. Overall, about a third of the papers dealt with one category of women's professional activity: sports performance. Fourteen papers during this period reported studies in which women were exposed to pain or cold at various stages of their cycles in order to determine pain threshold variation. Most of the papers on the effects of working conditions on the menstrual cycle came either from CINBIOSE or from Eastern Europe. The only paper on working conditions and premature menopause came from Poland.[49]

Thus, little of the research in this area was concerned with protecting the health of women workers. Yet most European and North American women of reproductive age now do paid work, and 30 to 90 percent of menstruating women report lower abdominal and lower back pain associated with their menstrual periods.[52]

Some of the reason for this lack of interest lies in the researchers' attitudes toward dysmenorrhea, which reflect a lack of respect for women's reports of health problems not experienced by men. For example, after reporting that beginning airline hostesses underwent unfavorable changes in the menstrual cycle 3.5 times as often as favorable changes, researchers commented: "There is not enough information to explain the pathophysiology of dysmenorrhea. The

TABLE 17: Results of a Search of the Medline Database (menstr-
× work, menstr- × environment)

	1983–1986	1987–1990	1991–1994	Total
Number of articles on work and menstruation	11	11	16	38
Effects of paid work on the cycle	36%	18%	62%	42%
Effects of exerting physical effort on the cycle	9%	64%	12%	26%
Effects of cycle phase on the ability to do work or exert physical effort	55%	18%	25%	32%
Total	100%	100%	100%	100%

frequent association of dysmenorrhea with other [sic] neurotic symptoms is indicative of its psychological origin."[51] Earlier researchers had been more frank: "In the course of the discussions which form an integral part of the annual medical examination of Hostesses [sic] it has become evident that some of these girls have become rather anxious because of [articles in the lay press on the effects of flying on air hostesses]. . . . Let us consider the assertion that flying, particularly in jets, has a definitely adverse effect on the menstrual function of hostesses. . . . It can be seen that the greatest deterioration occurred in regularity, followed by dysmenorrhea. The former is not at all surprising [in view of the known effects of jet lag on men's biorhythms]; the latter, however, is not a measurable entity but is highly subjective and it is just here that the psychological aspect may be of the greatest importance."[52] In other words, menstrual pain reports are not to be trusted.

This contempt for women's suffering was reflected in the tone of the comments we received from peer review committees our requests for funds to study the effects of working conditions on dysmenorrhea. We have, in fact, never been funded for any of our work on menstrual problems, despite our four published studies on the subject. Recall that, of nine projects we presented as a research program to the Institute for Research in Occupational Health and Safety, the only one refused on the grounds of insufficient priority and relevance was the one on menstrual problems. Surely this is an error, if only because menstrual pain can confuse reports on the prevalence of back pain, the "bread and butter" of occupational health.[53]

It is unfortunate that menstrual problems are understudied. If we want information about women's reproductive health, menstrual health is the most accessible parameter. In a given workplace, most women have a menstrual cycle, and about one in seven of those are menstruating at a given time. By contrast, less than 5 percent of women in the workplace become pregnant in a given year,[54] and only a small proportion have outcomes like prematurity, miscarriage, or low birthweight. Infertility is even harder to study, since relatively few women in the workplace are trying to conceive, and since the researcher must detect an event that does *not* take place. Researchers in infertility also need to know exactly what the couple is doing in order to conceive, requiring them to be even "nosier" than those who ask about menstruation.

So research into the effects of work on the menstrual cycle might ease the monthly pain of many women and could contribute to improving reproductive health. But there was no mention of menstruation in the 177 pages of the 1986 "state-of-the-art review" on occupational reproductive hazards. The only reference to menstruation in the 1993 "state-of-the-art review" on the occupational health of women workers was a mention that, in the past, menstruation was wrongly thought to disable women. The 1994 "state-of-the-art review" on reproductive hazards showed signs of progress, but discussion of occupational exposures that affect the menstrual cycle occupied one page (out of 196), and there was no mention of menstrual pain.

Again, the reason is probably tied to women's wish to remain invisible as women in the workplace. We know from experience that any clear identification of ourselves as women will probably not bring us any advantage and will probably hurt us. A supermarket checkout clerk interviewed by Angelo Soares described with embarrassment, how her femaleness gave a hostile supervisor an opportunity to humiliate her:

"When we work standing up, there are periods that are hard for a woman, I think, also to go to the bathroom. . . . I have had to go home because they wouldn't let me go there. There are some times of the month . . . I found it hostile, it's unpleasant. It's a lack of understanding, it doesn't happen all the time, once a month is all."[55]

Conclusion

The checkout clerk's plaintive description of how her needs as a woman were ignored in the workplace is similar in tone to stories we heard from and about pregnant and nursing women. Men and women in the workplace appear to believe that women who wish to work should take care of their peculiar states on their own. An American scientist described to me at a convention the difficulties her technician faced when she was forced by economic necessity to return to work a week after a cesarean birth. The technician was particularly uncomfortable, said the scientist, when she was perched on a high stool reading microscope slides. It did not seem to have occurred to the scientist to allow her to take some time off or even to get her a more comfortable chair. The scientist just felt sorry for her technician, who was having some personal problems.

11

Science and Real Life

■ ■ ■

Women have terrible problems getting compensated for workplace injuries and illnesses. Scientists appear to have little to do with the success of their claims, which depends more on employer–employee dynamics and the relative eloquence of each side's doctors. But scientists do contribute to the social process whereby women are disadvantaged. Scientific activity has given a veneer of objectivity to some social attitudes that have hurt women workers. Studies are quoted to justify inappropriate labor standards, denial of compensation, and inadequate prevention practices. In turn, workplace policies and interests, as well as stereotyped ideas of women's social role and biological nature, influence scientists' choices of subjects to study and the results they obtain.

Union health and safety representatives often insist to me that women are not the only workers who have a hard time getting compensated. Men's jobs are dangerous, and male workers often find it hard to receive compensation. Men also have terrible stories to tell about their treatment at the hands of compensation boards. I am arguing, not that women's suffering is worse than men's, but that it is less visible. It is hidden behind an illusion of easy, clean working conditions. It is concealed by supervisors who do not take women seriously and by women who do not want to endanger their jobs in a context where they are already second-class workers. A union health and safety representative explained why women were reluctant to claim: "Some work two days a week and are sole-support mothers. They need their two days a week .... 'I'll lose my job, already I don't have many hours, I need my pay.' ... If you succeed in getting them to the Appeal Board you practically have to pull the words out of their mouths, they don't want to come, and when they do come, they're all mixed up. They're so scared it's unbelievable."

In the occupational health system, women find themselves in a man's world, where their biology, their jobs, and their social situation are alien to those who will judge them. The agents and conditions they suffer from have not been shown to be dangerous, the organs affected can be shameful to talk about, and their word is doubted. In this confrontational situation, embarrassing details of their personal lives can be brought up.

The absence of relevant research data contributes to this situation. The interaction between scientists and the workplace affects women's health most directly and obviously in three areas of labor standards: exposure standards, compensation practices, and workplace policies. I present here some analyses of how these practices hurt women and show where and how women and their work should be included.

Exposure Standards

Workplace standards are suggested or legislated for exposure to chemicals, radiation, noise, and, to some extent, physical effort. Chemical exposure limits have often been guided by the American Conference of Governmental Industrial Hygienists (ACGIH), a nongovernmental body with great influence in the United States and elsewhere. Standards for exposure to ionizing radiation have usually been suggested by international commissions and legislated nationally. Permitted levels of exposure to noise vary by state and province. Limits for physical effort have been suggested by the U.S. National Institute of Occupational Health, and pan-European standards are also being developed.

Many standards are inappropriate for women's physiology and they do not include conditions present in women's work. In addition, they are often inappropriate for all workers, since they may be irrelevant to real-life workplace situations.

STANDARDS FOR CHEMICALS AND RADIATION

Various authors have criticized the process whereby chemical standards are created from the point of view of workers in general. After carefully examining the evidence used to establish standards for many chemical carcinogens, Castleman and Ziem have criticized those standards as based on insufficient evidence and on unverified experiments.[1] They show that chemical companies had an undue influence on the process of standard-setting. In another study, they find that the scientists who served on the Threshold Limit Value (TLV) Committee of ACGIH, whose suggested standards are used in most countries, may experience conflicts of interest.[2]

"TLV committee members can and do earn a substantial fraction of their incomes as industrial consultants, while publishing only their university affiliations in the TLV booklet. ACGIH has no policy either restricting TLV committee membership in such cases or requiring public disclosure of consulting work for financially interested parties. Similarly, there is no policy restricting the chemicals assigned to TLV committee members because of conflicts of interest through employment, consulting, and research grants."[3]

Other scientists have complained about direct industrial influence on the chemical standards used by the U.S. Occupational Safety and Health Administration (OSHA).[4] OSHA is charged with enforcing limits but tolerates levels of chemicals even higher than those suggested by the TLV committee.[5] In Canada and Québec, chemical standards are usually based on the U.S. procedures.[6]

Thus, standards for chemical exposures may be too lax in general. From the point of view of women workers specifically, three problems emerge. First, women and women's physiology have been excluded from studies used to establish the standard. Studies on human exposures have usually been done in industries that are heavily male. Since humans cannot be experimentally exposed to chemicals, most experiments have been done with animals. No one wants humans exposed to toxins for testing purposes, but applying animal-derived information to humans requires a certain amount of guesswork. The extrapolation procedure rarely includes factors relating to sex differences when, as is usual, male animals have been used.

Even when industrial exposures of humans have been considered, few women are involved. Little consideration has been given to variations in human characteristics that can influence reactions to toxins.[7] Body weight is particularly important, since the effects of a given environmental concentration of toxin may differ according to size.[8] Since women are usually smaller, industrial exposure standards based on larger people may be too high for them.

Second, pregnant women's concerns have not been handled appropriately during standard-setting. On the one hand, women may need some kind of special consideration during pregnancy, since the respiratory rate increases during pregnancy and exposure to chemicals is greater at a given air concentration. On the other hand, women do not want to be "protected" out of their jobs.

This conflict comes up repeatedly with respect to limits on the exposure of pregnant women to ionizing radiation. During a discussion of permissible levels sponsored by the Atomic Energy Commission of Canada, I heard diverse reactions from women workers and their representatives. Some argued that the existing limits are too high to protect the fetus; others said that lowering the levels was unnecessary and would only harm women's access to employment. Each side had scientific support.

The debate was hot, but the problem of protecting women's access to employment was never addressed directly, and no proposal was made that would incorporate job protection explicitly into the standards.[9] Neither side mentioned that the mere existence of exposure limits does not protect most workers exposed to radiation under real-life conditions, or that such conditions could involve special risks for fetuses, whose growing cells are especially susceptible. The reason relates to the way radiation exposure is monitored in the workplace. Radiation workers usually wear a dosimeter clipped to their clothing. In the case of the female hospital and laboratory workers who make up the majority of those exposed to radiation, the dosimeter is sent away to be read every three months (two weeks in the case of a pregnant woman), and the results arrive several weeks later. If the dose is too high, there is an investigation to see whether the result is an error or a real effect.[10] So a pregnant worker exposed to an excessive dose only learns about it several weeks after the fact. (A nonpregnant worker may be alerted even later.) Although any overexposed workers may then be reassigned in order to limit their dose, it is too late to prevent any damage to the fetus from the excessive exposure. Many scientists think fetuses may be damaged at very low exposure levels.[11]

For workers we have studied, the exposure pattern did not usu-

ally involve constant low-level exposure, but rather single accidental exposure, as when inexperienced, hurried doctors turned on
radiation-emitting equipment while the technician was still in the
patient's field. Spills of radioactive liquid could lead to other doses.
This type of exposure cannot be prevented by the use of dosimeters,
which only give information after the fact. Nuclear power plant
workers in Québec (almost all male) use dosimeters that signal immediately signal if workers are overexposed, but these dosimeters
are not available to the (mostly female) workers in most hospitals.
Hospital radiotherapy technicians we studied had been exposed to
higher levels of radiation than nuclear power plant workers.[12]

Thus, tightening regulations on the exposure of pregnant or potentially pregnant women to radiation without attention to job protection
probably limits women's access to well-paying jobs without substan-
tially lowering their risk of exposure. The recurring proposals to lower
exposure limits for radiation therefore appear inappropriate, especially
when we consider the dearth of information on standards for other exposures. According to the Massachusetts Coalition for Occupational
Safety and Health, few chemicals have been tested for reproductive
toxicity, and only four of the 500 chemical exposure standards set by
OSHA have been set to prevent reproductive damage (lead, benzene,
dibromodichloropropane, and ethylene oxide).[13]

The third problem is that working conditions usually experienced
by women may not be covered by exposure standards at all. Industrial
standards for chemicals are most often devised for those produced by
chemical companies for use in manufacturing and may not include
those to which women in some occupations are exposed. Until recently, there was little awareness of hairdressers, cleaners, or even
health care workers as chemical workers. In addition, women exposed
to chemicals from factories are increasingly working as "entrepre-
neurs" in their own homes, doing subcontracted work or telework,
where they have no access to information or, in many cases, coverage.

STANDARDS FOR PHYSICAL EFFORT

Chapter 3 showed that the databases used to derive standards for physical effort increasingly include women workers. However, the trans-
formation from data set to standards has not often been considered
from a gender perspective. As Joan Stevenson points out, scientists
have considered data on women's and men's biological capacities by

merging their few data on women with larger data sets on men. Divergencies between women and men are drowned, but the scientists are enabled to say that their conclusions are based on studies of both genders.[14]

The standards are designed for work involving the type of effort found in traditional men's jobs: lifting heavy weights. Some women's jobs do involve this type of effort, especially when the weights are people. For example, Llungberg and colleagues compared the physical demands of nurses' aides and warehouse workers. They found that although the warehouse workers moved much more weight, the nurses' aides moved weights during longer periods, in more awkward positions, and with more risk of having to react suddenly while lifting (as when a patient made an unexpected movement). These difficulties, they concluded, accounted for higher work accident rate observed among the nurses' aides.[15] Carrying people falls within the NIOSH guidelines on lifting weights.[16] An ergonomic analysis of typical lifting tasks performed by nursing assistants showed that very high levels of pressure were exerted on the lower spine by routine tasks involving even average-size patients.[17] These workers lifted or repositioned patients an average of 52 times per eight-hour shift in addition to doing other tasks that put pressure on the spine. Preschool teachers and day care workers, whose environment is designed for children and not for the workers, must lift dozens of 10–20 kilogram children per day.[18] Home care workers lift and reposition patients in their homes, which are not set up to facilitate this type of effort.

It is easy to see that this work could endanger health, even though it is not necessarily regarded as weightlifting in the same sense as loading a truck or laying bricks. A task that requires employees to lift 20-kilogram boxes several times in an hour is considered to be a manual materials handling task and is recognized as such. Equipment is provided, the work station is examined, and the worker is trained in handling weights. Increasingly, employers are conscious that such procedures should be introduced with regard to women's traditional work handling people. It was noted in a recent ergonomics journal that lifting children in a day care center can surpass the NIOSH standard and that the workload should be changed.[19]

Despite an attempt to introduce gender-fair guidelines for manual lifting tasks, no standards have been developed for the physical exertions typical of jobs traditionally assigned to women. Most of the jobs usually done by women and called "light work" do not fall under the

NIOSH guidelines. As a union health and safety activist told us, "It looks like nothing, that job [garment work]; it's true that it's not a manual job and it's not like a repairman who climbs telephone poles; it's less spectacular."

Parameters of women's work that should be regulated include the number of repetitions, the duration of static effort, and the fit between employee stature and the dimensions of equipment, tools, and work stations. Even though we know that highly repetitive movement is associated with musculoskeletal problems, the number of repetitions is not regulated in North America. In Brazil, a government regulation limits secretaries to 8,000 keystrokes per hour. In Canada, Billette and colleagues found that data entry clerks had workloads of up to 20,000 keystrokes per hour.[20] Walking is rarely considered as repetitive movement, and there is no limit to the total distance walked in a day. Hospital workers, waitresses, and cleaners, among others, may run from the beginning to the end of their shifts.

Static effort, exerted without movement, is invisible and has not been regulated. Many jobs men do involve dynamic effort, which is exerted when muscles are contracted during movement. Dynamic effort is visible: a box is lifted, a nail is hammered. Static effort is exerted when muscles are maintained in a contracted state for long periods, as in standing without moving. This type of effort creates musculoskeletal and circulatory problems by interfering with circulation.[21] Cleaning jobs (reaching to dust high surfaces, bending over toilets) often require this type of prolonged, uncomfortable posture.

Standing, a characteristic of many women's jobs, is an example of static effort. Many women in factories or services in North America (sales clerks, hairdressers, tellers, cashiers) are required to stand for long periods, resulting in back and other musculoskeletal problems. In fact, their workplaces are often designed so that it is impossible for them to sit down. Our research on bank tellers showed that although the workers stood for long periods in front of the wicket, they were forced to take half-steps frequently, about every 1.8 minutes. The placement of the cash drawer, for example, required them to step back every time they had to give out money. They had to step sideways for the computer and to the other side for the calculator. These little steps were not sufficient to prevent leg pain, but they did make it impossible to work sitting down. In Europe and Latin America, these workplaces have been designed for sitting, and bank tellers, cashiers, and salespeople work sitting down.

The lack of standards for static effort has to another consequence for women in North America. Legal limits for heat exposure are based on studies carried out in very hot workplaces (refineries, smelters) and take into account the dynamic muscular, heat-generating work typical of such workplaces. One day, my colleague Donna Mergler got a call from a union of laundry workers. They found the laundry unbearable in the summer, when the temperature reached 30° C (86° F). Several had fainted from the heat. However, the employer told them that the temperature was appropriate for the type of work they were doing, classified as "light work" under government guidelines.

The 30° temperature is in fact insufficient to produce specific heat-related illness. However, observations showed that the laundry workers were working quickly, manipulating tons of wet sheets every day. Under such conditions the static effort combined with low-level dynamic effort puts stress on the heart.[22] Mergler and her collaborators found that cardiac strain in women laundry workers exceeded recommended levels 40 percent of the time during warm summer months, and was similar to levels recorded for miners. They succeeded in getting the work reclassified from "light" to "moderate" and the temperature limit dropped to 27°.

As was pointed out in Chapter 7, poor fit between the worker's body and the dimensions of the work station is a particular problem for women. Many spaces are designed for men's dimensions. Pregnant women in fixed working postures are particularly hurt by the absence of clear guidelines for the physical parameters of their work stations. Jeanette Paul and collaborators have reviewed a number of scientific studies and suggest that many pregnant women have musculoskeletal problems because they cannot adjust their work position properly as pregnancy develops.[23] The researchers measured work stations and showed that the height of the working surface is a critical factor for the comfort and safety of pregnant workers. Because this is not normally taken into account when designing work stations, they point out that many work stations become quite uncomfortable as the abdomen grows. They make the cogent point that pregnancy may be brief and temporary for the individual worker, but it is a permanent characteristic of organizations that employ many women.[24] Therefore, such workplaces, such as hospitals and offices, could and should develop work stations at which pregnant women can sit comfortably while working.

Compensation Practices

The compensation system was designed to deal with the classic occupational injury: the worker who breaks a leg through a fall from a scaffolding. Such workers have to take a few weeks off to recover. Their salary is replaced for the time they are off, and they also receive money for treatment and any rehabilitation that is necessary. If they go back to work and suffer a relapse, they will probably be compensated for the new period of time off. Their families will be compensated if they die from the injury. If they are disabled so that they are unable to earn as much money as before, they will be given some compensatory amount. If they cannot do their previous jobs, money is available for retraining.

Male workers do not find it easy to gain compensation, but women workers are especially disadvantaged because of sexism and because of systemic problems. Katherine Lippel and Diane Demers have demonstrated that sexism is rife in the Québec compensation system. As mentioned in earlier chapters, these researchers have found that women are less likely than men to be compensated for similar stress problems. In addition, they found that women who are unable to do their routine household tasks because of a work injury are less likely than men to receive money to pay someone to replace them. Women's household tasks are not considered to be urgent or to require qualified replacement help. Finally, they found that women invalided out of their jobs are reoriented toward a much smaller list of new jobs than men, despite the fact that the disabled women generally have more education. Half of women are reoriented into the two fields of office work and sales, while only one-fifth of men are reoriented into the two top men's fields (management and clerical work).[25]

Systemic discrimination also prevents women from being compensated at the same levels as men. If we compare the sewing machine operator with a sore shoulder to the construction worker with a broken leg, we can be sure that he will receive more money than she will. The primary reason is, of course, salary: the construction worker will receive more than twice as much money as the sewing machine operator because his salary is higher. Generally, since compensation is paid at 90 percent of salary rates and women are paid much less than men, they are compensated at much lower levels (although men receive on average a lower percentage of their salary, being more apt to reach the maximum compensation level).

The sewing machine operator will also receive less because of the relative difficulty of compensating industrial diseases (more common among women) compared with industrial accidents (more common among men). She will find it harder to prove that her sore shoulder was acquired in the workplace, especially since investigators will probably be able to find that she routinely does some domestic task that puts pressure on the same structures. It will be much more obvious that the construction worker broke his leg on the job.

The sewing machine operator will be compensated for only a part of the time she is in pain, because compensation is linked to the ability to work for pay. It takes a long time for her to become so disabled that she is unable to work, although she may suffer pain every day while working. While she is suffering, she is not eligible for compensation. And if she takes early retirement because of her suffering, she will receive no compensation.

The system is also ill-adapted for women because it is designed to compensate single, extended periods of injury. As pointed out in Chapter 10, evidence is accumulating that severe menstrual pain is associated with work at too-low temperatures (around 0° C or 32° F). But the system is not designed to compensate workers who need to take one or two days off work every month for 30 years. Each absence is treated separately, and compensation must be decided for each.

Finally, the system disadvantages workers of both sexes when it erroneously defines many jobs done by women as "light work." In Québec and other jurisdictions, employers are encouraged by the Occupational Health and Safety Commission to limit the period of compensation for injured workers by transferring them temporarily to jobs considered to require little effort. Because of their image as easy jobs, "women's work" is often used for such temporary assignments for both women and men, although the physical requirements may be intense. These temporary assignments to "light work" may in fact slow workers' recovery from injury.[26]

Workplace Policies Affecting Family Roles

As shown in Chapter 1, women are still responsible for most domestic tasks. Although not part of health and safety legislation, workplace policies on balancing work and family roles have an enormous effect on women's health.

Health and safety legislation and practice usually recognize what workers need to survive and keep working. Employers are required to provide rest breaks, water fountains, toilets, and lunchtimes. But because regulations have evolved in relation to an older lifestyle when men were wage-earners with wives at home, the need to meet family responsibilities has not been included in labor standards. Workers, usually women, who must arrange child care, care of elderly relatives, meal production, laundry, housecleaning, and other chores in order to work, bear this burden and increased time pressure without help from the employer.

It is traditional to treat the paid work day as a time-limited phenomenon. The worker is expected to arrive at work in a rested condition, put in a totally concentrated work day, and be restored in the home environment. Any occupational injuries can ideally be attributed to either the home or the work sphere because there is no overlap between the two. Exposure standards are often based on a standard involving 8 hours of work and 16 hours of rest.

Increased sharing of the domestic and paid workload between the sexes makes these concepts obsolete. Most parents and those involved in elder care cannot count on 16 hours of rest and restoration after their work day. Exposure standards should be adjusted to take account of this reality. Standards for shift work must also be rethought, given that commonly used schedules often leave workers with little free time in common with other members of their families.

Recently, researchers have been examining other issues that arise in adapting the workplace to workers with family responsibilities, such as the need for parent–child or parent–childcare worker communication in emergencies.[27] In Switzerland, researchers are developing computer-aided systems to sort workers according to their of shift preferences and take these into account in scheduling.[28]

Older Women and the Workplace

As described in Chapter 7, many workplaces have informal policies that protect older workers who may no longer be able to assume the same workload as before. The workplace does not accommodate older women the way it does older men. Two European studies have shown that whereas men's working conditions improve as they get older, women's do not.[29] For example, in our study of train cleaners, chrome polishing (a very easy task done standing up) was assigned to men close to retirement age, because the co-workers and foremen did not think they could do the tasks usually assigned to men; such as driving the water truck or carrying bags of refuse. However, women even older were required to continue cleaning 150 or more toilets per day, a task that required rapid posture changes and spending a quarter of the time in a crouched position. Even a note from her doctor saying she was unable to do this task because of a back problem was not sufficient to keep one 40-year-old woman from being threatened with disciplinary proceedings if she did not clean toilets. A 64-year old woman told me there was no way she could avoid the toilet cleaning job, even though her permanently bowed back showed the effects of many years in a bent position. The extreme strength and endurance requirements of this job were invisible, so the workers' back problems were not relieved.[30]

Are Standards Important?

In addition to asking that standards and policies include women and their jobs, we can also question the entire standards-based approach to prevention in the workplace. Many conditions do not lend themselves to a standard-setting process: awkward movements, complex tasks, and stress. It is not easy to figure out how to limit the number of cantankerous clients a teller should have to deal with, the width of the smile that should be required of a waitress, the acerbity of the tone of a supervisor. More flexible approaches are required.

In British Columbia, the Workers' Compensation Board proposed a forward-looking draft ergonomics regulation that included no specific standards. It would have provided that employers identify factors (a long list was attached) that might "expose workers to a risk of adverse health effect." The employer would then have been required to eliminate or "minimize the risk of adverse health effect to workers."[31] The spirit of the legislation, unfortunately blocked by employer opposition, was to propose proactive steps to prevent injury. Such an alternative approach to health promotion would also be possible in the case of other hard-to-define exposures.

The importance of a more global approach became clear to us in our work with teachers. In order to identify stressful working conditions, we observed the work of primary school teachers, 82 percent of whom are women. Teachers have a high level of mental stress; David and Payeur reported that 90 percent of teachers found their task to be heavy, and 74 percent found it stressful.[32] Teaching is among the occupations with a significantly elevated risk of suicide.[33]

Our investigation into the working conditions of primary school teachers found that no single dramatic stressor could be isolated.[34] Instead, we found a combination of rather difficult conditions, particularly for those in areas with poor and immigrant children. Teaching is a fast-paced activity, since teachers must keep up with the attention span of children accustomed to the rhythm and excitement of television. The average duration of a communication from teachers to first graders is nine seconds, rising to 14 in the fourth grade. At the same time as they teach academic material, teachers seek opportunities to inculcate behavior standards, give emotional support, and maintain attention. Often when we asked the teachers why they had called on a particular child or asked such-and-such a question, they replied with five or six reasons for the same action (I called on Mary to encourage her, to quiet the boy sitting next to her, to teach Jimmy that if he cries out he won't get called on . . .).

This intense mental activity took place under exacting physical conditions. Teachers stand almost all of the time in order to keep the children's attention. Teachers with very young children spent 10 percent of the class time bent over in positions that are hard for the back. All this activity often took place in an unacceptable physical environment with too-low humidity and too-high temperatures, making it even more difficult to maintain concentration and discipline.

Teachers also worked outside the classroom, doing an average of 15 hours per week of preparation, correction, and coaching. Those with problem children took more time. One teacher met with a child in difficulties 26 times in one month. A case of incest took all fall to resolve, and at the Christmas holiday the teacher became ill and went on sick leave.

Little support was available. Teachers were isolated in their individual classrooms, with little time available to help each other with problem situations. Days intended for staff development were taken up by packaged material imposed by the employer (the regional school commission) and could not be used to share experiences. The employer and the public attacked teachers in the press when they requested more free time to communicate with one another, to develop their own materials, to write with psychologists, and to learn new techniques.

Teachers agreed with our description of their working conditions but did not see what to do about them. A health and safety representative told us he could not see how our study could help him. "In all you said, there is nothing I can tell the Occupational Health and

Safety Commission. If I say teachers have to work at 28 degrees [82° F], they'll laugh at me. They are used to workers in refineries next to ovens at thousands of degrees."

He was right. The occupational health and safety system is ill-adapted to situations where the relationship between aggressors and occupational illness is complex and multifaceted. An aggressor-by-aggressor, standard by standard approach will improve working conditions, but it sidesteps the many important health and safety problems due to the accumulation of low levels of different aggressors.

Conclusions

Unions are increasingly aware that they have to go beyond forcing observance of TLVs and getting compensation for broken legs. Many are trying to develop proactive prevention programs using a problem-solving approach. Women are too often absent from this process. They have been reluctant to get involved in health and safety activities, possibly because they feel incompetent. They see health and safety as an area where technical skills and expertise are critical. Unfortunately, those with the "appropriate" technical skills are often ignorant of the effects of women's jobs on their health. Lately, unions have tried to unite members from their women's committees and health and safety committees in special activities around risks in women's jobs.

12

Changing Science for Women Workers

■ ■ ■

I wrote most of this last chapter at the 1996 International Congress on Occupational Health (ICOH) in Stockholm, attended by some 4,000 occupational health specialists. Before the previous (1993) ICOH meeting in France, Laval University researcher Romaine Malenfant wrote to the organizers suggesting that there be a session on women and work. The president of the congress replied that since equality between the sexes had been achieved in France, no special session was necessary! In Sweden in 1996, this attitude was no longer dominant: there were three groups of presentations on gender and occupational health, plus a major address on the subject. For the first time, the organizers even found money to invite and pay the expenses of international experts on women and work, and to provide simultaneous translation into English and French. Hundreds of people attended these events. Interesting papers on women and work were also presented in sessions on heart disease, ergonomics, and work organization.

In Stockholm, there were some hints at progress on another front: that of worker participation in research. For the first time, a major plenary speech dealt with this subject: Rene Loewenson based her talk on Italian, Latin American, and African experiences with inviting workers to identify health problems and risky conditions. Several other scientists presented papers whose aim, object, and effect was to promote better health for working people. We heard about the importance of limiting monotonous and Taylorized[1] work, uncomfortable postures, and dangerous chemicals.

Despite such encouraging evidence of progress, I present in this chapter my feeling that scientists in occupational health are still missing some important points that feminists and women workers have been trying to make. Occupational health scientists have not fully profited from feminist insights into how to do research and report results. In this chapter I tell some stories about how research results are reported in nonfeminist and feminist scientific meetings. How results are communicated is an important part of scientific culture and informs us about how results are gathered. I end the book with some suggestions for changing the research climate in occupational health.

A Feminist at an ICOH Meeting

Despite progress toward the inclusion of women workers' concerns, most of ICOH 1996 resembled earlier meetings. The sex of workers often went unidentified, some conditions often found among women were ignored, thus biasing results, and gender was usually adjusted for rather than being taken into account. In the exhibit hall, safety boots and protective clothing appeared to be in large sizes, and the workers and work portrayed came primarily from men's jobs. Progress appeared to be spotty and attributable to specific organizers, and I wondered whether the next congress, in Singapore, would include any attempts to address women's concerns.

Company doctors and consultants outnumbered workers and union people more than 10 to one. Many if not most papers could not even indirectly contribute to improving workers' health. The medical director of a large U.S. corporation felt free to insult doctors who testify in hearings that workers' back pain is due to their jobs; he called them "prostitutes" and "hired guns" without being interrupted or opposed.

I gave two talks at the conference: an invited paper on women and work, given to an audience mainly composed of women, and a paper I submitted myself, given to a mixed audience. My experience with the latter presentation illustrates some of what I see as current challenges in occupational health science.

Our work with the bank tellers' union has been probably the most satisfying experience I have had as a researcher. First, the union is exceptionally enlightened. For example, it was successful in persuading its members to promote employment of the maximum number of people rather than safeguarding higher wages for the majority, as some other unions have done. It is run by a happy mix of women and men, with the women holding most of the important positions, as befits their proportion of the membership. Second, the collaboration was exciting and stimulating; the union involved itself critically and actively at every stage. We were initially referred to this union by the very competent head of women's affairs at the national level of the union. We met with members of the local union executive and were impressed by their energy and devotion. When we asked them to pick some representative grass-roots workers to be interviewed about their working conditions, they initiated a discussion of criteria for choosing the workers and generated a list of seven, corresponding to the major differences in working conditions: part-time/full-time, poor/rich area, high/low proportion of immigrants, mother/not, many/not many robberies, Montréal/suburbs, residential/commercial clientele.

They then recruited a group that represented these categories, people who turned out to be hard-working, cooperative, and intelligent. With the group, we worked out priorities for the research project. They identified their most important health risks: prolonged standing (they spend over 80 percent of the day on their feet and have back and leg problems), bank robberies (the average Montréal teller had been robbed five times), and pressure to sell bank services (the company had just started to require tellers to reach individual quotas for sales of credit cards, special accounts, etc.). The executive then negotiated entry into the bank branches for our observations and interviews.

We (Ana Maria Seifert, Lucie Dumais, and I) also worked hard. We observed work for 90 hours in six branches and interviewed tellers and supervisors to understand their problems. We used this information to derive a questionnaire, which was administered to 305 tellers. Because of the active involvement of this union and the information we got from the interviews and observations, we were especially proud of our questionnaire. We felt we fully understood the context of the responses, which made much more sense to us than the results from questionnaires we had devised for other workplaces before knowing as much about the job.

At the end of the project, we had figured out the working conditions and made, we thought, good suggestions. We understood why the workers could not work sitting down even on those rare occasions when stools were provided (the wicket was not designed for sitting). We understood the pressures that made branch managers less than empathetic about tellers' fear and distress after a robbery. We became aware of the importance of collaboration and teamwork among tellers and realized why the bank's technique of promoting competition between them was a bad idea, even from a management point of view.

We wrote a detailed, 100-page single-spaced report, which the tellers condensed to 25 more easily understandable pages. They incorporated our suggestions into their strategy for negotiating better working conditions. They invited us to present the results to the general assembly of bank workers, where we were given a standing ovation that brought tears to our eyes. Warmed and touched by the tellers' reactions, we felt ready to go from this friendly atmosphere to the colder, more critical audience of our scientific peers.

I could not present the whole study for the English-language group in Stockholm, because it was more accustomed to a single-subject, single-discipline approach, and, anyway, I was only allowed 15 minutes. I therefore chose to present just the part of the study dealing with bank robberies. We entitled the paper "Fear and distress among bank tellers after a robbery" and asked for it to be included in a session on violence at work. The context of bank work was important—not only the working conditions associated statistically with psychological distress among tellers, but also how the tellers and their supervisors felt after a robbery and how this related to other processes going on at the bank. For example, the tellers' job was changing from an accounting and money-managing function to sales, with resulting changes in the relationships between tellers, clients, and supervisors. In addition to the statistical analysis, I intended to fill my presentation with quotations so as to give a good idea of the feelings of the tellers (90 percent women) and their supervisors (85 percent men) and the strategies each group used to deal with their emotions after a robbery. The audience needed to understand how the sexual division of labor led to problems in preventing distress among tellers who had been robbed.

I faced the prospect of reporting my results with trepidation. Dealing with scientists en bloc in these scientific meetings is a tremendous challenge to the ego. We reveal our underbelly to our "peers," who have social permission to jump on it in the name of guaranteeing quality in scientific investigation. Since there are about two men for every woman present (four per woman among the *invited* speakers at the Stockholm conference), the tone of interaction is combative, modeled on football and wrestling. During my years in more theoretical branches of biology, I, like others, protected myself from criticism and ensured my mental health during scientific meetings by what passes for scientific rigor: doing experiments over and over and making sure I had missed no possible alternative explanation of my results. I was astonished at first when my colleague Nicole Vézina told me that she was sustained during her presentations to scientists by images of workers' reactions to her results. I tried this during the conference in Stockholm, with limited success.

I found on arrival at the conference that I had been put into a session on "post-traumatic stress syndrome," a medical diagnosis. This change meant that I was in a group who took a medical and diagnostic approach to stress rather than the prevention approach of the violence workshop. The papers before mine presented statistical studies linking performance on standard psychological tests to reactions to stressful events. Few data on gender were presented, and the audience had no sense of who the affected workers were. In this sense the session was not unusual in the biomedical sciences, where traditions of objectivity and distance from the subjects of research are believed to guarantee high-quality data.

Fresh from contact with the tellers, my style was much more personal and my content less focused than my listeners were used to. I felt out of place, and my paper evoked little applause and no questions. After the talk a psychiatric consultant from California explained to me gently that I should have used the same data-gathering techniques as the speaker before me: a standardized questionnaire. His tone was that of a missionary explaining the gospel to a "savage." His strictures were repeated by a Swedish woman, also a consultant for employers. The worst blow fell when a friend from Chicago, a progressive doctor, reacted to my presentation as if no statistics had been presented at all: the fact that I had talked about emotions had distracted him from the conclusions of the research. He did mention that my style was "sort of sweet." That evening, it took about three hours for my friend Dorothy to persuade me that I was not terminally stupid and naive, that my way of presenting might have had some value after all.

The consultant subsequently sent me a publication describing the relevant regulations for the state of California and recommended medical treatment for post-traumatic stress disorder. All the suggested treatments were individually based and were explicitly aimed at "assisting the employee to return to a more functional status and ultimately to some type of employment." None addressed workplace conditions.

This incident pointed up for me the differences between our approach and those usually accepted in the English-language scientific literature, the major publications in occupational health. First, I had talked about emotions and used emotion-laden language to convey what the tellers and directors were feeling after the robberies. This is out of place in a scientific meeting. The Canadian scientist Peggy Tripp-Knowles, in the film *Asking Different Questions: Women and Science*,[2] describes an experience similar to mine when she introduced her feelings about trees and the environment in a scientific presentation to environmental scientists. She felt as if she had done something really wrong. In the first chapter of *The Politics of Women's Biology*, Ruth Hubbard points out that scientists learn early to depersonalize their reactions.[3] We are taught to report facts out of context. "Scientific writing implicitly denies the relevance of time, place, social context, authorship and personal responsibility."[4]

Second, I established a context for the research presentation rather than trying to maintain, as do most presentations and publications, that the objective and scientific results obtained are independent of the reasons the questions were asked. None of the other presentations supplied any.

Third, I showed the link between research results and suggested action in a way that the other papers in that session did not. It was important to us that our project result in change for the tellers, so we chose the priorities with them, rather than basing our choice of subjects to investigate on the scientific literature. The listening scientists found this approach naive, since it did not appear to be grounded in scientific questions as theirs were. Although researchers like Laurell in Mexico, Berlinguet in Italy, Laville and Teiger in France, and Loewenson in Zimbabwe have been building theory for decades on the link between research and action in occupational health, researchers in North America, England, Asia, and non-Latin Western Europe have not usually included these perspectives.

However, some of these attitudes seem to be changing, and this was apparent elsewhere at the conference, at least among Scandinavians. Swedish researchers explained to me that they had been wondering how to translate their widely respected research results into concrete, effective changes in the workplace. It was this preoccupation that led them to invite Rene Loewenson to give her plenary lecture on worker participation in research.

Even though I was disappointed by the reception of my paper, my experiences at the Stockholm meeting left me with the impression that it is a good time for change in occupational health science. Under pressure from feminists and worker advocates, open-minded scientists are taking a look at some of their assumptions and practices.

The Conduct of Science

One tool for change might be an alternative set of guidelines for guaranteeing rigor and respect in those sciences that touch directly on human life. Margrit Eichler's ground rules for nonsexist science practices have been adopted by one of the major granting agencies in Canada.[5] Beyond insisting on including women as subjects and scientists, Eichler has asked for consideration of issues specific to women in such technical areas as defining the research question, choice of research subjects, and data analysis.[6] She has applied her analysis to medical research, where she has found sexism in these areas.[7] In particular, she insists that researchers be sensitive to gender-specific issues, a sensitivity that may lead to considering women and men either separately or together. For example, she inveighs against treating families as a unit, when "women and men tend to participate differentially in decisions that affect the household and the family,"[8] but she also condemns asking different questions regarding women's and men's roles in the family.[9]

Applied to the occupational health literature, Eichler's approach enabled us to see that the proportion of study subjects of each sex should be reported and explained, that titles and summaries of articles dealing only with males should make that limitation visible, and that data on men and women should be analyzed separately if there is reason to suppose gender is important.[10]

Building on these guidelines, we noticed important problems in the reporting of information about women and men, such as work schedules and job content (see Chapter 1 for more detail). In our study of how scientists examine absence for sickness, we realized that they had ignored the role of some women-specific phenomena such as menstrual pain and increased use of prescription drugs such as Valium, while perhaps overemphasizing others such as family responsibilities.

We have also, somewhat timidly compared with our colleagues in the social sciences, questioned the conventional approaches to data-gathering. Other feminists have attacked fundamental issues surrounding the relationship of research subjects and researchers, the relative value of qualitative and quantitative techniques. We have just begun to do this for occupational health research.[11] I set down here some of what I think we have learned, as a starting point for reform.

Before setting out my proposed agenda for change in occupational health, I have to point out that questions of race and ethnicity are entirely absent. I have lived almost all my adult life in French Québec, where these questions are presented very differently from the rest of North America: the French–English difference overshadows all others. I cannot generalize from my experiences, so I do not feel able to say anything here about how race should be treated in occupational health science elsewhere.[12]

GETTING GOOD INFORMATION

To summarize some of the points made in earlier chapters, we should:

- gather information relevant to women's occupational health and analyze it in such a way that the health problems and their sources become visible
- improve the database for women's occupational health (job indications on death certificates and in government and hospital records)
- develop sensitivity to the implications of employment segregation for data collection (e.g., awareness that different health problems may result from different task assignments)
- ensure use of data-gathering instruments that have been validated with and standardized for both sexes
- move toward recording accident statistics based on hours worked rather than on numbers of individual workers
- use measures complementary to accident statistics in order to identify risky jobs; include qualitative interview methods
- extend interest in women's reproductive health beyond fetal protection to include fertility, sexuality, early menopause, and menstrual disorders
- improve record-keeping on absences due to sick leave.[13]

TOWARD GENDER SENSITIVITY

The sexual division of paid and unpaid labor makes it easy to confuse sex differences with differential exposures due to sex-typed working conditions. The procedure normally used to untangle them, "adjusting for gender," is unsatisfactory for two reasons. As Mergler has shown,[14] it is useless when professions almost exclusively male are compared with those almost exclusively female: only when we are sure that men and women have similar working conditions (and not just the same job title) can the procedure be used at all.[15] Second, it obscures the specificities of women's and men's working and family lives. In a study of sickness absence among French poultry processors, we found very different results when we analyzed data on men and women separately and together.[16] Therefore, I suggest that information on occupation and health be disaggregated and analyzed by age, race, sex, and whatever other variables may be relevant.

However, as Stellman and Bertin have pointed out, care should be taken when doing such analyses. If data are indiscriminately analyzed by sex (or race, etc.), statistically significant male/female (or black/white) differences will be found in 5 percent of all analyses, by the very definition of statistical significance (that level which only appears by chance in 5 percent of cases). Attention must be paid to the mechanisms underlying male/female differences, whether they are biological or attributable to the work or home environment.[17]

GETTING GUIDANCE FROM WORKERS

Occupational health scientists are beginning to recognize that interesting research questions are raised by workers.[18] At the ICOH meeting, a Danish specialist in occupational heart disease told me that all his early studies arose from contacts with workers, and all had succeeded in identifying problems that had later been validated by more conventional methods.

Most workers exposed to industrial hazards eventually become aware that something is wrong. Many times they are able to make changes right away, asking the employer to fix a machine that is too hard to use, install a more comfortable chair, or reduce the workspeed. This procedure is easier when there is a joint worker–management health and safety committee and an active union.

Sometimes the effects of working conditions are invisible, as with genetic effects from chemicals and radiation. Early signs may not be picked up, and workers may lack the expert knowledge needed to identify the risks with precision. Mergler tells a story about workers who knew very well that there was a problem in their plant because they kept fainting. However, they thought the problem was only that the plant was too hot, whereas Mergler was able to show that the heat increased the concentration of some solvents in the air, accounting for the effects.

Workers need scientists when they are not sure of the cause of their problem or when they cannot make the employer listen. Sometimes they need scientists because the employer has already brought in a scientist who rejects the workers' ideas about their health problems. Few contexts give workers access to scientific expertise, since their financial resources are usually limited. However, this situation is improving. A report from the Federation of Humanities and Social Sciences, now being considered by the Canadian government, proposes setting up 25 centers to facilitate community access to science. In the United States, the Loka Institute in Amherst, Massachusetts, has created a network of those interested in community-based science.[19]

EXPERTISE

Scientists who accept that workers must play an important role in controlling occupational health research have to deal with issues relating to expertise. This is not a new question for feminist researchers, since questions of knowledge versus experience have been central to the development of feminist research.[20] Respect for women's experiences and perceptions has been proposed as a central element of feminist research methodologies (in, for example, Shulamit Reinharz's encyclopedic *Feminist Methods in Social Research*).[21]

Practices of involving and respecting workers' knowledge pose a problem in occupational health, where an immediate money value is attached to credibility. If the worker is believed, she will be paid for her work accident or (in the case of dangerous work) for pregnancy leave. If not, the employer and government will profit financially. In this situation, a lot of attention is paid to who has the right to define illness and disability. Arguments over expertise occupy a large place in compensation cases. We and others have been threatened with lawsuits and prosecution for "illegal medical practice" for merely reporting to workers what they themselves have told us in questionnaires.

We have often been puzzled about how to act. On the one hand, we are grateful to workers who have been valuable sources of information and inspiration, and we would like to see their input recognized. On the other, we are not yet in a political position where we can question the official stance of objectivity in our reports and papers.[22] We are already marginal in our approach to occupational health because we are women, we work with unions, and we are not doctors. Underplaying our qualifications has proved risky in situations opposing us to employer-paid experts. When we question established research methods, other scientists tend to think we have failed to understand them properly because of our weird background. Both because we are women and because we use nontraditional language about workers, we may be treated with less respect by both workers and employers. For example, we are called by our first names, while other experts are referred to by their titles: this can be dangerous in compensation hearings.[23] We have not yet successfully resolved the contradiction between insisting on respect for our expertise and avoiding mystification of that expertise.

Yet moving the center of expertise from the scientist to the worker and validating workers' perceptions are processes critical to enabling workers to change their conditions. Much of our research has been done with the hospital workers' unions, where our educational sessions are contradicted by authoritative statements from employer representatives who are doctors. We once gave a session in a hospital radiology department. Halfway through the session, the room was so hot and humid that it was hard to continue (the temperature was 25°C, or 77°F). When we raised this point, workers laughed at us and said it was always like that in their department. They had taken up the problem with their department head, who had explained to them that they felt hot because they were women, since the men did not feel uncomfortable. According to this physician, the women's biology was making them react abnormally to comfortable temperatures. We suggested that one reason for the difference between male and female perceptions of comfort might be that the doctors did not share with technicians the extensive physical manipulation of patients, almost all of whom had to be transferred manually from stretchers to radiography tables and back. Our interpretation seemed quite plausible to the technicians, but they felt unable to defend it to their department head by themselves.

These experiences led us to think that a transfer of power as well as knowledge from us to the women workers was a necessary step in improving working conditions. Our partnership with the women's committees of the trade unions is intended to allow workers to systematize and validate their own experience of their workload. Because the project is being coordinated by the union women's committees, results can be used to focus suggestions for change in the workplace. Our project aims to give them tools to recognize and to promote recognition of their workload so that they will feel entitled to create conditions for better health.

DISTANCE FROM WORKERS AND SCIENTIFIC RIGOR

In her talk on participatory approaches in occupational health, Rene Loewenson said, "It is NOT [her emphasis] the aim of this paper to argue that participatory approaches have an exclusive or superior role in generating new occupational health knowledge and practice, but that they may be more appropriate and effective than nonparticipatory approaches in certain circumstances."[24] She went on to discuss whether or not participatory research is scientific and gave a careful résumé of methodological questions in participatory research. Although most conventional scientists who presented data also enumerated limitations to their applicability or reliability, I did not hear any other speakers question whether their work was "scientific." Loewenson felt forced to do this, I think, because she knew she might be attacked. But the fact that only she did this may have led listeners to believe that scientists doing participatory research were *less* scientific.

Separation of science and politics is a canon of Western science, but it may be impossible. Scientists are supposed to produce objective data. As private citizens, they may have opinions, but nothing is supposed to interfere with their objectivity. However, I do not think there are any neutral researchers in areas as laden with controversy as occupational health. Everyone has an ideology, not just those who differ from the mainstream. In this book I try to show that ideology concerning women workers affects many choices made in the conduct of research, from the questions asked to technical details of data analysis.

Although scientists can and should try to be aware of their ideological positions and the influence these can have on their studies, no one can claim to produce choice-free research, and in that sense the pursuit of objective science is an illusion. Given this, it is important that the word "objective" not be used as a club to beat scientists whose ideas are not in the mainstream. In other words, it seems to me that the ideology of scientists only becomes obvious when it is not shared by critics. Choosing to study why workers smoke seems ideological to me, motivated by a wish to blame the victim, but not choosing to study the influence of shared office space on exposure to indoor air pollutants. Other scientists would take the opposite view.

Institutions being what they are, raising the question of whether our work is ideologically or scientifically based, while leaving aside the question of whether others' is, leaves the impression that only our rigor is to be contested. This is unwise and unjust. We can combat this tendency by forcing other scientists to be more rigorous.

EMOTIONS AND SCIENTISTS

At the plant where I did my very first study of occupational health, workers told us in a matter-of-fact tone that they had to go on leave for several weeks before they could go to the dentist because the phosphate ore to which they were exposed weakened their jaws so much that they could not be safely manipulated. We were upset at this evidence of health damage and showed it. The (all-male) workers seemed to be irritated by our reaction because they had already made the choice to keep on with their dangerous, uncomfortable jobs for the sake of their families and their self-respect. A bunch of romantic young middle-class women had no business getting upset in their place.

At the end of the study, the same workers chose not to go on with the research but to use our preliminary results to support a demand for improved ventilation. The employer promised to change the ventilation system if we withdrew, and the workers accepted. We were, again, upset. We thought the workers should have kept on with our study so as to demonstrate the full effects of the dust and make their bargaining position stronger. Again, we had to learn that it was up to the workers to decide what they wanted to do about what were, after all, their own working and living conditions.

We had a similar learning experience with the telephone operators, one which I personally found even harder. Because I had been a single parent with young children, I empathized with their superhuman attempts to cope with balancing work and family needs. It seemed to me that their work schedules had brought several near a breakdown. In fact, one of our 30 subjects committed suicide shortly after the end of the study. My emotions about the schedules showed in one meeting and, I think, made workers feel that we looked down on them for accepting these jobs. Again, we had to learn to accept the choices made by the telephone operators in the situations they faced. In the socio-economic conditions prevailing in Montréal in 1996, there were few alternatives to clinging to one's job, whatever the stresses.

I now think that we should keep trying to put ourselves in the workers' place and getting distressed by terrible working conditions, but we should make it clear that we have no opinion on whether it is a good idea to work for employer X or Y, or on what terms, since we do not have to live with the consequences or confront the alternatives. Although it is important to use our intersubjectivity as a source of information and energy for our research, it is equally important not to let our empathy with workers slide into overidentification with their interests. Only they are in a position to decide what action is best for them. This is why we choose to work with unionized workers, who have a forum in which they can make these decisions democratically and the strength to act on them.

Changing Conditions of Production and Dissemination of Knowledge

RIGOR IN REPORTING RESULTS

When scientists start from problems as perceived by workers, they may run into trouble with those who take more conventional approaches. Occupational health science, like environmental science, pharmacology, public health, reproductive health, and many other sciences, is a battleground of conflicting interests. A scientific approach can involve important political and economic implications. A clear example is the choice between large sample size and detail on exposure. Some scientists, primarily epidemiologists, think that statistical significance at the 0.05 level is critical to producing reproducible results and is therefore essential to the practice of good science. They are impressed with large samples. They accept the resulting loss of detail on exposures and the possibility of not identifying a real risk. Other scientists, primarily toxicologists and ergonomists, think that detailed information on exposures is critical to producing coherent results and is essential to the practice of good science. They want to use smaller samples and get more exposure information on each individual. They accept an increased risk of losing statistical significance.[25]

Whether they be epidemiologists or ergonomists, employer-friendly scientists will discount all but the most reproducible, statistically significant results while worker-friendly scientists will do studies even at small workplaces where a "definitive" study could never be done. Like the choices not to include women or people of color, to adjust data for sex or social class, these decisions and their consequences are almost never explained in the scientific literature. Although the *American Journal of Industrial Medicine* and other publications have started to insist that scientists identify their own direct financial interest in occupational health studies, nothing obliges scientists to disclose ideological choices or indirect financial interests (for example, a consultant's reluctance to alienate potential clients).

Ratcliffe and Gonzalez-del-Valle[26] suggest that rigorous research should involve a clear statement of the elements leading to problem identification and definition and a description of relationships to all stakeholders. Improving reporting practices and requiring scientists to state their ideologies at the outset would improve the quality of research.

"POLITICS" SHOULD NOT BE A DIRTY WORD

Scientists are sometimes thought to be above politics, but many scientists have learned otherwise. The week before the Stockholm meeting, I had organized a workshop on ergonomics and the sexual division of labor at the 1996 meeting of French-language ergonomists in Brussels. Problems and struggles surrounded this workshop, the first ever with a feminist flavor in this group. There was a struggle in the organizing committee to get the workshop into the program, and it was probably not accidental that it was finally scheduled to coincide with a plenary session with a popular speaker, the only activity during the conference that conflicted with a plenary session.

One of the authors was forbidden to come by her superior, a French public official, who told her that her proposed communication did not conform to the image he wished his service to project. In Brussels, the other speakers and I cornered the official and asked him to provide us with more information about his decision. Why was our colleague not allowed to present data about the work schedules and generally bad conditions of supermarket checkout clerks? He said that he had two objections. First, his service was primarily concerned with accidents, and her study provided no information about accidents. We did not believe this was the real reason, because he had allowed her to do the study in the first place and accidents had never been an issue in that workplace. The other reason invoked was that the study was not scientific. Repeatedly pressed to explain why, he pointed out that the title was political: "Flexible schedules in large distribution centers: A bad deal reserved for women" ("Horaires flexibles dans la grande distribution: Un mauvais lot réservé aux femmes"). It was, he said, a title more appropriate for a tract or a newspaper than for a scientific communication.

In other words, the author of a very political act—excluding the author of a communication from a scientific meeting—was reproaching a scientist for being political because of a title, when she had produced data on little-known risks in a little-understood profession. The word "political" was being used to identify an act of resistance. We did not accept his interpretation and, in fact, discussed it during the workshop. Participants praised us for having one of the most interesting workshops in the meeting.

The incident raised the consciousness of some ergonomists and, I think, helped in the ongoing struggle to have worker-friendly, feminist perspectives recognized for their scientific contributions to ergonomics. What I learned from this experience was that old-fashioned organizing and political tactics are needed, in scientific organizations as elsewhere. We made progress because we were organized and gave each other solid support. Scientific organizations are just as subject to political struggle as any others.

CULTURAL, PHYSICAL, SOCIAL, AND EMOTIONAL CONTEXTS FOR STUDY RESULTS

Sometimes I do not plan ahead and find myself immersed in head-bending sequences of activities. During one such seven-week period in the fall of 1996, I presented data on bank tellers to (in order): French-speaking industrial psychologists, English-speaking health psychologists, French-speaking feminist researchers, French-speaking ergonomists, English-speaking occupational health scientists, English-speaking social scientists and occupational health scientists; English-speaking community activists; French-speaking union health and safety activists. I also met with some Spanish-speaking professors of occupational health because of our joint program on women's occupational health in Latin America. The process of adapting presentations to these diverse audiences made me aware of the differences in the various cultures. Only before one audience did it feel illegitimate to present the social context in which the tellers worked: the English-speaking occupational health group. For the French-language ergonomists, I could present the global study on the bank tellers, together with our proposed solutions. I knew that, because of their French academic tradition, this group of ergonomists would be favorable to a global approach, and would think it appropriate to talk about standing posture, bank robberies, and pressure to sell at the same time, since the problems were interrelated. (Some of the precautions taken to prevent robberies meant that it was hard to do the teller's job sitting down, pressure to compete with other tellers in selling bank products undermined the solidarity needed to face the threat of robbery.) On the other hand, feminist perspectives were entirely new and alien to this group.

Similarly when our study on teachers came out, I presented it first to English-language occupational health scientists and then to French-language ergonomists. Again, I felt much more at ease presenting the context of the work process in the French-language milieu, and believed that presenting the context with my new information made the reports more complete and understandable. But I had to watch my words in the French group, since any identification of the sex of workers is an innovation.[27]

English-speaking occupational health scientists are probably the one group in the world with the most influence on the health of workers. The fact that English has become the language of science is lucky for us English speakers, but it has kept us from knowing very much about the more political approaches to occupational health that have developed in Europe and Latin America. English-language courses and textbooks in occupational health should make these other perspectives more available.

Creating a Favorable Context for Research

One of the pleasanter scientific meetings I have attended was a meeting of the Society for Menstrual Cycle Research (SMCR) in Montréal in 1995, attended by about 200 researchers from North America, mostly women. Data were presented on subjects from social attitudes toward menstruation to pain and suffering. New information was shared on endocrinology, psychology, and occupational health. Social and medical scientists were well represented, and both agreed on the necessity to involve women at all stages of research projects, from decisions on funding to orientation of research directions. The atmosphere—unlike that of other meetings involving natural scientists—inspired presenters to discuss their own feelings about their research. I spoke on occupational effects on the menstrual cycle and felt empowered by the scientists' relaxed attitudes: I was not afraid to ask questions or reveal my ignorance. I learned that the SMCR had been created by women's health activists and scientists to establish links between scientific knowledge and women's need for knowledge.

I thought that the warmth and openness of the SMCR meeting was an aberration until I went to the Women, Work and Health meeting in Barcelona organized by Carme Valls-Llobet, a Spanish endocrinologist with the city health service. Seven hundred researchers from 37 countries shared a similar atmosphere of sharing and exchange. Almost all researchers presented their data clearly and carefully, showing they were aware that other participants might not speak their language or might come from other fields. Women journalists came to interview scientists and ended up confiding their health and safety problems and, in at least one case, crying with the researcher over how it felt to be a woman in a man's job. The meeting ended with a folk dance on the steps of the convention center, with most of the researchers joining in.

I contrast this picture with the more traditional scientific meetings where people are afraid to show weakness and only the most courageous or those whose fame places them beyond attack will make controversial statements or ask naive questions. I cannot believe that the atmosphere of fear, rivalry, and predation that surrounds most of these meetings is good for scientific progress.

Changing scientific institutions will not be easy, but there has been progress in recent years. Advances have almost always come from creating alternative associations rather than by working through the accepted professional groups. The international Gender and Science and Technology association, the Association for Women in Science, and the Canadian Association for Women in Science, among others, are devoted to making science more woman-friendly. The Canadian government has set up a chair for women in science and technology at the University of New Brunswick, and four more chairs will soon be added. The Women's Health Initiative in the United States has created forums where women's concerns can be addressed.

This penetration from without must be complemented by forces working within scientific associations. Few scientific societies have allowed women to form officially recognized groups, and those that ex-

ist are often more devoted to advancing the careers of women as individuals than to changing the face of science. It is very hard for
women (or any other group, such as people of color) to influence a
professional society without giving the impression that they are un-
professional. The women's caucus of the American Public Health Association has been an exception, an important influence in making scientists more gender-sensitive. The context where this could happen
was created by means of a great deal of work on the part of progressive scientists. A similar effort is called for in occupational health.

TOWARD A BALANCE BETWEEN BIOMEDICAL
AND SOCIAL SCIENCE

In Stockholm, I spoke at another session, with invited presentations
about women, work, and occupational health. I was the only biomedical scientist who spoke, the others being social scientists who
studied women and work. I felt supported by the feminist perspectives and the warmer tone of the session, but not by the content. Few
occupational health specialists came, and I was afraid that some people in the session did not understand the occupational health problems they were discussing. One speaker presented as examples of
intervention in occupational health: breast cancer screening in the
workplace; a system whereby bank supervisors would refer workers
with mental health problems to psychologists; and interventions to
prevent domestic violence. These did not sound like occupational
health problems to me. In fact, the intervention at the bank scan-
dalized me because it took no notice of the mental health problems
that were rooted in the bank's own working conditions.

Thus, occupational health scientists and their perspectives were
absent from the sessions specifically about gender. At the same time,
in the mainstream occupational health sessions, few papers included
a gender analysis. In the format of a scientific meeting (15-minute
presentations, five minutes for discussion), it was hard to make
points about the specific relevance of gender to research results,
even though I felt that many results were invalid or not believable
because of the exclusion of gender-specific concerns. To many scientists, these social-science-based concerns seem too "soft" to be
part of real science; to persuade them otherwise would take longer
than the five minutes allowed, and require me to take a difficult, "illegitimate" position outside the context of the session. Biomedical

and social scientists were not really communicating, and I felt unable to bridge the gap.

When Canadian feminist researchers in occupational health held our own meetings in 1993 and 1994, the differences in culture and style between biomedical and social scientists were striking. Biomedical scientists presented data, usually quantitative, while social scientists were not ashamed to give opinions and syntheses. One sociologist remarked, after listening to an epidemiologist read tables relating disease to domestic workload, "I have never heard so many facts with so little meaning!" Most of the biomedical scientists present also found the presentations of their social science colleagues to be rather thin: so many ideas with no facts to back them up! Since the format permitted more exchange than was possible in Stockholm, we were able to overcome these attitudes to some extent and profit from each others' approaches. I think that more such efforts would be an important way to get occupational health scientists to understand more about social divisions relevant to their work, and for social scientists to understand the importance of details of occupational exposures and illnesses.

EASIER ACCESS TO BECOMING A HEALTH SCIENTIST

If we look at the effects of scientific research, we quickly notice that some scientists in fact help women workers and others hurt. When we ask who has done research that has improved women's health, and where, we notice that it is not randomly distributed with respect to sex, country, and context. Although many women have done antiwomen research and some men have produced important research helpful to women workers, probably a statistical analysis would shown that women scientists have often been alert to dangers affecting women workers.

It is easy to see that the work of Barbara Silverstein, Laura Punnett, Åsa Kilbom, Erika Viikari-Juntura, Susan Stock, and others has helped women get recognition for musculoskeletal disorders and that the insistence of some male researchers that only machines can diagnose carpal tunnel syndrome has hurt them. This concentration of women scientist on the side of the angels is not just chance.

In other words, some scientists have ideologies and work in contexts that favor woman-friendly and worker-friendly research, and others do not. Although the impetus for studying women has often come from nonunion sources, the ability to see through some of the biased language surrounding women's work is, I think, related to union experience and, particularly, to contact with women workers. The importance of unions in influencing occupational health research should not be underestimated, although the influence may be indirect. The recent gains in the recognition of musculoskeletal diseases are attributable largely to scientists in Scandinavia, the United States, and Québec. The Scandinavian workforce is over 90 percent unionized, and health and safety are a concern of all. Many of the U.S. and Québec scientists have done their research with the help of unions or in contexts where unions contribute to the choice of problems to be studied.

Jeanne Stellman, a chemist who has done perhaps more than any other scientist in North America in recent times to promote recognition of risks in work generally and in women's work in particular,[28] came from the union movement. She was the health and safety officer for the Oil, Chemical and Atomic Workers' Union. She became interested in women's work because of contacts with other progressive women scientists, such as Vilma Hunt. At this writing she is directing the publication of—and trying to integrate women's concerns into—the *Encyclopedia of Occupational Health and Safety*, published by the International Labor Organization (a joint labor-employer-sponsored branch of the United Nations).[29]

In France, union contacts were also important in developing the ideas of the ergonomics experts who trained me, and they heavily influenced such thinkers as Christophe Dejours, the father of work psychodynamics.[30] Union contacts are now an important source of support for scientists who produce results unwelcome to employers.[31] In Venezuela, the Center for the Study of Occupational Health (CEST) at the University of Carabobo, under the leadership of Oscar Feo, set up associations with trade unions and associated itself with a union-based worker education center and with the local women's center. The CEST now publishes the only peer-reviewed occupational health journal in South America, *Salud y Trabajo*, which regularly reports new perspectives in occupational health.

In the United States, the strength of unions in Michigan has created a labor-friendly research program in environmental and industrial health; it trained Barbara Silverstein and Laura Punnett, among others, who have done pioneering work on MSDs. In Québec, collaboration with the union enabled Chantal Brisson to do the first rigorous demonstration that sewing machine operators are likely to suffer long-term disability. Thus, contact with the union movement and especially with workers has given scientists new ideas for research that has, in turn, helped workers.

The stimulation of feminist ideas has been equally important. Although not all those who have produced results that have helped women workers are feminists, research results helpful to women workers have often come from countries and contexts where their specific needs are acknowledged. Women's studies and feminist studies networks, although they rarely involve natural scientists, contribute to a university context where issues can be raised and cross-fertilization can take place.

It is therefore important for the quality of research in occupational health to create contexts where woman-friendly and worker-friendly research can be done.

FAIRNESS TO NON-PH.D. RESEARCHERS

Most scientific workers are probably women. As Ruth Hubbard puts it, In "the ivory (that is, white) towers in which science gets made, one can find lots of people from the working and lower-middle classes, but they are technicians, secretaries and clean-up personnel."[32] A sharp class divide separates "support staff" from those who are considered to be scientific workers. The attitudes involved are quite clear. When I was a student in the late sixties and early seventies, a professor once explained to me that while professors were not supposed to sleep with their students, "Your technician is fair game." In fact, one professor was well known for sexually harassing and terrorizing his technicians, while nothing was done. I presume the reason for the differential code is that even women students are, at least potentially, professors-in-training, while support staff are not in the same social class. There are no career paths through which technicians can advance. They can produce years of important research results, sometimes with minimal supervision, but they can never receive a promotion and can certainly never become professors.[33] Any recognition of their role in the production of knowledge is entirely dependent on the good will of their supervisors.

In academia, support staff put up with conditions of employment that are unknown in industry, probably because they are supposed to get their satisfaction from being associated with the production of knowledge. Because of the evanescent nature of research funds, research technicians at my university are given no job security at all, even after 20 years of service. Despite years of battle, they have no pension fund and are excluded from most of the fringe benefits provided by their union's collective agreement. (They are, however, members of an industrial trade union with a collective agreement that protects them from arbitrary firing and guarantees them a reasonable salary. This is not the case for most North American scientific workers.)

In order for this situation to change, universities and granting agencies would have to work together to devise career plans for technicians that would make them independent of the grant-getting ability of their supervisors. Such a plan would have to allow them to specialize in a new field so that they would be able to work for different supervisors.

CONTEXTS FAVORING KNOWLEDGE ABOUT WOMEN'S WORK AND HEALTH

In this book, I have tried to show that scientific institutions make it difficult to get information about women in general and working women in particular. In the normal course of their work, scientists have little contact with working women's problems and few ways to find out about their needs for research. Most women, for their part, have few contacts with scientists and no idea what use scientific research could be to them.

The few exceptions to this social isolation provide indicators of how things should develop. I am, of course, particularly proud of my own university's approach: since 1978, we have been doing research in collaboration with women workers. Because of the constraints on us and on them, we cannot say that our research agenda is entirely driven by women's questions; rather, it represents a compromise between the needs of women and other workers and the requirements of academia, granting agencies, employers, and unions. Still, if we define feminist research as research that responds to questions asked by women and advances the status of women in society, we have been engaged in feminist research for more than 15 years. Through these experiences we have been forced to think differently and to act differently. This came about through an agreement between a group of trade unions and University of Québec.

The Université du Québec à Montréal was founded in 1969 with a mandate to serve the Québec community, including "those sectors of

the community not usually served by universities." The theory was
that workers as taxpayers have the right to benefit from the knowledge of public supported personnel such as university professors. The
university signed agreements in 1976 with two of the three major
Québec unions, the CSN[33] and the FTQ,[34] and in 1991 a similar agreement with the third, the CEQ,[35] providing resources for responding to
union requests: released time for professors who participate in educational activities and university seed money for research.[36] A similar
agreement was signed in 1981 with a consortium of women's groups.[37]
These arrangements have made it part of our jobs to participate in
union-organized workshops on work and health, to give courses on
women's health at the women's health center, to produce information
on noise, radiation, and solvents, to work with the unions' women's
committees to write brochures on protection of pregnant women,
women's occupational health, and health risks for women in nontraditional jobs, to carry out research in response to needs expressed by
workers, and to provide expert testimony in litigation involving occupational health.

During the 1970s, professors at the Université du Québec à Montréal joined the CSN. We negotiated clauses in our collective agreement recognizing work done in the context of the university–union
relationship. Our work in occupational health is carried on as part
of our regular workload (for 45 hours of teaching in unions we can
be released from 45 hours of university teaching), making many
professors available to work with unions. The unions benefit from
the prestige and perquisites of professors' status, such as access to
university services and grants. Union-initiated research, which is
often received with hostility by the scientific community, *must* be
recognized by our employer, at the risk of grievance procedures in
the context of our collective agreement.

Several features of the university–union agreement have been
important in making it productive: explicit recognition of the power
imbalance between career researchers and community groups, with
structures in place to guarantee that the needs of both are recognized throughout the entire project; title to the research results held
by the researcher and by the initiating organization; seed money for
feasibility studies, often necessary given the radically new questions
posed by community groups; and guarantees of scientific credibility
through peer review. Although peer-review committees need to be
sensitized to the specific difficulties of community-based research,

they provide an important quality guarantee to the community group and help maintain the scientific credibility of the researchers.

COMMUNITY INPUT AND SCIENTIFIC GRANTS

Two Québec granting agencies incorporate representatives from labor or community groups in the determination of funding. The Québec Institute for Research in Occupational Health and Safety incorporates representatives from labor and management into determination of grants; the two sides explicitly and openly negotiate to fund research that they consider important. This process paradoxically appears to allow for *less* research bias in funding, since the practical consequences of the projects are put on the table at the outset.

During one period, one of the labor representatives was in charge of women's affairs for her union, and we were able to get funding for some feminist studies. However, since her departure we (and the union women's committees) have turned to the Québec Council for Social Research, which incorporates community representatives into its decision-making processes. The council has funded a study of the impacts and consequences of methods used to reconcile family and professional responsibility, initiated by the FTQ union, and a study of ways to make women's work more visible, in partnership with women's committees from all three unions.

These institutions have allowed us to build relationships with women workers. Over the years, we have been able to count on support and orientation from union members, from health and safety committees, and from the very active women's committees of the three major trade unions in Québec. With them, we have come to a better understanding of the needs of working women, and provided information that has been helpful to them. Their solidarity has been a source of strength to us over many years, and their insights have been invaluable. From the cleaner who explained to us why "light work" was heavier than "heavy work" to the technicians who told us why time-and-motion studies were not a good way to organize radiotherapy treatments to the factory workers who made us understand why being able to go to the bathroom when you need to is an important health practice,[39] workers have constantly put us in touch with real occupational health problems. If our colleagues had similar opportunities and information, perhaps they would change the rules for occupational health research. They might be more able to believe in workers' accounts of risks and symptoms, and become convinced that it is important to protect their health.

Conclusion

A growing number of researchers are interested in involving workers in their studies of occupational health. At the same time, feminist researchers have been developing ways to listen to women. Finally, science critics have been contributing to our understanding of science as a social institution.

Meanwhile, in the real world, unions have been organizing around occupational health and safety issues and feminists have been promoting change in the ways women's health is fostered and protected. We hope that all these tendencies will come together to produce democratic, reflexive science that will be more effective in producing knowledge and, ultimately, improving the health of women workers.

Notes

■ ■ ■

PREFACE

1. Pukkala, E., Auvinen, A. and Wahlberg, G. (1995) Incidence of cancer among Finnish airline cabin attendants, 1967–1992. British Medical Journal 311: 649–652.

2. Courville, J., Vézina, N. and Messing, K. (1992) Analyse des facteurs ergonomiques pouvant entraîner l'exclusion des femmes du tri des colis postaux. Le travail humain 55: 119–134.

3. The case of Société canadienne des postes et Corbeil et Grégoire-Larivière (1994) Commission d'appel en matière de lésions professionnelles de Québec, 285.

4. People with Turner's syndrome have only one X chromosome, instead of two like women or one X and one Y like men. They are characterized by short stature, absence of gonads (no ovaries or testes), and physical underdevelopment. The appearance of their external genitals leads to their being defined as female at birth. The fact that they have no penis has led some scientists to claim that being the female is the "basic sex"—that is, the sex that occurs in the absence of the second chromosome. See, for example, the work of developmental biologist Susumu Ohno.

5. Hubbard, R. (1996) Gender and genitals: constructs of sex and gender. Social Text 14: 157–165.

6. This point is especially well made in Lewontin, R., Rose, S. and Kamin, L. J. (1984) Not in Our Genes. Pantheon, New York.

7. Colker, R. (1994) Pregnant Men: Practice, Theory and the Law, p. 132. Indiana University Press, Bloomington.

CHAPTER 1

1. This chapter is not intended to be a review of job segregation but rather a brief explanation of why occupational health scientists need to look specifically at women's work. Job segregation has been extensively researched in many countries by (among many others): Joan Acker, Pat Armstrong, Harriet Bradley, Cynthia Cockburn, Hélène David, Heidi Hartmann, Helena Hirata, Kaisa Kauppinen, Danièle Kergoat, Barbara Reskin, Sylvia Walby.

2. Tomaskovic-Devey, D. (1993) *Gender and Racial Inequality at Work*. ILR Press, Ithaca.

3. Statistics Canada (1995) *Women in Canada: A Statistical Report*, p. 86. No. 89–503 E. Statistics Canada, Ottawa.

4. Employment and Earnings report for 1994 obtained from the U.S. Bureau of Labor Statistics. This figure is not strictly comparable to the Canadian figure, since it comes from annual averages of weekly median earnings rather than yearly average earnings. The Canadian figure is about a year older. The most recent trend is toward widening rather than narrowing the gap between women and men in both countries.

5. Employment and Earnings report for 1995 obtained from the U.S. Bureau of Labor Statistics.

6. The literature on the vertical segregation phenomenon was recently reviewed by Catherine Hakim (1996) in *Key Issues in Women's Work: Female Heterogeneity and the Polarisation of Womens Employment*. Athlone, London. For a discussion of hierarchical position, see Karasek, R. and Theorell, T. (1990) *Healthy Work: Stress, Productivity, and the Reconstruction of Working Life*. Basic Books, New York. The situation of bank tellers is examined in Siefert, A.M., Messing, K., and Dumais, L. (1997) Star wars and strategic defense initiatives: work activity and health symptoms of unionized bank tellers during work reorganization. International Journal 396 of Health Services 27 (3): 455–477.

7. Statistics Canada (1995) *Women in Canada: A Statistical Report*, p. 64, No. 89–503 E. Statistics Canada, Ottawa.

8. Advisory Group on Working Time and the Distribution of Work (1994) *Report*, p. 21. No. MP43–336/1994. Ministry of Supplies and Services, Ottawa.

9. Armstrong, P. and Armstrong, H. (1994) *The Double Ghetto: Canadian Women and Their Segregated Work*, 3d ed., pp. 50–54. McClelland and Stewart, Toronto.

10. Statistics Canada (1994) *Women in the Labour Force*, table 2.5. No. 75–507 E. Statistics Canada, Ottawa.

11. Ibid. table 6.8.

12. Walters, V., Beardwood, B., Eyles, J. and French, S. (1995) Paid and unpaid work roles of male and female nurses. In Messing, K., Neis, B. and

Dumais, L. (Eds.), *Invisible: Issues in Women's Occupational Health and Safety / Invisible: La santé des travailleuses*, pp. 125–149. Gynergy Books, Charlottetown.

13. Guberman, N., Maheu, P. and Maillé, C. (1994) *Travail et soins aux proches dépendants*, pp. 27–29. Éditions Remue-mémage, Montréal.

14. Statistics Canada (1994) *Women in the Labour Force*, table 2.6.

15. Ibid., table 2.11.

16. Rubin, C. H., Burnett, C. A., Halperin, W. E. and Seligman, P. J. (1993) Occupation as a risk identifier for breast cancer. American Journal of Public Health 83: 1311–1315.

17. Carpentier-Roy, M.-C. (1991) *Organisation du travail et santé mentale chez les enseignantes et les enseignants du primaire et du secondaire*. Centrale de l'enseignement du Québec, Québec.

18. Statistics Canada (1995) *Women in Canada*, p. 82.

19. Bouchard, J.-A. (Ed.) (1984) *Les effets des conditions de travail sur la santé des travailleuses*. Confédération des syndicats nationaux, Montréal.

20. Soares, A. (1995) Les (més)aventures des caissières dans le paradis de la consommation: Une comparaison Brésil-Québec. Ph.D. thesis. Department of Sociology, Université Laval, Québec.

21. Armstrong and Armstrong (1994) *The Double Ghetto*, p. 34–37

22. CINBIOSE (1995) *Quand le travail "léger" pèse lourd: Vers la prévention dans les emplois des femmes*. Université du Québec à Montréal, Montréal.

23. Dumais, L., Messing, K., Seifert, A. M., Courville, J. and Vézina, N. (1993) Make me a cake as fast as you can: Determinants of inertia and change in the sexual division of labour of an industrial bakery. Work, Employment and Society 7 (3):363–382.

24. Mergler, D., Brabant, C., Vézina, N. and Messing, K. (1987) The weaker sex? Men in women's working conditions report similar health symptoms. Journal of Occupational Medicine 29: 417–421. Courville, J., Dumais, L. and Vézina, N. (1994) Conditions de travail de femmes et d'hommes sur une chaîne de découpe de volaille et développement d'atteintes musculo-squelettiques. Travail et santé 10 (3): S17–S23. Messing, K., Saurel-Cubizolles, M.J. Kaminski, M. and Bourgine, M. (1992) Menstrual cycle characteristics and working conditions in poultry slaughterhouses and canneries. Scandinavian Journal of Work, Environment, and Health 18:302–309. Messing, K., Saurel-Cubizolles, M. J., Kaminski, M. and Bourgine, M. (1993) Factors associated with dysmenorrhea among workers in French poultry slaughterhouses and canneries. Journal of Occupational Medicine 35: 493–500.

25. Vézina, N., Chatigny, C. and Messing, K. (1994) A manual materials handling job: Symptoms and working conditions among supermarket cashiers. Chronic Diseases in Canada 15 (1):17–22.

26. Messing, K. (in press). Hospital trash: Cleaners speak of their role in disease prevention. Medical Anthropology Quarterly.

27. From the official task descriptions at the Montréal Heart Institute (1994).

28. Ibid.

29. Kauppinen-Toropainen, K., Kandolin, I. and Haavio-Mannila, E. (1988) Sex segregation of work in Finland and the quality of women's work. Journal of Organizational Behavior 9: 15–27.

30. Paoli, P. (1992) *First European Survey on the Work Environment 1991–1992*, pp. 126–128. European Foundation for the Improvement of Living and Working Conditions, Dublin.

31. Teiger, C. and Plaisantin, M.-C. (1984) Les contraintes du travail dans les travaux répétitifs de masse et leurs conséquences sur les travailleuses. In Bouchard, J.-A. (Ed.), *Les effets des conditions de travail sur la santé des travailleuses*, pp. 33–68. Confédération des syndicats nationaux, Montréal.

32. Vézina, N., Courville, J. and Geoffrion, L. (1995) Problèmes musculosquelettiques, caractéristiques des postes de travailleurs et des postes de travailleuses sur une chaîne de découpe de dinde. In Messing et al. (1995) *Invisible*, pp. 29–61.

33. Karasek and Theorell (1990) *Healthy Work*.

34. Hall, E. M.(1989) Gender, work control and stress: A theoretical discussion and an empirical test. International Journal of Health Services 19: 725–745.

35. Hochschild, A. (1983) *The Managed Heart*, p. 14 (definition), p. 171 (airline attendants). University of California Press, Berkeley.

36. Messing, K., Dumais, L., Courville, J., Seifert, A. M. and Boucher, M. (1994) Evaluation of exposure data from men and women with the same job title. Journal of Occupational Medicine 36 (8): 913–917.

37. Because the work force was overwhelmingly male, many men worked with only male colleagues and could not answer the question.

38. Cockburn, C. (1991) *Brothers: Male Dominance and Technological Change*, 2d ed. Pluto Press, London.

39. Stafford, A. (1991) *Trying Work: Gender, Youth and Work Experience*. University of Edinburgh Press, Edinburgh.

40. For example, for a discussion of the experiences of women in the army, see: Enloe, C. (1988) *Does Khaki Become You? The Militarization of Women's Lives*, chap. 5. Pandora, London.

41. Seifert, A. M., Messing, K. and Dumais, L. (1996) *Les caissières dans l'oeil du cyclone: Analyse de l'activité de travail des caissières de banque*. CINBIOSE, Montreal. Seifert, A. M., Messing, K. and Dumais, L. (1997) Star wars and strategic defense initiatives: Work activity and health symptons of unionized bank tellers during work reorganization. International Journal of Health Services 27 (3): 455–477.

42. Robinson, A. (1995) *Travailler, mais à quel prix!* pp. 30, 105–108.

Cahiers de recherche du Groupe de recherches et d'etudes multidisciplinaires sur les femmes (GREMF), Université Laval, Québec.

CHAPTER 2

1. Wagener, D. K. and Winn, D. W. (1991) Injuries in working populations: Black–white differences. American Journal of Public Health 81: 1408–1414. Robinson, J.C. (1989) Trends in racial equality and inequality and exposure to work-related hazards, 1968–1986. American Association of Occupational Health Nurses (AAOHN) Journal 37: 56–63. Pines, A., Lemesch, C. and Grafstein, O. (1992) Regression analysis of time trends in occupational accidents (Israel 1970–1980). Safety Science 15: 77–95. Laurin, G. (1991) *Féminisation de la main d'oeuvre: Impact sur la santé et la sécurité du travail.* Commission de la santé et de la sécurité du Québec, Montréal.

2. National Institute of Occupational Safety and Health (1993) *Fatal Injuries to Workers in the United States, 1980–1989.* National Institute of Occupational Safety and Health, U.S. Department of Health and Human Services, Cincinnati.

3. Root, N. (1981) Injuries at work are fewer among older employees. Monthly Labor Review (March): 30–34. Keyserling, M. (1983) Occupational injuries and work experience. Journal of Safety Research 14: 37–42.

4. Motard, L. and Tardieu, C. (1990) *Les femmes ça compte,* chap. 2. Publications du Québec. Kempeneers, M. (1992) *Le travail au féminin.* Presses de l'Université de Montréal, Montréal.

5. Depending on the industry, women may have a lower, greater, or equal rate compared to men. See: Oleske, D. M., Brewer, R. D., Doan, P. and Hahn, J. (1989) An epidemiologic evaluation of the injury experience of a cohort of automotive parts workers: A model for surveillance in small industries. Journal of Occupational Accidents 10: 239–253 (lower rate). Tsai, S. P., Bernacki, E. J. and Dowd, C. M. (1989) Incidence and cost of injury in an industrial population. Journal of Occupational Medicine 31: 781–784 (lower rate). Wilkinson, W. E. (1987) Occupational injury at a midwestern health science center and teaching hospital. AAOHN Journal 35: 367–376 (greater rate). McCurdy, S. A., Schenker, M. B. and Lassiter, D. V. (1989) Occupational injury and illness in the semiconductor manufacturing industry. American Journal of Industrial Medicine 15: 499–510 (greater rate). Neuberger, J. S., Kammerdiener, A. M. and Wood, C. (1988) Traumatic injuries among medical center employees. AAOHN Journal 36: 318–325 (greater rate). Jensen, R. and Sinkule, E. (1988) Press operator amputations: Is risk associated with age and gender? Journal of Safety Research 19: 125–133 (equal rate).

6. Lippel, K. (1995) Watching the watchers: How expert witnesses and

decision-makers perceive men's and women's workplace stressors. In Messing, K., Neis, B. and Dumais, L. (Eds.), *Invisible: Occupational Health Problems of Women at Work / Invisible La Sauté des travailleuses*, pp. 265–291. Gynergy Books, Charlottetown.

7. Statistics Canada, 1995. *Women in Canada*, p. 43. No. 89–503 E. Statistics Canada, Ottawa.

8. Silman, A. J. (1987) Why do women live longer and is it worth it? British Medical Journal 293: 1211–1212.

9. Guyon, L. (1996) *Derrière les apparences: Santé et conditions de vie des femmes*, p. 346. Ministère de la santé et des services sociaux, Québec. Silman (1987) Why do women live longer?

10. Statistics Canada (1995) *Women in Canada*, p. 45. Verbrugge, L. M. and Patrick, D. L. (1995) Seven chronic conditions: Their impact on US adults' activity levels and use of medical services. American Journal of Public Health 85 (2): 173–182.

11. Statistics Canada (1995) *Women in Canada*, chap. 4.

12. Ibid. p. 52. Verbrugge and Patrick (1995). Seven chronic conditions.

13. Gervais, M. (1993) *Bilan de santé des travailleurs québécois*. Institut de recherche en santé et en sécurité du travail du Québec, Montréal.

14. Primary school teachers in one of our studies attributed their allergies and skin problems to certain types of chalk.

15. Akyeampong, E. B. (1992) L'absentéisme. Tendances sociales canadiennes 25: 25–28.

16. Bourbonnais, R. and Vinet, A. (1990) L'absence pour maladie chez les infirmières et quelques indicateurs de charge de travail. In Brabant, C. and Messing, K. (Eds.), *Sexe faible ou travail ardu: recherches sur la santé des travailleuses*, pp. 87–101. Cahiers de l' Association canadienne-française pour l'avancement des sciences (ACFAS) 70. ACFAS, Montréal pp. 87–101. Bourbonnais, R., Vinet, A., Vézina, M. and Gingras, S. (1992) Certified sick leave as a non-specific morbidity indicator: A case-referent study among nurses. British Journal of Medicine 49: 673–678.

17. Courville, J., Dumais, L. and Vézina, N. (1994) Conditions de travail de femmes et d'hommes sur une chaîne de découpe de volaille et développement d'atteintes musculo-squelettiques. Travail et santé 10 (3): S17–S23.

CHAPTER 3

1. Vézina, N., Courville, J. and Geoffrion, L. (1995) Problèmes musculo-squelettiques, caractéristiques des postes de travailleurs et des postes de travailleuses sur une chaîne de découpe de dinde. In Messing, K., Neis, B. and Dumais, L. (Eds.), *Invisible: Issues in Women's Occupational Health / Invisible: la santé des travailleuses*, pp. 29–61. Gynergy Books, Charlottetown.

2. Ibid.

3. Bradley, H. (1989) *Men's Work, Women's Work.* University of Minnesota Press, Minneapolis.

4. *Dufour, L. et al. c. Centre Hospitalier St-Joseph de la Malbaie (1992),* Commission des affaires sociales. No. 240–53–000001–918. *Syndicat des employé-es de l'hôpital St-Sacrement (Belzile, Bergeron) c. Hôpital St-Sacrement.* (1990), Commission des affaires sociales. Nos. 30450–30451.

5. Chaffin, D. B., Herrin, G. D. and Keyserling, W. M. (1978) Pre-employment strength testing. Journal of Occupational Medicine 20: 403–408. Karvonen, M. J., Jukk, A. T., Viitasalo, P. V., Komi, J. N. and Tuulikki, J. (1980) Back and leg complaints in relation to muscle strength in young men. Scandinavian Journal of Rehabilitation Medicine 12: 53–59.

6. See especially: Bacchi, C. L. (1990) *Same Difference.* Allen and Unwin, St. Leonard's. Armstrong, P. and Armstrong, H. (1991) *Theorizing Women's Work,* chap. 2. Garamond Press, Toronto (contains an interesting discussion of the concepts of sex and gender). Hubbard, R. (1990) *The Politics of Women's Biology.* Rutgers University Press, New Brunswick.

7. For a fuller discussion, see Hubbard, R. and Wald, E. (1993) *Exploding the Gene Myth.* Beacon Press, Boston.

8. See Fausto-Sterling, A. (1992) *Myths of Gender,* revised Ed. Basic Books, New York.

9. Pheasant, S. (1986) *Bodyspace,* p. 45. Taylor & Francis, London.

10. Ibid. chaps. 3 and 4.

11. The following discussion is based on Messing, K. and Stevenson, J. (1996) A Procrustean bed: Strength testing and the workplace. Gender, Work and Organization 3 (3): 156–167.

12. Snook, S. M. and Ciriello, V. M. (1991) The design of manual handling tasks: Revised tables of maximum acceptable weights and forces. Ergonomics 34 (9): 1197–1213. Snook, S. M. and Ciriello, V. M. (1974) Maximum weights and work loads acceptable to female workers. Journal of Occupational Medicine 16: 527–534.

13. Mital, A. (1983) The psychophysical approach in manual lifting: A verification study. Human Factors 25 (5): 485–491. Mital, A. (1984) Maximum weights of lift acceptable to male and female industrial workers for extended shifts. Ergonomics 27: 1115–1126.

14. Froberg, K. and Pederson, P. K. (1984) Sex differences in endurance capacity and metabolic response to prolonged heavy exercise. European Journal of Applied Physiology 52: 446–480.

15. Wells, C. L. (1985) *Women, Sport and Human Performance.* Human Kinetics Publishers, Champaign.

16. Laubach, L. (1976) Comparative muscular strength of men and women. Aviation, Space and Environmental Medicine 47: 534–542.

17. Falkel, J. E., Sawka, M. N., Levine, L. et al. (1986) Upper body exercise performance: Comparison between women and men. Ergonomics 29:

145–154. Falkel, J. E., Sawka, M. N., Levine, L. and Pandolf, K. B. (1985) Upper to lower body muscular strength and endurance ratios for women and men. Ergonomics 28: 1661–1670.

18. Fothergill, D. M., Grieve, D. W. and Pheasant, S. T. (1991) Human strength capabilities during one-handed maximum voluntary exertions in the fore and aft plane. Ergonomics 34 (5): 563–565.

19. Fransson, C. and Winkel, J. (1991) Hand strength: The influence of grip span and grip type. Ergonomics 34 (7): 881–892.

20. Stevenson, J. M., Bryant, J. T., Greenhorn, D.R., Smith, J. T., Deakin, J. M. and Surgenor, B. (1990) The effect of lifting protocol on comparison with isoinertial lifting performance. Ergonomics 33 (12): 1455–1469.

21. Stevenson, J. M., Greenhorn, D. R., Bryant, J. T., Deakin, J. M. and Smith, J. T., (1996) Selection test fairness and the incremental lifting machine. Applied Ergonomics 27: 45–52.

22. Stevenson, J. M., Bryant, J. T., Greenhorn, D. R., Deakin, J. M. and Smith, J. T. (1995) Development of factor-score-based models to explain and predict maximal box-lifting performance. Ergonomics 38 (2): 292–302.

23. Ayoub, M. M., Denado, J. D., Smith, J. L., Bethea, N. J., Lambert, B. K., Alley, L. R., and Duran, B. S. (1982) *Establishing Physical Criteria for Assigning Personnel to Air Force Jobs: Final Report.* Air Force Office of Scientific Research Contract No. F 49620–79C–0006. Texas Technical University, Lubbock.

24. Misner, J. E., Boileau, R. A. and Plowman, S. A., (1989) Development of placement tests for firefighting. Applied Ergonomics 20 (3): 218–224.

25. Laurin G. (1992) *Féminisation de la main d'oeuvre: Impact sur la santé et la sécurité du travail.* Commission de la santé et de la sécurité du travail du Québec, Montréal. Calculated from fig. 4.1.1, p. 63.

26. Courville, J., Vézina, N. and Messing, K. (1992) Analyse des facteurs ergonomiques pouvant entraîner l'exclusion des femmes du tri des colis postaux. Le travail humain 55: 119–134.

27. Procrustes was an evil Greek giant who made his victims lie in a bed. If they were too short for the bed, he stretched them to fit. If they were too tall, he chopped off the excess.

28. Tancred, P. and Messing, K. (1996) Et si les femmes avaient le contrôle de la technologie? Recherches féministes 9 (1): 1–14.

29. Chabaud-Rychter, D. (1996) L'innovation industrielle dans l'électroménager: Conception pour l'usage et Conception pour la production. Recherches féministes 9 (1): 15–37.

30. Al-Haboubi, M. H. (1992) Anthropometry for a mix of different populations. Applied Ergonomics 23 (3): 191–196. Lest we North Americans be tempted to imagine that the faraway origins of this paper are responsi-

ble for its exclusion of women, I also refer the reader to a Canadian paper whose summary begins: "A comprehensive series of variables that describe the essential three dimensional characteristics of the human foot is presented together with descriptive statistics derived from a diverse civilian population (N = 1197), representing a wide age range (18–85 years) and randomly selected in terms of physical demands placed upon the foot in the course of a normal working day." The words "comprehensive," "essential," and "diverse" did not seem to the authors or editors incongruent with the total exclusion of women, which was not mentioned in the title or summary or explained in the paper. Hawes, M. R. and Sovak, D. (1994) Quantitative morphology of the human foot in a North American population. Ergonomics 37 (7): 1213–1226.

31. Braid, K. *Covering Rough Ground.* (Victoria, British Columbia: Polestar Book Publishers, 1991), p. 14.

32. Messing, K., Chatigny, C. and Courville, J. (1996) L'invisibilité du travail et la division léger/lourd dans l'entretien sanitaire: Impact sur la santé et la sécurité du travail. Objectif prévention 19 (2): 13–16.

33. Vézina, N., Tierney, D. and Messing, K. (1992) When is light work heavy? Components of the physical workload of sewing machine operators which may lead to health problems. Applied Ergonomics 23: 268–276.

34. Courville, J., Vézina, N. and Messing, K. (1991) Analysis of work activity of a job in a machine shop held by ten men and one woman. International Journal of Industrial Ergonomics 7: 163–174.

35. Saurel-Cubizolles, M.-J., Bourgine, M. Touranchet, A. and Kaminski, M. (1991) *Enquête dans les abattoirs et les conserveries des régions Bretagne et Pays-de-Loire: Conditions de travail et santé des salariés.* Rapport à la Direction Régionale des Affaires Sanitaires et Sociales des Pays-de-Loire. Institut de science et recherche médical (INSERM) Unité 149, Villejuif.

36. Vézina, N., Chatigny, C. and Messing, K. (1994) A manual materials handling job: Symptoms and working conditions among supermarket cashiers. Chronic Diseases in Canada 15 (1): 17–22.

37. Seifert, A. M., Messing, K. and Dumais, L. (1996) *Les caissières dans l'oeil du cyclone: Analyse de l'activité de travail des caissières de banque.* CINBIOSE, Montreal.

38. Saurel-Cubizolles, Bourgine, Touranchet, and Kaminski (1991) Enquête dans les abattoirs.

39. Messing, K., Haëntjens, C. and Doniol-Shaw, G. (1993) L'invisible nécessaire: L'activité de nettoyage des toilettes sur les trains de voyageurs en gare. Le travail humain 55: 353–370.

40. Brabant, C., Bédard, S. and Mergler, D. (1989)Cardiac strain among women laundry workers engaged in sedentary repetitive work. Ergonomics 32: 615–628.

CHAPTER 4

1. Hubbard, R. (1990) *The Politics of Women's Biology,* p. 23. Rutgers University Press, New Brunswick.

2. Etkowitz, H., Kemelgor, C., Neuschatz, M., Uzzi, B. and Alonzo, J. (1994) The paradox of critical mass for women in science. Science 266: 51–54.

3. Ibid.

4. Weaver, J. L. and Garrett, S. D. (1983) Sexism and racism in the American health care industry: A comparative analysis. In Fee, E. (Ed.), *Women and Health,* pp. 79–104. Baywood, Farmingdale. Sanmartin, C. and Snidel, L. (1993) Profile of Canadian physicians: Results of the 1990 Physician Resource Questionnaire. Canadian Medical Association Journal 149: 977–984.

5. Dagg, A. I. (1990) Women in science—Are conditions improving? In Ainley, M. G. *Despite the Odds: Essays on Canadian Women and Science,* pp. 337–347. Vehicule Press, Montréal.

6. Angier, N. (1991) Women swell ranks of science but remain invisible at the top. New York Times, May 21.

7. Rossiter, M. (1982) *Women Scientists in America.* Johns Hopkins University Press, Baltimore.

8. Ainley (1990) *Despite the Odds.*

9. The extensive literature on determinants of success in science has been recently summarized in Sonnert, G. (1996) *Who Succeeds in Science? The Gender Dimension.* Rutgers University Press, New Brunswick.

10. Tannen, D. (1994) *Gender and Discourse.* Oxford University Press, New York. Tannen D. (1994) *Talking from 9 to 5: Women and Men in the Workplace.* Avon Books, New York.

11. Cole, J. R. and Zuckerman, H. (1987) Marriage, motherhood and re-search performance in science. Scientific American 56 (2): 119–125. Sonnert (1996). *Who Succeeds.*

12. The value of the Canadian dollar varies between 70 and 80 percent of the U.S. dollar. In 1996 it was worth about $0.75 U.S. Unless otherwise noted, U.S. and Canadian dollar amounts will be quoted without conversion in the currency of the country referred to.

13. Blumenthal, D., Causino, N., Campbell, E. and Louis, K. S. (1996) Relationships between academic institutions and industry in the life sciences—An industry survey. New England Journal of Medicine 334 (6): 368–373.

14. Association of Canadian Medical Colleges (1996) *Canadian Medical Education Statistics,* table 70–71. Association of Canadian Medical Colleges, Ottawa.

15. Messing, K. and Mergler, D. (1986) Determinants of success in ob-taining grants for action-oriented research in occupational health. Com-

munication presented at the annual meeting of the American Public Health Association, Las Vegas, September 28–October 1.

16. Messing, K. (1991) *Occupational Health and Safety Concerns of Canadian Women: A Review.* Labour Canada, Ottawa. Messing, K. (1993) Doing something about it: Priorities in women's occupational health. In *Proceedings of the Round Table on Gender and Occupational Health,* pp. 155–161. Health Canada, Ottawa.

17. The Women's Bureau of Health Canada sponsored a research round table in 1992 which was well attended by government, university, employer, and union researchers and interveners from Newfoundland to British Columbia. See Health Canada, (1993). *Proceedings of the Round Table on Gender and Occupational Health. Health Canada, Ottawa, Ont., Canada.* The U.S. Women's Health Research Office has recently advocated for research on women's occupational health. In 1993 it sponsored the first research conference on women and occupational cancer. Together with the Women's Health Bureau of Health Canada, it also sponsored the Canada–U.S. Health Forum in August 1996, where occupational health was a subject of study and policy suggestions.

18. Medical Research Council of Canada (1994) *Report of the Advisory Committee on Women's Health Research Issues,* pp. 8–9. Cited in Status of Women Canada (1995) *Setting the Stage for the Next Century: The Federal Plan for Gender Equality,* p. 36. No. SW21–15/1995. Status of Women Canada, Ottawa.

19. We were once refused a grant on the grounds that our work was too applied, insufficiently related to basic science objectives. We replied by quoting long sections of the granting agency's own appeal for projects, which clearly and emphatically stated that applied work should be funded. We were told to submit our grant proposal again the following year. Our new proposal was rejected on the same grounds. We then submitted the same proposal without the applied part: the request was enthusiastically accepted and funded and in fact was among the five top-ranked proposals.

20. Ste-Marie, G. (1992) La recherche scientifique au Canada: Un trafic déloyal. Le Devoir. May 23.

21. Glantz, S. J. and Bero, L. A. (1994) Inappropriate and appropriate selection of "peers" in grant review. Journal of the American Medical Association 272 (2): 114–116.

22. Information for this section comes from my own experience as an outside evaluator for seven Canadian and Québec granting agencies in the natural and social sciences and as a member of five granting committees in Canada and Québec.

23. Garfunkel, J. M., Ulshen, M. H., Hamrick, H. J. and Lawson, E. E. (1994) Effect of institutional prestige on reviewers' recommendations and editorial decisions. Journal of the American Medical Association 272 (2): 137–138.

24. I almost never see people of color at scientific meetings and can only imagine how difficult it must be for those few who attend.

25. Garfunkel et al. (1994) Effect of institutional prestige.

26. This conclusion is based on data presented in Gilbert, J. R., Williams, E. S. and Lundberg, G. D. (1994) Is there gender bias in JAMA's peer review process? Journal of the American Medical Association 272 (2): 139–142. Copyright 1994, American Medical Association. I present here their data in a different form.

	Male reviewers' recommendations	
	Immediate Rejection	Other
Articles written by men	487	986
Articles written by women	169	254
Total	656	1240

$\chi^2 = 6.90, p < 0.01$

	Female reviewers' recommendations	
	Immediate Rejection	Other
Articles written by men	102	192
Articles written by women	36	102
Total	138	294

$\chi^2 = 3.20, 0.05 < p < 0.10$

27. It is difficult to ascribe sex to the authors of published papers because usually only first initials are published. I still remember how surprised and dismayed my parents were not to see my full name on my first published paper. "They can't even tell you're a girl!" said my feminist mother.

28. This is one reason why employers in the United States have been anxious to restrict women's access to nontraditional jobs, which they suspect of causing reproductive damage. A fetus cannot be covered by workers' compensation, and a malformed child could sue an employer for millions of dollars.

29. A historical and political treatment of workers' compensation can be found in Lippel, K. (1986) *Le droit des accidentés du travail à une indemnité: Analyse historique et critique.* Thémis, Montréal.

CHAPTER 5

1. This chapter is not intended to review the extensive literature on women as subjects of biological and medical research and on the social context of science, but merely to situate occupational health scientists in their com-

munity. For a wider discussion see (among many, many others): Lesley Doyal, Margrit Eichler, Anne Fausto-Sterling, Michel Foucault, Stephen Jay Gould, Donna Haraway, Sandra Harding, Ruth Hubbard, Richard Lewontin, Dorothy Nelkin, Londa Schiebinger, Nancy Tuana. The Spring/Summer 1996 issue of the journal *Social Text* contains a discussion of many currents in this field.

2. Ratcliffe, J. W. and Gonzalez-del-Valle (A.) 1988. Rigor in health-related research: Toward an expanded conceptualization. International Journal of Health Services 18 (3): 361–392.

3. In fact, women's domestic work overload is often used as a reason for refusing compensation. An employer presented evidence in a recent musculoskeletal injury case purporting to show that the woman had in fact injured herself by carrying heavy loads in her kitchen.

4. Tremblay, C. (1990) Les particularités et les difficultés de l'intervention préventive dans le domaine de la santé et de la sécurité des femmes en milieu de travail. Communication presented at the 58th Annual Meeting of the Association canadienne-française pour l'avancement des sciences, Université Laval, Québec, May 14.

5. Carlan, N. and Keil, M. (1995) Developing a proposal for a working women's health survey. In Messing, K., Neis, B. and Dumais, L. (Eds.), *Invisible: Issues in Women's Occupational Health / Invisible: La santé des travailleuses*, p. 295. Gynergy Books, Charlottetown.

6. Broerson, J. P. J., van Dijk, F. J. H., Weel, A. N. H. and Verbeek, J. H. A. M. (1995) The atlas of health and working conditions by occupation. 1. Occupational ranking lists and occupational profiles from periodical occupational health survey data. International Archives of Occupational and Environmental Health 67: 325–335.

7. Greenberg, G. N. and Dement, J. M. (1994) Exposure assessment and gender differences. Journal of Occupational Medicine 36 (8): 907–912.

8. Zahm, S. H., Linda, M. P., Lewis, D. R., Ward, M. H. and White, D. W. (1994) Inclusion of women and minorities in occupational cancer epidemiological research. Journal of Occupational Medicine 36 (8): 842–847.

9. Stock, S. R. (1993) *Gastric Cancer and Occupation: A Review of the Literature.* Industrial Disease Standards Panel, Toronto.

10. Block, G., Matanoski, G., Seltser, R. and Mitchell, T. (1988) Cancer morbidity and mortality in phosphate workers. Cancer Research 48: 7298–7303. This is only one of many, many examples.

11. Semenciew, R., Morrison, H., Riedel, D., Wilkins, K., Ritter, L. and Mao, Y. (1993) Multiple myeloma mortality and agricultural practices in the prairie provinces of Canada. Journal of Occupational Medicine 35: 557–561.

12. In 1988–1990, only 11 of 86 claims for psychological and psychosomatic pathologies were accepted, according to Vézina, M., Cousineau, D., Mergler, D., Vinet, A. and Laurendeau, M.-C. (1992) *Pour donner un sens au travail* p. 109. Gaëtan Morin Éditeur, Boucherville. This compilation excludes post-traumatic stress disorders and other event-related compensation.

13. Lippel, K. (1993) *Le stress au travail: Indemnisation des atteintes à la santé en droit québécois, canadien et américain*, p. 228. Éditions Yvon Blais, Cowansville. The data cited come from appeal decisions. This book contains a full discussion of the difficulties involved in compensation claims for stress-related disability.

14. Lippel, K. (1995) Watching the watchers: How expert witnesses and decision-makers perceive men's and women's workplace stressors. In Messing, Neis, and Dumais (1995) *Invisible* pp. 265–291.

15. Harber, P., Bloswick, D., Penna, L., Beck, J., Lee J. and Baker, D. (1992) The ergonomic challenge of repetitive motion with varying ergonomic stresses. Journal of Occupational Medicine 34: 518–528.

16. Gilboa, R., Al-Tawil, N. G. and Marcusson, J. A. (1988). Metal allergy in cashiers. Acta Dermatovenereologica 68 (4): 317–324.

17. Gutek, B. (1995) *The Dynamics of Service*, pp. 122–123. Jossey-Bass, San Francisco.

18. White, J. (1993). *Sisters and Solidarity*, p. 168. Thompson Educational Publishing, Toronto.

19. Seifert, A. M., Demers, C., Dubeau, H. and Messing, K. (1993) HPRT-mutant frequency and lymphocyte characteristics of workers exposed to ionizing radiation on a sporadic basis: A comparison of two exposure indicators, job title and dose. Mutation Research 319: 61–70.

20. The fact that each worker has many mutant cells means that smaller populations can be compared effectively. Hundreds of workers are required for a comparison of disease incidence, while we have published in the scientific literature comparisons of mutant cells involving 25 workers. See Messing, K., Seifert, A. M., Ferraris, J., Swarz, J. and Bradley, W. E. C. (1989) Mutant frequency of radiotherapy technicians appears to reflect recent dose of ionizing radiation. Health Physics 57: 537–544.

21. Siemiatycki, J., Dewar, R., Lakhani, R., Nadon, L., Richardson, L. and Gérin, M. (1989) Cancer risks associated with 10 organic dusts: Results from a case-control study in Montréal. American Journal of Industrial Medicine 16: 547–567.

22. Goldberg, M. S. and Labrèche, F. (1996) Occupational risk factors for female breast cancer: A review. Occupational and Environmental Medicine 53: 145–156.

23. Messing, K. (1988) Union-initiated research in genetic effects of workplace agents. Alternatives: Perspectives on Technology, Environment and Society 15 (1): 14–18.

24. A search of the 1990–1995 Medline database using the terms *restaurant* or *waitress* or *food service* x *health* or *epidemiol** or *illness* or *back pain* or *back injur** turned up 23 references, none of which dealt with waitresses' health (21 were about health problems acquired from eating in restaurants).

25. Guo and colleagues found, for example, that health care workers, maids, cleaners, hairdressers, checkers, designers, and waitresses reported

an excess of 50 percent or more back pain compared with other women workers. Of the studies reviewed, 78 had been done on health care workers, one on cleaners, and none on hairdressers, maids or (according to my own literature search) waitresses. For medical scientists, it may be easier to gain access to a hospital workplace than to get consent from a restaurant owner. However, hospitals employ cafeteria and housekeeping staff who could be studied as easily as nurses. See Guo, H.-R., et al. (1995) Back pain among workers in the United States: National estimates and workers at high risk. *American Journal of Industrial Medicine* 28: 591–602

26. The following section draws for its examples of orthodoxy on Monson, R. R. (1980) *Occupational Epidemiology*. CRC Press, Boca Raton.

27. Messing, K., Saurel-Cubizolles, M.-J., Kaminski, M. and Bourgine, M. (1992) Menstrual cycle characteristics and working conditions in poultry slaughterhouses and canneries. Scandinavian Journal of Work, Environment and Health 18: 302–309

28. Hsairi, M., Kauffmann, F., Chavance, M. and Brochard, P. (1992) Personal factors related to the perception of occupational exposure: An application of a job exposure matrix. International Epidemiology Association Journal 21: 972–980

29. Vézina, N. 1986 Le travail en ambiance froide dans la découpe de volailles, Laboratoire de physiologie du travail et ergonomie. Ph.D. thesis in ergonomics. Conservatoire National des Arts et Métiers and Université de Paris-Nord, Paris.

30. Hall, E. M. (1989) Gender, work control and stress: A theoretical discussion and an empirical test. International Journal of Health Services 19: 725–745.

31. Stevenson, J., Greenhorn, D. R., Bryant, J. T., Deakin, J. M. and Smith, J. T. (1996) Selection test fairness and the incremental lifting machine. Applied Ergonomics 27: 45–52. Strength testing issues are further discussed in Messing, K. and Stevenson, J. (1996) Women in procrustean beds: Strength testing and the workplace. Gender, Work and Organization 3 (3): 156–167.

32. Blishen, B. R., Carroll, W. K. and Moore, C. (1987) The 1981 socioeconomic index for occupations in Canada. Canadian Review of Sociology and Anthropology 24: 465–488. Heller, R. F., Williams, H. and Sittampalam, Y. (1984) Social class and ischaemic heart disease: Use of the male:female ratio to identify possible occupational hazards. Journal of Epidemiology and Community Health 38: 198–202.

33. Some social class influences on health may be mediated through common family-revenue-dependent factors such as nutrition, but others may be specific to the individual situation, such as job parameters.

34. Rosenstock, L., Logerfo, J., Heyer, N. J. and Carter, W. B. (1984) Development and validation of a self-administered occupational health history questionnaire. Journal of Occupational Medicine 26 (1): 50–54. Joffe, M.

(1992) Validity of exposure data derived from a structured questionnaire. American Journal of Epidemiology 135 (5): 564–570.

35. Guo, H.-R., Tanaka, S., Cameron, L. L., Seligman, P. J., Behrens, V. J., Ger, J., Wild, D. K. and Putz-Anderson, V. (1995) Back pain among workers in the United States: National estimates and workers at high risk. American Journal of Industrial Medicine 28: 591–602.

36. Raphael, K. (1987) Recall bias: A proposal for assessment and control. International Journal of Epidemiology 16 (2): 167–170.

37. MacKenzie, S. G. and Lippman, A. (1989) An investigation of report bias in a case-control study of pregnancy outcome. American Journal of Epidemiology 129: 65–75.

38. I thank Alain Lajoie for collecting articles that were useful for this discussion.

39. Wiktorin, C., Karlqvist, L. and Winkel, J. (1993) Validity of self-reported exposures to work postures and manual materials handling. Scandinavian Journal of Work, Environment and Health 19: 208–214.

40. Hays, M., Saurel-Cubizolles, M.-J., Bourgine, M., Touranchet, A., Verge, C., Kaminski, M. (1996) Conformity of workers' and occupational health physicians' descriptions of working conditions. International Journal of Occupational and Environmental Health 2: 10–17.

41. Behrens, V., Seligman, P., Cameron, L., Mathias, T. and Fine, L. (1994) The prevalence of back pain, hand discomfort and dermatitis in the US working population. American Journal of Public Health 84 (11): 1780–1785.

42. Many waitresses in Québec (unlike other jurisdictions) are unionized.

43. The second most frequent refers to our feminism. A critique of one of our articles on feminist perspectives in occupational health began, "This emotional article . . . " Readers are invited to consult the following article to see whether they think it had an emotional tone. We think the emotion was the reviewer's! See Messing, K., Dumais, L. and Romito, P. (1993) Prostitutes and chimney sweeps both have problems: Toward full integration of the two sexes in the study of occupational health. Social Science and Medicine 36: 47–55.

44. Deguire, S. and Messing, K. (1995) L'étude de l'absence a-t-elle un sexe? Recherches féministes 8 (2): 9–30.

45. Akyeampong, E. B. (1992). L'absentéisme. Tendances sociales canadiennes 25: 25–28.

CHAPTER 6

1. Hagberg, M., Morgenstern, H. and Kelsh, M. (1992) Impact of occupations and job tasks on the prevalence of carpal tunnel syndrome. Scandinavian Journal of Work, Environment and Health 18: 337–345, table 2.

2. Messing, K., Tissot, F., Saurel-Cubizolles, M.-J., Kaminski, M., and Bourgine, M. Sex as a variable can be a surrogate for some working conditions: Factors associated with sickness absence. Journal of Occupational and Environmental Medicine, accepted for publication.

3. Not only women are affected. Any powerless group (among which workers and women are well represented) may have the burden of proof placed on it without explicit justification.

4. Shilts, R. (1987) *And the Band Played On.* Penguin Books, New York.

5. Moher, D., Dulberg, C. S. and Wells, G. A. (1994) Statistical power, sample size and their reporting in randomized controlled trials. Journal of the American Medical Association 272 (2): 122–124.

6. Needleman, H. L. (1990) What can the study of lead teach us about other toxicants? Environmental Health Perspectives 86: 183–189. Messing, K. (1990) Environnement et santé: La santé au travail et le choix des scientifiques. In Bourgeault, G. (Ed.), *L'avenir d'un monde fini: Jalons pour une éthique du développement durable,* pp. 107–110. Cahiers de recherche éthique, no. 15. Editions Fides, Saint-Laurent.

7. Heller, R. F., Williams, H. and Sittampalam, Y. (1984) Social class and ischaemic heart disease: Use of the male:female ratio to identify possible occupational hazards. Journal of Epidemiology and Community Health 38: 198–202.

8. There is also an implicit assumption that working-class men have jobs that are less stressful for the heart than upper-class men. This is probably wrong. Other studies show that men of the upper social classes are less likely than working-class men to have heart disease related to their jobs. See, for example: Cassou, B., Derrienec, F., Lecuyer, G. and Amphoux, M. (1986) Déficience, incapacité et handicap dans un groupe de retraités de la Région Parisienne en relation avec la catégorie socio-professionnelle. Reveu d'épidémiologie et santé publique 34: 332–340.

9. Rossignol, M., Suissa, S. and Abenhaim, L. (1992) The evolution of compensated occupational spinal injuries. Spine 17 (9): 1043–1047.

10. This interpretation is borne out by a study of workers in the same jurisdiction who were referred to a rehabilitation center. Those who returned to work quickly were more likely to work in situations that allowed them to take unscheduled breaks. See Infante-Rivard, C. and Lortie, M. (1996) Prognostic factors for return to work after a first compensated episode of back pain. Occupational and Environmental Medicine 53: 488–494.

11. Brodeur, P. (1992) Enemies of the people. New Solutions (Summer): 6–10.

12. Greenberg, G. N. and Dement, J. M. (1994) Exposure assessment and gender differences. Journal of Occupational Medicine 36 (8): 907–912.

13. Needleman, H. L. (1992) Salem comes to the National Institutes of Health: Notes from inside the crucible of scientific integrity. Pediatrics 90 (6): 977.

14. I have never had to fear job loss for political reasons because of the strong union at my university. The relatively stronger unions give Québec and to some extent Canadian researchers more freedom than their U.S. counterparts.

15. Lippel, K. (1992) L'incertitude des probabilités en droit et médecine. Revue de droit Université de Sherbrooke 22 (2): 445–472.

CHAPTER 7

1. Kraut, A. (1994) Estimates of the extent of morbidity and mortality due to occupational diseases in Canada. American Journal of Industrial Medicine 25: 267–278. MSDs are still responsible for a relatively small amount of the total payout for occupational accidents and injuries in North America, the lion's share of which goes to accidents. According to the U.S. Bureau of Labor Statistics (cited in CTD News [1996] 5(1):1), about 5 percent of nonfatal occupational illnesses and accidents are MSDs. It is, however, hard to calculate the true incidence of MSDs because in some jurisdictions it is easier to get them recognized as accidents than as diseases.

2. For a comprehensive review of the English-language literature on work-related MSDs, with definitions of the major problems and discussion of the state of research, see: Hagberg, M., Silverstein, B., Wells, R., Smith, M. J., Hendrick, H. W., Carayon, P. and Pérusse, M. (1995) Work-Related Musculoskeletal Disorders: A Reference Book for Prevention. Taylor & Francis, London.

3. Laurin, G. (1991) Féminisation de la main d'oeuvre: Impact sur la santé et la sécurité du travail, pp. 64–69. Commission de la santé et de la sécurité du travail, Montréal.

4. Andersson, R., Kemmlert, K. and Kilbom, A. (1990) Etiological differences between accidental and nonaccidental occupational overexertion injuries. Journal of Occupational Accidents 12: 177–186.

5. Lortie, M. (1987) Structural analysis of occupational accidents affecting orderlies in a geriatric hospital. Journal of Occupational Medicine 29: 437–444.

6. Guo, H.-R., Tanaka, S., Cameron, L. L., Seligman, P. J., Behrens, V. J., Ger, J., Wild, D. K. and Putz-Anderson, V. (1995) Back pain among workers in the United States: National estimates and workers at high risk. American Journal of Industrial Medicine 28: 591–602.

7. Vézina, N., Tierney, D. and Messing, K. (1992) When is light work heavy? Components of the physical workload of sewing machine operators which may lead to health problems. Applied Ergonomics 23: 268–276.

8. Punnett, L., Robins, J. M., Wegman, D. H. and Keyserling, W. M. (1985) Soft tissue disorders in the upper limbs of female garment workers.

Scandinavian Journal of Work, Environment and Health and 11: 417-425. Silverstein, B. A., Fine, L. J. and Armstrong, T. J. (1987) Occupational factors and carpal tunnel syndrome. American Journal of Industrial Medicine 11: 343–358. Silverstein, B. A., Fine, L. J. and Armstrong, T. J. (1986) Hand wrist cumulative trauma disorders in industry. British Journal of Industrial Medicine 43: 779–784.

9. English, C. J., Maclaren, W. M., Court-Brown, C., Hughes, S. P. F., Porter, R. W., Wallace, W. A., Graves, R. J., Pethick, A. J. and Soutar, C. A. (1995) Relations between upper limb soft tissue disorders and repetitive movements at work. American Journal of Industrial Medicine 27: 75–90.

10. Brisson, C., Vinet, A. and Vézina, M. (1989) Disability among female garment workers. Scandinavian Journal of Work, Environment and Health 15: 323–328.

11. Saurel-Cubizolles, M.-J., Bourgine, M., Touranchet, A., and Kaminski, M. (1991) *Enquête dans les abattoirs et les conserveries des régions Bretagne et Pays-de-Loire: Conditions de travail et santé des salariés*, p. 46. Rapport à la Direction Régionale des Affaires Sanitaires et Sociales des Pays-de-Loire. Institute national de science et recherche medical (INSERM) Unité 149, Villejuif, France, p. 46.

12. Hagberg et al. (1995) *Work-Related Musculoskeletal Disorders*, p. 24.

13. Stock, S. R. (1992) Epidemiology of work-related musculoskeletal disorders of the neck and upper limbs: A response. American Journal of Industrial Medicine 21: 899–901.

14. Guo et al. (1995) Back pain, p. 600. Reid, J., Ewan, C. and Lowy, E. (1991) Pilgrimage of pain: The illness experiences of women with repetition strain injury and the search for credibility. Social Science and Medicine 32 (5): 601–612.

15. Tarasuk, V. and Eakin, J. M. (1995) The problem of legitimacy in the experience of work-related back injury. Qualitative Health Research 5 (2): 204–221.

16. An industrial accident is defined as "a sudden and unforeseen event" in the Québec legislation.

17. English et al. (1995) Relations.

18. Silverstein et al. (1986) Hand wrist. Punnett et al. (1985) Soft tissue.

19. Hagberg et al. (1995) *Work-Related Musculoskeletal Disorders*, chap. 4, reviews many factors involved in determining exposure.

20. Silverstein et al. (1987) Occupational factors.

21. Chatigny, C., Seifert, A. M., Messing, K. (1995) Repetitive movements in a non-repetitive task: A case study. International Journal of Occupational Safety and Ergonomics 1 (1): 42–51.

22. Stock (1992) Epidemiology.

23. Seifert, A. M., Messing, K. and Dumais, L. (1996) *Les caissières dans l'oeil du cyclone: Analyse de l'activité de travail des caissières de banque.* CINBIOSE, Montréal.

24. Saurel-Cubizolles et al. (1991) Enquête dans les abattoirs, p. 42.

25. Paoli, P. (1992) *First European Survey on the Work Environment 1991–1992*, pp. 126–128. European Foundation for the Improvement of Living and Working Conditions, Dublin.

26. Courville, J., Vézina, N. and Messing, K. (1992) Analyse des facteurs ergonomiques pouvant entraîner l'exclusion des femmes du tri des colis postaux. Le travail humain 55: 119–134.

27. Seifert, A. M., Messing K., and Dumais, L. (1997) Star wars and strategic defense initiatives: Work activity and health symptoms of unionized bank tellers during work reorganization. International Journal of Health Services 27 (3): 455–477.

28. Silverstein et al. (1986) Hand wrist.

29. Murata, K., Araki, S., Okajima, F. and Saito, Y. (1996) Subclinical impairment in the median nerve across the carpal tunnel among female VDT operators. International Archives of Occupational and Environmental Health 68: 75–79.

30. Courville, J., Dumais, L. and Vézina, N. (1994) Conditions de travail de femmes et d'hommes sur une chaîne de découpe de volaille et développement d'atteintes musculo-squelettiques. Travail et santé 10 (3): S17–S23.

31. See, for example, the polemic between Drs. Susan Stock and Peter Nathan in the pages of the American Journal of Industrial Medicine in 1992.

32. Lucire, Y. (1986) Neurosis in the workplace. Medical Journal of Australia 145: 323–327.

33. US, Canadian companies resisting CTD comp claims. CTD News 4 (10): 2.

34. Nathan, P. A. (1992) Hand and arm ills linked to life style. Letter to the New York Times, April 7.

35. Canakis, A. (1995) Mouvements répétitifs: La problématique. Littérature scientifique. Document distributed during a colloquium on "Les mouvements répétitifs: À quelles conditions représentent-ils un risque de lésions professionnelles?" organized by Robert Gilbert, Olivier Laurendeau, and François LeBire in collaboration with Canada Post Corporation and held in Montréal, December 1.

36. Reviewed by Bongers, P. M., de Winter, C. R., Kompier, M. A. J. and Hildebrandt, V. H. (1993) Psychosocial factors at work and musculoskeletal disease. Scandinavian Journal of Work Environment and Health 19: 297–312. Leino, P. and Magni, G. (1993) Depressive and distress symptoms as predictors of low back pain, neck-shoulder pain and other musculoskeletal morbidity. Pain 53: 89–94. Mäkelä, M., Heliövaara, M., Sievers, K., Impivaara, O., Knekt, P. and Aromaa, A. (1991) Prevalence, determinants and consequences of chronic neck pain in Finland. American Journal of Epidemiology 134: 1356–1367.

37. Rossignol, M., Suissa, S. and Abenaim, L. (1992) The evolution of compensated occupational spinal injuries. A three-year follow-up study. Spine 17 (9): 1043–1047, p. 1046.

38. Abenaim, L. and Suissa, S. (1987) Importance of economic burden of occupational back pain: A study of 2,500 cases representative of Québec. Journal of Occupational Medicine 22: 670–674.

39. Spitzer, W. O., LeBlanc, F. E., Dupuis, M., Abenhaim, L., Bélanger, A. Y., Bloch, R., Bombardier, C., Cruess, R. L., Drouin, G., Duval-Hesler, N., Laflamme, J., Lamoureux, G., Nachemson, A., Pagé, J. J., Rossignol, M., Salmi, L. R., Salois-Arsenault, S., Suissa, S. and Wood-Dauphinée, S. (1987) Scientific approach to the assessment and management of activity-related spinal disorders: A monograph for clinicians. Spine 12 (7S): S1–S59.

40. Spitzer, W. O. (1993) Low back pain in the workplace: Attainable benefits not attained. British Journal of Industrial Medicine 50: 383–388, p. 385.

41. Some of the possible flaws in this theory have been discussed by Ison, T. (1986) The therapeutic significance of compensation structures. Canadian Bar Review 64 (4): 605–637.

42. Waddell, G., Newton, M., Henderson, I., Somerville, D. and Main, C. J. (1993) A fear-avoidance beliefs questionnaire (FABQ) and the role of fear-avoidance beliefs in chronic low back pain and disability. Pain 52: 157–168.

43. Flodmark, B. T. and Aase, G. (1992) Musculoskeletal symptoms and type A behaviour in blue collar workers. British Journal of Industrial Medicine 49: 683–687.

44. Linton, S. J. and Kamwendo, K. (1989) Risk factors in the psychosocial work environment for neck and shoulder pain in secretaries. Journal of Occupational Medicine 31 (7): 609–613.

45. Viikari-Juntura, E., Vuori, J., Silverstein, B. A., Kalimo, R., Kuosma, E. and Videman, T. (1991) A life-long prospective study on the role of psychosocial factors in neck-shoulder and low-back pain. Spine 16 (9): 1056–1061.

46. Karasek, R. and Theorell, T. (1991) *Healthy Work: Stress, Productivity, and the Reconstruction of Working Life.* Basic Books, New York. Theorell, T., Harms-Ringdahl, K., Ahlberg-Hulten, G. and Westin, B. (1991) Psychosocial job factors and symptoms from the locomotor system: A multicausal analysis. Scandinavian Journal of Rehabilitation Medicine 23 (3): 165–173.

47. Faucett, J. and Rempel, D. (1994) VDT-related musculoskeletal symptoms: Interactions between work posture and psychosocial work factors. American Journal of Industrial Medicine 26: 597–612.

48. Leino, P. and Magni, G. (1993) Depressive and distress symptoms as predictors of low back pain, neck-shoulder pain and other musculoskeletal morbidity: A 10-year follow-up of metal industry employees. Pain 53: 89–94.

49. Hagberg, M., Morgenstern, H. and Kelsh, M. (1992) Impact of occupations and job tasks on the prevalence of carpal tunnel syndrome. Scandinavian Journal of Work, Environment and Health 18: 337–345, table 2.

50. Stetson, D. S., Albers, J. W., Silverstein, B. A. and Wolfe, R. A. (1992) Effects of age, sex, and anthropometric factors on nerve conduction measures. Muscle and Nerve 15: 1095–1104.

51. Dieck, G. S. and Kelsey, J. L. (1985) An epidemiologic study of the

carpal tunnel syndrome in an adult female population. Preventive Medicine 14: 63–69.

52. Voitk, A. J., Mueller, J. C., Farlinger, D. E. and Johnston, R. U. (1983) Carpal tunnel syndrome in pregnancy. Canadian Medical Association Journal 128: 277–281.

53. De Krom, M., Kester, A., Knipschild, P. and Spaans, F. (1990) Risk factors for carpal tunnel syndrome. American Journal of Epidemiology 132 (6): 1102–1110.

54. Cannon, L. J., Bernacki, E. J. and Walter, S. D. (1981) Personal and occupational factors associated with carpal tunnel syndrome. Journal of Occupational Medicine 23 (4): 255–258.

55. Mäkelä et al. (1991) Prevalence, determinants and consequences.

56. Paul, J. A. (1993) *Pregnancy and the Standing Working Posture: An Ergonomic Approach.* Coronel Laboratory, University of Amsterdam, Amsterdam. Paul, J. A. van Dijk, F. J. H. and Frings-Dresen, M. H. W. (1994) Work load and musculoskeletal complaints during pregnancy. Scandinavian Journal of Work, Environment Health and 20: 153–159. Paul, J. A. and Frings-Dresen, M. H. W. (1994) Standing working posture compared in pregnant and non-pregnant conditions. Ergonomics 37 (9): 1563–1575.

57 Schumacher, H. R., Dorwart, B. B. and Korzeniowshki, O. M. (1985) Occurrence of De Quervain's tendinitis during pregnancy. Archives of Internal Medicine 145 (11): 2083–2084.

CHAPTER 8

1. Stellman, J. M. and Henefin, M. S. (1983) *Office Work Is Dangerous for Your Health.* Pantheon Books, New York.

2. Statistics Canada (1994) *Women in the Labour Force,* table 2.8. No. 75–507E. Statistics Canada, Ottawa.

3. Stellman and Henefin (1983) *Office Work.*

4. Billette, A. and Piché, J. (1987) Health problems of data entry clerks and related job stressors. Journal of Occupational Medicine 29: 942–988.

5. Reviewed by Ong, C.-N., Chia, S.-E., Jeyaratnam, J. and Tan, K.-C. (1995) Musculoskeletal disorders among operators of visual display terminals. Scandinavian Journal of Work, Environment and Health 21: 60–64.

6. Karlqvist, L., Hagberg, M. and Selin, K. (1994) Variation in upper limb posture and movement during word processing with and without mouse use. Ergonomics 37 (7): 1261–1267.

7. Hagberg, M., Morgenstern, H. and Kelsh, M. (1992) Impact of occupations and job tasks on the prevalence of carpal tunnel syndrome. Scandinavian Journal of Work, Environment, and Health 18: 337–345.

8. Roman, E., Beral, V., Pelerin, M. and Hermon, C. (1992). Spontaneous abortion and work with visual display units. British Journal of Industrial Medicine 49: 507–512.

9. Bentur, Y. and Koren, G. (1991) The three most common occupational exposures reported by pregnant women: An update. American Journal of Obstetrics and Gynecology 165 (2): 429–437.

10. Lindbohm, M.-L., Hietanen, M., Kyyrönnen, P., Sallmén, M., von Nandelstadh, P., Taskinen, H., Pekkarinen, M., Ylikoski, M. and Hemminki, K. (1992) Magnetic fields of video display terminals and spontaneous abortion. American Journal of Epidemiology 136 (9): 1041–1051.

11. Statistics Canada (1994) Women in the Labour Force, graph 8.2.

12. David, H. and LeBorgne, D. (1983) Au Québec: La santé et la sécurité des travailleuses. In Stellman, J. M. (Ed.), La santé des femmes au travail, pp. 299–349. Éditions Parti Pris, Montréal.

13. Statistics Canada (1994) Women in the Labour Force, graph 8.2.

14. Stenberg, B. and Wall, S. (1995) Why do women report "sick building symptoms" more often than men? Social Science and Medicine 40 (4): 491–502.

15. Skov, P., Valbjorn, O. and Pederson, B. V. (1989) The Danish indoor climate study group: Influence of personal characteristics, job-related factors and psychosocial factors on the sick building syndrome. Scandinavian Journal of Work, Environment and Health 15: 286–295. Skov, P., Valbjorn, O. and Pedersen, B.V. (1990). The Danish indoor climate study group: Influence of indoor climate on the sick building syndrome in an office environment. Scandinavian Journal of Work, Environment and Health 16: 363–371. Norback, D., Michel, I., Widstrom, J. (1990) Indoor air quality and personal factors related to the sick building syndrome. Scandinavian Journal of Work, Environment and Health 16: 121–128. Hodgson, M. J., Frohliger, J., Permar, E., Tidwell, C., Traven, N. D., Olenchock, S. A. and Karpf, M. (1991). Symptoms and microenvironmental measures in nonproblem buildings. Journal of Occupational Medicine 4: 527–533. Harrison, J., Pickering, C. A. C., Faragher, E. B., Austwick, P. K. C., Little, S. A. and Lawton, L. (1992) An investigation of the relationship between microbial and particulate indoor air pollution and the sick building syndrome. Respiratory Medicine 86: 225–235. Norback, D., Torgen, M. and Edling, C. (1990) Volatile organic compounds, respirable dust, and personal factors related to prevalence and incidence of sick building syndrome in primary schools. British Journal of Industrial Medicine 47: 733–741. Kelland, P. (1992) Sick building syndrome, working environments and hospital staff. Indoor Environment, 1: 335–340. Mendell, M. J. and Smith, A. H. (1990) Consistent pattern of elevated symptoms in air conditioned office buildings: A reanalysis of epidemiologic studies. American Journal of Public Health 80: 1193–1199. Menzies, R., Tamblyn, R., Farant, J-P., Hanley, J., Nunes, F. and Tamblyn, R. (1993) The effect of varying levels of outdoor-air supply on the symptoms of sick building syndrome. New England Journal of Medicine 328: 821–827. Franck, C., Bach, E. and Skov, P. (1993) Prevalence of objective eye manifestations in people working in office buildings with different prevalences of the

sick building syndrome compared with the general population. International Archives of Occupational Environmental Health 65: 65–69. Stenberg, B., Eriksson, N., Mild, K. H. L., Höög, J., Sandström, M., Sundell, J. and Wall, S. (1995) Facial skin symptoms in visual display terminal workers. A case-referent study of personal, psychosocial, building- and VDT-related risk indicators. International Journal of Epidemiology 24 (4): 796–803. Nelson, N., Kaufman, J. D., Burt, J. and Karr, C. (1995) Health symptoms and the work environment in four nonproblem United States office buildings. Scandinavian Journal of Work, Environment and Health 21: 51–59. Stenberg and Wall (1995) Why do women report.

    16. Menzies et al. (1993) Effect of varying levels.

    17. Harrison et al. (1992) Investigation of relationship.

    18. Nelson et al. (1995) Health Symptoms.

    19. Hodgson et al. (1991) Symptoms. Menzies et al. (1993) Effect of varying levels Stenberg and Wall (1995) Why do women report.

    20. Kelland (1992) Sick building syndrome.

    21. Stenberg et al. (1995) Facial skin symptoms.

    22. Nelson et al. (1995) Health symptoms.

    23. This is Cullen's definition, discussed in Rest, K. M. (1992) Advancing the understanding of multiple chemical sensitivity (MCS): Overview and recommendations from an AOEC workshop. Toxicology and Industrial Health 8: 1–50.

    24. Kipen, H. M., Hallman, W., Kelly-McNeil, K. and Fiedler, N. (1995) Measuring chemical sensitivity prevalence: A questionnaire for population studies. American Journal of Public Health 85 (4): 574–577.

    25. Davidoff, A. L. and Fogarty, L. (1994) Psychogenic origins of multiple chemical sensitivities syndrome: A critical review of the research literature. Archives of Environmental Health 49 (5): 316–325.

    26. Ibid.

    27. Kreiss, K. (1990) The sick building syndrome: Where is the epidemiologic basis? American Journal of Public Health 80 (10): 1172–1173.

    28. Stenberg and Wall (1995) Why do women report, p. 501.

    29. Macintyre, S. (1993) Gender differences in the perceptions of common cold symptoms. Social Science and Medicine 36: 15–20.

    30. Brabant, C., Mergler, D. and Messing, K. (1990) Va te faire soigner, ton usine est malade: La place de l'hystérie de masse dans la problématique de la santé des travailleuses. Santé mentale au Québec 15: 181–204.

    31. Levine, R. J. (1984) Mass hysteria: Diagnosis and treatment in the emergency room. Archives of Internal Medicine 144: 1945–1946.

    32. Guidotti, T. L., Alexander, R. W. and Fedoruk, M. J. (1987) Epidemiological features that may distinguish between building-associated illness outbreaks due to chemical exposure or psychogenic origin. Journal of Occupational Medicine 29: 148–150. Salvaggio, J. E. (1994) Psychological aspects of

"environmental illness," "multiple chemical sensitivity," and building-related illness. Journal of Allergy and Clinical Immunology 94: 366–370.

33. Salvaggio (1994) Psychological aspects, p. 369.

34. Yassi, A., Weeks, J. L., Samson, K. and Raber, M. B. (1989) Epidemic of "shocks" in telephone operators: Lessons for the medical community. Canadian Medical Association Journal 140: 816–820.

35. Ong et al. (1995) Musculoskeletal disorders.

36. Stenberg and Wall, Why do women report, p. 105.

CHAPTER 9

1. Bellerose, C., Lavallée, C. and Camirand, J. (1994) *Enquête sociale et de santé 1992–1993: Faits saillants*. Ministère de la santé et des services sociaux, Québec.

2. The Ilfeld Psychiatric Symptom Index is based on responses to 29 questions such as (my translation of the French version): "During the last 7 days, have you felt dizzy or had the impression that you were about to faint? Have you felt tense or under pressure?" It does not measure pathology but rather signs of malfunctioning that may predict eventual pathology. See Ilfeld, F. W. (1976) Methodological issues in relating psychiatric symptoms to social stressors. Psychological Reports 39: 1251–1258.

3. Guyon, L. (1996) *Derrière les apparences: Santé et conditions de vie des femmes*, p. 144. Ministère de la santé et des services sociaux, Québec. Guyon reports that work protects against psychological distress for single-parent mothers and for women who live alone, but that women who combine work with husbands and children are in significantly more distress than those who just keep house. Vézina, M., Cousineau, M., Mergler, D., Vinet, A. and Laurendeau, M.-C. (1992) *Pour donner un sens au travail*, p. 142. Gaëtan Morin Éditeur, Boucherville.

4. Vézina et al. (1992) *Pour donner un sens au travail*, pp. 84–86.

5. Billette, A. and Bouchard, R. (1993) Pool size, job stressors and health problems: A study of data entry clerks. International Journal of Human–Computer Interaction 5 (2): 101–113.

6. Seifert, A. M., Messing, K. and Dumais, L. (1996) *Les caissières dans l'oeil du cyclone: Analyse de l'activité du travail des caissières de banque*. Cinboise Montréal. Seifert, A. M., Messing, K. and Dumais, L. (1997) Star-wars and strategic defense initiatives: Work activity and health symptoms of unionized bank tellers during work reorganization. International Journal of Health Services 27 (3), 455–477.

7. See discussion in Lippel, K. (1993) *Le stress au travail*, p. 167. Éditions Yvon Blais, Cowansville.

8. Cox, T., Thirlaway, M. and Cox, S. (1984) Occupational well-being: Sex differences at work. Ergonomics 27 (5): 499–510.

9. Programme Abstracts (1996) Conference on Women, Health and Work, Barcelona, April 17–20.

10. Frankenhaeuser, M., Lundbergh, U. and Chesney, M. (1991) *Women, Work and Health: Stress and Opportunities.* Plenum Press, New York.

11. Verbrugge, L. M. and Patrick, D. L. (1995) Seven chronic conditions: Their impact on US adults' activity levels and use of medical services. American Journal of Public Health 85 (2): 173–182.

12. This discussion relies heavily on two sources: Frankenhaeuser, M. (1991) The psychophysiology of sex differences as related to occupational status. In Frankenhaeuser et al. (1991) *Women, Work,* pp. 39–61. Astrand, P.-O. and Rodahl, K. (1986) *Textbook of Work Physiology,* 3d ed., pp. 161–163, 498–501. McGraw-Hill, New York.

13. Johansson, J. A. and Nonas, K. (1994) Psychosocial and physical working conditions and associated musculoskeletal symptoms among operators in five plants using arc welding in robot stations. International Journal of Human Factors in Manufacturing 4 (2): 191–204.

14. Bongers, P. M., de Winter, C. R., Kompier, M. A. J. and Hildebrandt, V. H. (1993) Psychosocial factors at work and musculoskeletal disease. Scandinavian Journal of Work, Environment and Health, 19: 297–312, p. 297.

15. Sprout, J. and Yassi, A. (1995) Occupational health concerns of women who work with the public. In Messing, K., Neis, B. and Dumais, L. (Eds.), *Invisible: Issues in Women's Occupational Health,* pp. 104–124. Gynergy Books, Charlottetown.

16. Hochschild, A. (1983) *The Managed Heart,* p. 7. University of California Press, Berkeley.

17. Soares, A. (1996) Nouvelles technologies = nouvelles qualifications? Le cas des caissières de supermarché. Recherches féministes 9 (1): 37–56.

18. In 1994–1995, the popular press carried articles alerting U.S. women to their supposed greater danger of dying on the job from violent acts: 42 percent of women's occupational fatalities and only 19 percent of men's were due to violent acts. However, since men have many more occupational fatalities than women, a man is several times more likely to die from a violent act in the workplace than a woman is. Kedjidjian, C. B., (1996) Work can be murder for women. Safety and Health (March): 42–45.

19. Seifert et al. (1996) *Les caissières dans l'oeil du cyclone.* Seifert et al. (1997) Star wars.

20. Karasek, R. and Theorell, T. (1990) *Healthy Work: Stress, Productivity, and the Reconstruction of Working Life.* Basic Books, New York.

21. Walters, V., Beardwood, B., Eyles, J. and French, S. (1995) Paid and unpaid work roles of male and female nurses. In Messing et al. (1995) *Invisible,* pp. 125–149.

22. Maslach, C. and Jackson, S. E. (1986) *The Maslach Burnout Inventory Manual*, 2d ed., p. 1. Consulting Psychologists Press, Palo Alto.

23. Sperandio, J. C. (1988) *L'ergonomie du travail mental*, pp. 91–92. Masson, Paris.

24. A subjective estimate of combined physical, mental, and emotional load may be obtained from Karasek's Job Content Questionnaire, which seeks to assess workers' perceptions of their capacity to meet the demands of their jobs.

25. Gaskell, J. (1991) What counts as skill? In Fudge, J. and McDermott, P. (Eds.), *Just Wages: A Feminist Assessment of Pay Equity*, pp. 141–159. University of Toronto Press, Toronto.

26. Messing, K. In press. Hospital trash: Cleaners speak of their role in disease prevention. Medical Anthropology Quarterly.

27. Tannen, D. (1994) *Talking from 9 to 5: Women and Men in the Workplace*. Avon Books, New York. Tannen argues that women's ways of presenting their ideas put them at a disadvantage in an overwhelmingly male organizational culture. Women who express their ideas in ways more typical of men, however, are heavily criticized.

28. There is some evidence that women react less than men to undervaluation, possibly because their expectations are lower or because they are protected by their multiple roles from investing too much of their self-evaluation in their workplace experience. See Phelan, J. (1994) The paradox of the contented female worker: An assessment of alternative explanations. Social Psychology Quarterly 57 (2): 95–107.

29. Lippel, K. 1993. *Le stress au travail: Indemnsation des atteintes à la santé en droit québécois, canadien et américain.* pp. 53–60 Éditions Yvos Blais, Cowansville.

30. Lippel, K. (1995) Watching the watchers: How expert witnesses and decision-makers perceive men's and women's workplace stressors. In Messing et al. (1995) Invisible, pp. 265–291.

31. Hessing, M. (1993) Mothers' management of their combined workloads: Clerical work and household needs. Canadian Journal of Sociology and Anthropology 30 (1): 37–63.

32. Prévost, J. and Messing, K. (1995) *L'activité de conciliation des responsabilités familiales et professionnelles chez des téléphonistes qui concilient un horaire de travail irrégulier et la garde des enfants.* Report submitted to the Syndicat de la communication, de l'énergie et du papier. CINBIOSE, Montréal.

33. An article from the research team of Robert A. Karasek, the pioneering researcher into stress and heart disease, mentions (p. 179) that all the group's studies relating blood pressure to job strain had been done on men, although they intended to expand these studies. See Pickering, T. G., James, G. D., Schnall, P. L., Schlussel, Y. R., Pieper, C. F., Gerin, W. and Karasek, R. A. (1991) Occupational stress and blood pressure: Studies in working men and women. In Frankenhaeuser et al. (1991) *Women, Work* pp. 171–186.

34. Steingart, R. M. Packer, M., Hamm, P., Coglianese, M. E., Gersh, B., Geltman, E. M., Sollano, J., Katz, S., Moyé, L., Basta, L. L., Lewis, S. J., Gottlieb, S. S., Bernstein, V., McEwan, P., Jacobson, K., Brown, E. J., Kukin, M. L., Kantrowitz, N. E. and Pfeffer, M. A. (1991) Sex differences in the management of coronary artery disease. New England Journal of Medicine 325: 226–230.

35. Doyal, L. (1995) *What Makes Women Sick: Gender and the Political Economy of Health*, p. 17. Macmillian, London.

36. Fine, L. J. (1996) Editorial: The psychosocial work environment and heart disease. American Journal of Public Health 86 (3): 301–303.

37. Hall, E. M., Johnson J. V., Spratt, K., Griffith, J. and Curbow, B. (1996) Methodological problems in measuring work in women: Double exposure, career patterns and emotional labor. Proceedings of the International Congress on Work, Women and Health, pp. 134–143. Barcelona, April 17–20.

38. Steingart et al. (1991) Sex differences.

39. D'Hoore, W., Sicotte, C. and Tilquin, C. (1994) Sex bias in the management of coronary artery disease in Québec. American Journal of Public Health 84 (6): 1013–1015.

40. Leigh, J. P. (1991) A ranking of occupations based on the blood pressures of incumbents in the National Health and Nutrition Examination Survey I. Journal of Occupational Medicine 33 (8): 853–861.

41. Diastolic blood pressure is the smaller of the two numbers given when blood pressure is reported as, for example, 120/80.

42. Kristensen, T. S. (1989) Cardiovascular diseases and the work environment. Scandinavian Journal of Work, Environment and Health 15: 165–179.

43. Astrand and Rodahl (1986) *Textbook of Work Physiology*, p. 617.

44. Kristensen, T. S. (1991) Sickness absence and work strain among Danish slaughterhouse workers. Social Science and Medicine 32 (1): 15–27.

45. Moser, K. A., Fox, A. J., Goldblatt, P. O. and Jones, D. R. (1986) Stress and heart disease: Evidence of associations between unemployment and heart disease from the OPCS Longitudinal Study. Postgraduate Medical Journal 62: 787–789.

46. Waldron, I. (1991) Effects of labor force participation on sex differences in mortality and morbidity. In Frankenhaeuser et al. (1991) *Women, Work*, pp. 17–38.

47. Hazuda, H. P., Haffner, S. M., Stern, M. P., Knapp, J. A., Eifler, C. W. and Rosenhal, M. (1986) Employment status and women's protection against coronary heart diease. American Journal of Epidemiology 123 (4): 623–640. Haertel, U., Heiss, G., Filipiak, B. and Doering, A. (1992) Cross-sectional and longitudinal associations between high density lipoprotein cholesterol and women's employment. American Journal of Epidemiology 135 (1): 68–78.

48. Kwachi, I., Colditz, G. A., Stampfer, M. J., Willett, W. C., Manson, J. E., Seizer, F. E. and Hennekens, C. H. (1995) Prospective study of shift work and risk of coronary heart disease in women. Circulation 92 (11): 3178–3182.

49. Haynes, S. (1991) The effect of job demands, job control and new

technologies on the health of employed women. In Frankenhaeuser et al. (1991) *Women, Work*, pp. 157–169.

50. Theorell, T. (1991) Psychosocial cardiovascular risks—On the double loads in women. Psychotherapy Psychosomatics 55: 81–89.

51. Fouriaud, C., Jacquinet-Salord, M. C., Degoulet, P., Aimé, F., Lang, T., Laprugne, J., Main, J., Oeconomos, J., Phalente, J. and Prades, A. (1984) Influence of socioprofessional conditions on blood pressure levels and hypertension control. American Journal of Epidemiology 120 (1): 72–86.

52. Saurel-Cubizolles, M. J., Kaminski, M., Du Mazaubrun, C. and Bréart, G. (1991) Les conditions de travail professionnel des femmes et l'hypertension artérielle en cours de grossesse. Revue d'épidémiologie et santé publique 39: 37–43.

53. Krasek, R. (1994) *Job Content Questionnaire and User's Guide, Revision 1.12*. Department of Work Environment, University of Massachusetts, Lowell.

54. Hall, E. M. (1989) Gender, work control and stress: A theoretical discussion and an empirical test. International Journal of Health Services 19: 725–745.

55. Schnall, P. L., Landsbergis, P. A. and Baker, D. (1994) Job strain and cardiovascular disease. Annual Reviews of Public Health 15: 381–411.

56. Theorell, T. (1991) On cardiovascular health in women. In Frankenhaeuser et al. (1991) *Women, Work*, pp. 187–204.

57. Johnson, J.V. and Hall E. (1996) Dialectic between conceptual and causal inquiry in psychosocial work-environment research. Journal of Occupational Health Psychology 1(4):362–374.

58. Frankenhaeuser, M. (1991) The psychophysiology of sex differences as related to occupational status. In Frankenhaeuser et al. (1991) *Women, Work*, pp. 39–61.

59. Endresen, I. M., Vaernes, R., Ursin, H. and Tonder, O. (1987) Psychological stress factors and concentration of immunoglobulins and complement components in Norwegian nurses. Work and Stress 1 (4): 365–375.

60. Vaernes, R. J., Myrgre, G., Aas, H., Homner, T., Hansen, I. and Tonder, O. (1991) Relationships between stress, psychological factors, health and immune levels among military aviators. Work and Stress 5 (1): 5–16, p. 6.

61. Endresen et al. (1987) Psychological stress factors, p. 365.

62. Lippel (1995) Watching the watchers, p. 284.

63. Lippel, K. (1996) Workers' compensation and stress: Gender and access to compensation. Proceedings of the International Congress on Women, Work and Health, pp. 82–91. Barcelona, April 17–20.

64. Gervais, M. (1993) *Bilan de santé des travailleurs québécois*, p. 26. Institut de recherche en santé et en sécurité du travail du Québec, Montréal.

65. Ibid. p. 24

66. Boxer, P. A., Burnett, C. and Swanson, N. (1995) Suicide and occupa-

tion: A review of the literature. Journal of Occupational and Environmental Medicine 37 (4): 442–452.

67. Estryn-Behar, M., Kaminski, M., Pegne, E., Bonnet, N., Vaichère, E., Gozlan, C., Azoelay, S. and Giorgi, M. (1990) Stress at work and mental health status among female hospital workers. British Journal of Industrial Medicine 47: 20–28.

68. Work and Stress 9 (2/3), 1995.

69. Karasek and Theorell (1990) Healthy Work, pp. 177, 184–185.

70. An important exception has been the Swedish Institute for the Quality of Working Life, recently merged with the Institute for Occupational Health to form the National Institute for Working Life.

71. Matuszek, P. A. C., Quick, J. C. and Nelson, D. L. (1995) Women at work: Gender differences in distress. Abstracts from the American Psychological Association Conference on Work, Stress and Health '95: Creating Healthier Workplaces, p. 249. Washington, D.C., September 10–14.

72. Goldberg, P., David, S., Landre, M.-F., Fuhrer, R., Dassa, S. and Goldberg, M. (1993) An epidemiological study of depressive symptomatology and working conditions of prison staff. Proceedings of the 24th International Congress on Occupational Health, p. 110. Nice, September 26–Oct. 1.

73. Bassan, D., Moore, M. A. and Britt, T. W. (1995) Relationships between gender, discrimination, sexual harassment and depression. Communication presented at the American Psychological Association Conference on Work, Stress and Health '95: Creating Healthier Workplaces. Washington, D.C., September 12–14.

74. Hofschid, A. (1997) The Time Bind: When Work Becomes Home and Home Becomes Work. Henry Holt/Metropolitan Books, New York.

75. St-Jacques, Y., Vézina, N. and Stock, S. (1995) Apport de la démarche ergonomique à l'organisation du travail: L'aménagement d'un module de couture. Proceedings of the 27th Annual Conference of the Human Factors Association of Canada, pp. 43–48. Québec, October.

76. Kasl, S. V. and Serxner, S. (1992) Health promotion at the worksite. In Maes, S., Leventhal, H. and Johnston, M. (Eds.), International Review of Health Psychology, pp. 111–142. John Wiley and Sons, London. The authors note that North American employee assistance and workplace health promotion programs are particularly unlikely to pay attention to working conditions.

77. Heaney, C. A. (1995) Worksite stress reduction programs: Integrating health protection and health promotion approaches. Abstracts from the American Psychological Association Conference on Work, Stress and Health '95: Creating Healthier Workplaces, p. 85. Washington, D.C., September 12–14.

78. Frankenhaeuser (1991) Psychophysiology of sex differences.

79. Carayon, P., Yank, C. L. and Lim, S. Y. (1995) Examining the relationship between job design and worker strain over time in a sample of office workers. Ergonomics 38 (6): 1199–1211. Kasl and Serxner (1992) Health promotion.

80. Dejours, C. (1993) *Travail: Usure mentale.* Bayard, Paris.

81. Carpentier-Roy, M.-C. (1991) *Organisation du travail et santé mentale chez les enseignantes et les enseignants du primaire et du secondaire.* Centrale de l'enseingement du Québec, Québec.

82. Hirata, H. and Kergoat, D. (1988) Rapports sociaux de sexe et psychopathologie du travail. In Dejours, C. (Ed.), *Plaisir et souffrance dans le travail,* Vol. 2, pp. 131–163. Édition de l'AOCIP, Paris.

83. Carpentier-Roy, M.-C. (1991) *Corps et âme.* Éditions Liber, Montréal.

84. Ibid. chap. 3.

85. Essentialism is attributing characteristics to people based on their biological "nature," such as presuming that women are naturally motherly or men are naturally violent.

86. Teiger, C. (1996) Changer de regard sur les gestes et postures par la formation à l'analyse ergonomique du travail pour mieux prévenir les risques professionnels. Proceedings of the Annual Meeting of the Société d'ergonomie de langue française, vol. 1, pp. 282–289. Brussels, September 11–13.

87. Summarized in Wendelen, E. (1995) La formation des syndicalistes à l'ergonomie: L'interaction des politiques publiques, des pratique syndicales et de la recherche. Éducation Permanente 124: 49–58. An English summary is available in Safety Science 3(2/3): 181–182, 1996. Wigmore, D. (1996) Looking for clues to escape the Taylorist "ergonomic trap." Are participatory mapping and other visual tools a way to re-integrate work organisation and ergonomics? M.S. thesis. Work Environment Department, University of Massachusetts at Lowell, Lowell.

CHAPTER 10

1. Hemminki, K., Sorsa, M. and Vainio, H. (1985) *Occupational Hazards and Reproduction,* p. ix. Hemisphere Publishing Corporation, Washington, D.C.

2. Kenen, R. (1993) *Reproductive Hazards in the Workplace: Mending Jobs, Mending Pregnancies.* Hayworth Press, Binghampton.

3. Gold, E. B., Lasley, B. L. and Schenker, M. B. (1994) Preface. Occupational Medicine: State of the Art Reviews 9 (3): ix.

4. Shepard, T. H. (1995) *Catalog of Teratogenic Agents.* Johns Hopkins University Press, Baltimore.

5. Wakeford, R. (1995) The risk of childhood cancer from intrauterine and preconceptional exposure to ionizing radiation. Environmental Health Perspectives 103 (11): 1018–1925.

6. Infante-Rivard, C. (1995) Electromagnetic field exposure during pregnancy and childhood leukemia. Lancet 346: 177.

7. Lalande, N. M., Hétu, R. and Lambert, J. (1986) Is occupational noise exposure during pregnancy a risk factor of damage to the auditory system of the fetus? American Journal of Industrial Medicine 10: 427–435.

Nurminen, T. (1995) Female noise exposure, shift work and reproduction. Journal of Occupational and Environmental Medicine 37 (8): 945–950.

8. Goulet, L. (1987) Association between spontaneous abortion and ergonomic factors. Scandinavian Journal of Work, Environment and Health 13: 399–403.

9. Marbury, M. C. (1992) Relationship of ergonomic stressors to birthweight and gestational age. Scandinavian Journal of Work, Environment and Health 18: 73–83.

10. Nurminen (1995) Female noise exposure.

11. Stein, Z. A., Susser, M. W. and Hatch, M. C. (1986) Working during pregnancy: Physical and psychosocial strain. Occupational Medicine: State of the Art Reviews 1 (3): 405–409. Swan, S. H., Beaumont, J. J., Hammond, S. K., Von Behren, J., Green, R. S., Hallock, M. F., Woskier, S. R., Hines, C. J. and Schenker, M. B. (1995) Historical cohort study of spontaneous abortion among fabrication workers in the Semiconductor Health Study: Agent-level analysis. American Journal of Industrial Medicine 28 (6): 751–769.

12. Cherry, N. (1987) Physical demands of work and health complaints among women working late in pregnancy. Ergonomics 30 (4): 689–701.

13. Moore, K., Dumas, G. A. and Reid, J. G. (1990) Postural changes associated with pregnancy and their relationship with low-back pain. Clinical Biomechanics 5: 169–174. Saurel-Cubizolles, M.-J., Kaminski, M., Du Mazaubrun, C. and Bréart, G. (1991) Les conditions de travail professionnel des femmes et l'hypertension artérielle en cours de grossesse. Revue d'épidémiologie et santé publique 39: 37–43.

14. Katherine Lippel quotes an expert witness in a case of radiation exposure during pregnancy: "It's a case of a radiation-exposed worker who has inside her a member of the public: since the public cannot be exposed to more than 5 milliSieverts (of radiation) and the mother's body is considered to act as a barrier which reduces the dose by half, the radiation-exposed pregnant worker cannot be exposed to more than 10 milliSieverts so as to respect the limit of 5 milliSieverts for the public (foetus in this case)." Extract from the testimony in Hôtel-Dieu de St-Jérome et Chaput before the Commission d'appel en matière de lésions professionnelles, May 1995.

15. Massachusetts Coalition for Occupational Safety and Health (1992) Confronting Reproductive Health Hazards on the Job: A Guide for Workers, p. 39. MassCOSH, Boston.

16. Wilson, B. W. and Stevens, R. G. (1996) Occupational exposure to electronmagnetic fields: The case for caution. Applied Occupational and Environmental Hygiene 11 (4): 299–306.

17. Headopohl, D. M. (1993) Women workers. Occupational Medicine: State of the Art Reviews 8 (4).

18. Filkins, K. and Kerr, M. J. (1993) Occupational reproductive health risks. Occupational Medicine: State of the Art Reviews 8 (4): 733–754.

19. Saiki, C. L., Gold, E. B. and Schenker, M. B. (1994) Workplace pol-

icy on hazards to reproductive health. Occupational Medicine: State of the Art Reviews 9 (3): 541–550.

20. Kenen (1993) *Reproductive Hazards*, pp. 18–19.

21. Hochschild, A. (1989) *The Second Shift*, chap. 6. Avon Books, New York.

22. Malenfant, R. (1996) *Travail et grossesse: Peut-on laisser la maternité à la porte de l'entreprise?* p. 21. Éditions Liber, Montréal.

23. Kenen (1993) *Reproductive Hazards*, p. 211.

24. Ibid. Kenen points out that no one has suggested barring all women nurses from night shifts in hospitals or other hazardous situations in primarily female jobs. Draper, E. (1991) *Risky Business*. Cambridge University Press, Cambridge.

25. Saurel-Cubizolles, M.-J. and Romito, P. (1992) Mesures protectrices pour les femmes enceintes au travail. Revue française des affaires sociales 2: 49–65.

26. Paul, J. A. (1993) *Pregnancy and the Standing Working Posture: An Ergonomic Approach*. Coronel Laboratory, University of Amsterdam, Amsterdam.

27. Saurel-Cubizolles et al. (1991) Conditions de travail.

28. Romito, P. and Saurel-Cubizolles, M.-J. (1996) New mothers' depression in Italy and France: The role of the couple, employment and social factors. Communication presented at the Women, Work and Health Conference, Barcelona, April 19.

29. The leave is paid for through a special fund to which all employers contribute, whether or not they employ women. Employers are not required to improve the risky job site. Although they are encouraged to do so or to transfer workers, it is more convenient for most to send the worker home, at the Occupational Health and Safety Commission's expense. Thus, applications of the provisions on pregnancy constitute an exception to the principle of "elimination of risk at the source" underlying the rest of the Québec occupational health and safety law.

30. Lippel, K., Bernstein, S. and Bergeron, M.-C. (1995) *Le retrait préventif de la travailleuse enceinte ou qui allaite: Réflexions sur le droit et la médecine*. Les Éditions Yvon Blais, Cowansville.

31. Canada provides precautionary reassignment for federally regulated employees, but if the employee cannot be reassigned and must take leave, the weeks taken are subtracted from total allowable maternity leave.

32. Draper (1991) *Risky Business*, p. 65–66.

33. Castleman, B. and Ziem, G. (1988) Corporate influence on threshold limit values. American Journal of Industrial Medicine 13: 531–559.

34. Malenfant, R. (1992) *L'évolution du programme de retrait préventif de la travailleuse enceinte ou qui allaite. Pour une maternité sans danger, Axes de recherche.* Rapport du groupe de travail pour une maternité sans danger, pp. 5–44. Institut de recherche en santé et en sécurité du travail du Québec,

Montréal. Malenfant, R. (1993) Le droit au retrait préventif de la travailleuse enceinte ou qui allaite: À la recherche d'un consensus. Sociologie et sociétés 25 (1): 61–75.

35. Lippel et al. (1995) *Retrait Préventif,* p. 53.

36. McDonald, A. D., (1994) The "retrait préventif": An evaluation. Canadian Journal of Public Health 85 (2): 136–139.

37. Messing, K., Lippman, A., Infante-Rivard, C. and Vézina, N. (1988) *Les nouvelles normes sur le retrait préventif de la travailleuse enceinte.* Report of an ad-hoc committee, submitted to the CSN union, Montréal, September.

38. Vogel, L. (1990) Debating difference: Feminism, pregnancy and the workplace. Feminist Studies 16: 9–32

39. U.S. Congress, Office of Technology Assessment (1985) *Reproductive Health Hazards in the Workplace,* p. iii. OTA-BA-266. US Government Printing Office, Washington, D.C.

40. Ibid. pp. 246–247. The U.S. courts found that firing the technicians was discriminatory. In Québec, we lost the case for precautionary leave, but similar cases are still being fought out, with contradictory results.

41. Occupational Health and Safety Commission of Québec. (1996) *Annual Report 1995.* Québec.

42. McDonald (1994) "Retrait préventif."

43. This is not a very large proportion; in Italy and France, analogous provisions are used by 60 percent of pregnant women. Stellman, J. M. (1978) *Women's Work, Women's Health.* Pantheon, New York. Stellman, J., and Henefin, M. S. (1984) *Office Work Can Be Dangerous for Your Health,* chap. 1. Pantheon Books, New York. Stock, S. (1991) Workplace ergonomic factors and the development of musculoskeletal disorders of the neck and upper limbs. American Journal of Industrial Medicine 19: 87–107. Turcotte, G. (1992) How pregnant workers see their work, its risks and the right to precautionary leave in Québec. Women and Health 18 (3): 79–96.

44. Turcotte (1992) How pregnant workers see their work.

45. Narod, S. A., Douglas, G. R., Nestmann, E. R. and Blakey, D. H. (1988) Human mutagens: Evidence from paternal exposure? Environmental Molecular Mutagenesis 11: 401–415.

46. Whorton, M. D. (1986) Male reproductive hazards. Occupational Medicine State of the Art Reviews 1 (3): 375–379, p. 375. Lindbohm, M.-L., Hemminki, K., Bonhomme, M. G., Anttila, A., Rantala, K., Heikkila, P., and Rosenberg, M. J., (1991) Effects of paternal occupational exposure on spontaneous abortions. American Journal of Public Health 81: 1029–1033.

47. See for example Delaney, J., Lupton, M. J. and Toth, E. (1988) *The Curse: A Cultural History of Menstruation,* pp. 62–63 University of Illinois Press, Urbana.

48. Mergler, D., and Vézina, N. (1985). Dysmenorrhea and cold exposure. Journal of Reproductive Medicine 30: 106–111.

49. Stanosz, S., Kuligowski, D. and Pieleszek, A. (1995) Concentration

of dihydroepiandrosterone, dihydroepiandrosterone sulphate and testosterone during premature menopause in women chronically exposed to carbon disulphide. Medycyna Pracy 46 (4): 340.

50. Woods, N. F., Most, A. and Dery, G. K. (1982) Prevalence of premenstrual symptoms. American Journal of Public Health 72: 1257–1264. Sundell, G., Milsom, I., and Andersch, B. (1990) Factors influencing the prevalence of dysmenorrhea in young women. British Journal of Obstetrics and Gynaecology 97: 588–594 Pullon, S., Reinken, J. and Sparrow, M. (1988) Prevalence of dysmenorrhea in Wellington women. New Zealand Medical Journal, February 10: 52–54.

51. Iglesias, R. E., Terrés, A. and Chavarria, A. (1980) Disorders of the menstrual cycle in airline stewardesses. Aviation, Space and Environmental Medicine (May): 518–520.

52. Cameron, R. G. (1969) Effect of flying on the menstual function of air hostesses. Aerospace Medicine (September) 1020–1023.

53. Tissot, F. and Messing, K. (1995) Perimenstrual symptoms and working conditions among hospital workers in Québec. American Journal of Industrial Medicine 27: 511–522.

54. Calculated by combining two sources: Statistics Canada (1992) Census 1991: Le pays. No. 93–326. Statistics Canada, Ottawa. Québec Occupational Health and Safety Commission (1992) Annual Report, table 1. Québec.

55. Soares, A. S. (1995) Les (mes)aventures des caissières dans le paradis de la consommation: Une comparaison Brésil-Québec, p. 144. Ph.D. thesis. Department of Sociology. Laval University, Québec (my translation).

CHAPTER 11

1. Castleman, B. I. and Ziem, G. E. (1988) Corporate influence on threshold limit values. American Journal of Industrial Medicine 13: 531–559.

2. Ibid. Castleman, B. I. and Ziem, G. E. (1994) American Conference of Governmental Industrial Hygienists: Low threshold of credibility. American Journal of Industrial Medicine 26: 133–143.

3. Castleman and Ziem (1988) Corporate influence, p. 555.

4. Landrigan, P. J. and Perera, F. P. (1988) Controversy in the regulation of formaldehyde. American Journal of Industrial Medicine 14: 375–377. Nicholson, W. J. and Landrigan, P. J. (1989) Quantitative assessment of lives lost due to delay in the regulation of occupational exposure to benzene. Environmental Health Perspectives 82: 185–188.

5. Rekus, J. (1996) The real meaning of threshold limit values. Occupational Hazards (June) 45–46.

6. According to a letter sent to various scientists on January 24, 1994, and signed by Mark Goldberg and Yvette Bonvalot of the Department of Community Health in Montréal, over 90 percent of the Québec exposure limits were directly copied from ACGIH.

7. Sass, R. (1988) What's in a name? The occupational hygienist's problem with threshold limit values. American Journal of Industrial Medicine 14: 355–363.

8. Absorption is often proportional to body surface, and smaller people have a higher ratio of surface to volume.

9. Only a small minority of workers exposed to radiation in Canada are covered by the Québec law on precautionary reassignment.

10. Dosimeters used to be made of film, and the initial readings could be checked. They are now made of chemical sensors, so that they are more sensitive, but can only be read once. An extra-high reading, possibly due to errors in the procedure, cannot be checked.

11. Otake, M., Schull, W. J. and Neel, J. V. (1990) Congenital malformations, stillbirths and early mortality among the children of atomic bomb survivors: A reanalysis. Radiation Research 122: 1–11.

12. Seifert, A. M., Demers, C., Dubeau, H. and Messing, K. (1993) HPRT-mutant frequency and lymphocyte characteristics of workers exposed to ionizing radiation on a sporadic basis: A comparison of two exposure indicators, job title and dose. Mutation Research 319: 61–70.

13. Massachusetts Coalition for Occupational Safety and Health (1992) Confronting Reproductive Health Hazards on the Job: A Guide for Workers. MassCOSH, Boston.

14. Messing, K. and Stevenson, J. (1996) A Procrustean bed: Strength testing and the workplace. Gender, Work and Organization 3 (3): 156–167.

15. Llungberg, A-S., Kilbom, A., and Hägg, G. (1989) Occupational lifting by nursing aides and warehouse workers. Ergonomics 32 (1): 59–78.

16. Waters, T. R., Putz-Anderson, V., Garg, A. and Fine, L. J. (1993) Revised NIOSH equation for the design and evaluation of manual lifting tasks. Ergonomics 36 (7): 749–776.

17. Garg, A., Owen, B. D. and Carlson, B. (1992) An ergonomic evaluation of nursing assistants' jobs in a nursing home. Ergonomics 35 (9): 979–995.

18. Stock, S. (1995) A study of musculoskeletal symptoms in daycare workers. In Messing, K., Neis, B. and Dumais, L. (Eds.), Invisible: Issues in Women's Occupational Health / Invisible: La santé des Travailleuses. pp. 62–74. Gynergy Books, Charlottetown. Legault-Faucher, M. (1994) Educatrices et éducateurs de garderie: Faire grandir la prévention. Prévention au travail 71: 30–31.

19. Grant, K. A., Habes, D. J. and Tepper, A. L. (1995). Work activities and musculoskeletal complaints among preschool workers. Applied Ergonomics 26: 405–410.

20. Billette, A. and Piché, J. (1987) Health problems of data entry clerks and related job stressors. Journal of Occupational Medicine 29: 942–948.

21. This is the discomfort people experience when they visit a museum and spend a long time in front of each exhibit. It is even worse if the worker cannot take any steps at all from her position, as with some factory jobs.

22. Brabant, C., Bédard, S. and Mergler, D. (1989) Cardiac strain among women laundry workers engaged in sedentary repetitive work. Ergonomics 32: 615–628.

23. Paul, J., van Dijk, F. J. H. and Frings-Dresen, M. H. W. (1994) Work load and musculoskeletal complaints during pregnancy. Scandinavian Journal of Work, Environment and Health 20: 153–159.

24. Paul, J., Frings-Dresen, M. H. W., Sallé, H. J. A. and Rozendal, R. H. (1995) Pregnant women and working surface height and working surface areas for standing manual work. Applied Ergonomics 26 (2): 129–133.

25. Lippel, K. and Demers, D. (1996) L'invisibilité, facteur d'exclusion: Les femmes victimes de lésions professionnelles. Department of Legal Sciences, Université du Québec à Montréal, Montréal.

26. Courville, J., Dumais, L. and Vézina, N. (1994) Conditions de travail de femmes et d'hommes sur une chaîne de découpe de volaille et développement d'atteintes musculo-squelettiques. Travail et santé 10 (3): S17–S23.

27. Delaney-LeBlanc, M. (1993) Presentation. Proceedings of the Research Round Table on Gender and Workplace Health, pp. 85–88. June 22–23. Health and Welfare Canada, Ottawa.

28. Ramaciotti, D., Blaire, S. and Bousquet, A. (1994) Quels critères pour l'aménagement du temps de travail? Communication at the International Ergonomics Association. Toronto, August.

29. Saurel-Cubizolles M.J. Bourgine M., Touranchet, A., and Kaminski M. (1991) Enquête dans les abattoirs et les conserveries des régions Bretagne et Pays-de-Loire. Conditions de travail et santé des salariés, p. 46. Rapport à la the Direction régionale des affaires sanitaires et sociales des Pays-de-Loire. INSERM Unité 149, Villejuif, France. Kilbom, A., and Torgén, M. (1996) Do physical loads at work interact with interact with aging? Proceedings of the 25th International Congress of Occupational Health, vol. 2. p. 17, Stockholm, September 15–20.

30. Messing, K., Doniol-Shaw, G. and Haëntjens, C. (1993) Sugar and spice: Health effects of the sexual division of labour among train cleaners. International Journal of Health Services 23 (1): 133–146.

31. Workers' Compensation of British Columbia, Secretariat for Regulation Review (1994) Draft Ergonomics Regulations. Worker's Compensation Board of British Columbia, Richmond.

32. David, H. and Payeur, C. (1993) Différences et similitudes entre les enseignantes et les enseignants des commissions scolaires. Revue des sciences de l'éducation 19 (1): 113–131.

33. Boxer, P. A., Burnett, C. and Swanson, N. (1995) Suicide and occupation: A review of the literature. Journal of Occupational and Environmental Medicine 37 (4): 442–452.

34. Messing, K., Seifert, A. M. and Escalona, E. (1997). The 120-second minute: Using analysis of work activity to prevent psychological distress

among elementary school teachers. Journal of Occupational Health Psychology 2 (1): 45–62.

CHAPTER 12

1. Frederick W. Taylor reduced the work process to its component parts and parceled out operations to different workers. Instead of making a whole product, the worker repetitively makes a single part. See Taylor, F. W. (1947) *The Principles of Scientific Management.* Harper and Brothers, New York.

2. Basen, G. and Buffie, E. (1996) Asking Different Questions: Women and Science. Produced by Merit Jensen Carr, Artemis Productions, Signe Johansson and Margaret Pettigrew. Available from the National Film Board of Canada, Montréal.

3. Hubbard, R. (1990) *The Politics of Women's Biology,* chap. 1. New Brunswick, Rutgers University Press.

4. Ibid. p. 13.

5. Eichler, M. and Lapointe, J. (1985) *On the Treatment of the Sexes in Research.* Social Science and Humanities Research Council, Ottawa.

6. Eichler, M. (1992) Nonsexist research: A metatheoretical approach. Indian Journal of Social Work 53: 329–341. Eichler, M. (1991) *Non Sexist Research Methods: A Practical Guide.* Routledge, New York.

7. Eichler, M., Reisman, A. and Manace-Borins, E. (1992) Gender bias in medical research. Women and Therapy 12 (4): 61–70.

8. Eichler (1991) *Non Sexist Research Methods,* p. 115.

9. Ibid. p. 108.

10. Deguire, S. and Messing, K. (1995) L'étude de l'absence au travail a-t-elle un sexe? Recherches féministes 8 (2): 9–30.

11. Rene Loewenson and the epidemiology committee of the International Congress on Occupational Health are discussing many of these issues with occupational health researchers in 1997 and 1998 in meetings in Harare and Helsinki.

12. A good starting point is Nancy Krieger and Elizabeth Fee's paper on race and sex in public health, "Man-made medicine and women's health: The biopolitics of sex/gender and race/ethnicity," originally published in the International Journal of Health Services and reprinted in Fee, E. and Krieger, N. (1994) *Women's Health, Politics and Power: Essays on Sex/Gender, Medicine and Public Health.* Baywood Press, Amityville. In it, they explain exactly why race and sex are not biological determinants of health but rather social categories that are associated with environmental determinants of health.

13. This list is taken from my 1996 report to Health Canada entitled *Women's Occupational Health in Canada: A Critical Review and Discussion of Current Issues.*

14. Mergler, D. (1995) Adjusting for gender differences in occupational

health studies. In Messing, K., Neis, B. and Dumais, L. (Eds.), *Invisible: Issues in Women's Occupational Health and Safety/Invisible: La santé des travailleuses*, pp. 236–251. Gynergy Books, Charlottetown.

15. Mergler, D. Brabant, C., Vézina, N. and Messing, K. (1987) The weaker sex? Men in women's working conditions report similar health symptoms. Journal of Occupational Medicine 29: 417–421.

16. Messing K., Tissot, F., Saurel-Cubizolles, M-J., Kaminski, M., and Bourgine, M. Sex, a surrogate for some working conditions: Factors associated with sickness absence in French poultry slaughterhouses and canneries. Journal of Occupational and Environmental Medicine, in press.

17. Jeanne Stellman and Joan Bertin explained this to the U.S. Food and Drug Administration in a letter in 1996.

18. In fact, public health researchers in general are becoming aware that they can get useful information from lay people. See Popay, J. and Williams, G. (1996) Public health research and lay knowledge. Social Science and Medicine 42 (5): 759–768.

19. The Loka Institute and the Community Research Network were set up by the University of Massachusetts Extension. The address of the Loka Institute, which is playing a leading role in putting scientists in contact with the community through various forums, is: P.O. Box 355, Amherst, MA 01004; Internet: loka@amherst.edu.

20. Code, L. (1991) *What Can She Know? Feminist Theory and the Construction of Knowledge,* chap. 6. Cornell University Press, Ithaca.

21. Reinharz, S. (1992) *Feminist Methods in Social Research.* Oxford University Press, New York.

22. Patrizia Romito describes with wry humor the fate of one of her medical research papers, which was not detached enough for the American journal to which she submitted it: Romito, P. (1990) *Lavoro e salute in gravidanza,* pp. 13–23. Franco Angeli, Milan.

23. Nicole Vézina testified for the workers and Robert Gilbert for the employer in the case of *Société canadienne des postes et Diane Corbeil et Monique Grégoire-Larivière* Commission d'appel en matière de lésions professsionnelles, Dossiers 05775-61-8712, 10911-61-8902, 02380-61-8703. Both are fairly senior university professors with Ph.D.'s and published papers. However, only Gilbert was referred to as "Doctor" during the hearings and in the published decision.

24. Loewenson, R. (1996) Participatory approaches in occupational health research. Proceedings of the 25th International Congress on Occupational Health. Keynote Addresses, p. 73. Stockholm, September 15–20.

25. Getting detailed exposure information may in fact increase the likelihood of getting statistically significant results through better identification of the group at risk. See the example of restaurant workers Chapter 6.

26. Ratcliffe, J. W. and Gonzalez-del-Valle, A. (1988) Rigor in health-

related research: Toward an expanded conceptualization. International Journal of Health Services 18 (3): 361–392.

27. I wrote a paper on this problem for a seminar held by the research group Marché du Travail et Genre (MAGE). The subject has been hotly debated by ergonomists but was readily accepted by the French feminist sociologists in the MAGE group. See Messing, K. (1996) Le genre des "opérateurs": Un paramètre pertinent pour l'analyse ergonomique? Les Cahiers du MAGE 4: 45–60.

28. Stellman, J. M. and Daum, S. (1973) *Work Is Dangerous for Your Health.* Vintage Books, New York. Stellman, J. M. (1977) *Women's Work, Women's Health: Myths and Realities.* Pantheon Books, New York.

29. Stellman, J. M. (1993) Keynote overview. *Proceedings of the Round Table on Gender and Occupational Health,* pp. 3–7. Health Canada, Ottawa.

30. Dejours, C. (1993) *Travail: Usure mentale.* 2d ed. Bayard, Paris.

31. In 1996 Ellen Imbernon, an occupational health physician and epidemiologist, was fired by the French national electric and gas company for having insisted on her right to investigate workers' health without hindrance. The workers' representatives had the right to protest and did so publically.

32. Hubbard (1990) *Politics of Women's Biology,* p. 23.

33. I thank André Duchastel for sensitizing me to this problem.

34. Confédération des syndicats nationaux, a Québec union with 200,000 members, about half of whom are women.

35. Fédération des travailleuses et travailleurs du Québec, a Québec union with 350,000 members, about 30 percent of whom are women.

36. The Centrale de l'enseignement du Québec (CEQ) groups all of Québec's primary and secondary school teachers, as well as some junior college and university lecturers and professors and some support staff. It has a large majority of women members.

37. Comité conjoint UQAM-CSN-FTQ (1977) *Le protocole d'entente UQAM-CSN-FTQ: Sur la formation syndicale. Comité conjoint UQAM-CSN-FTQ (1988) Le protocole UQAM-CSN-FTQ: 1976–1986. Bilan et perspectives.* Both available from Services aux collectivités, Université du Québec à Montréal, CP 8888, Succ. Centre-ville, Montréal, Québec, H3C 3P8, Canada. Messing, K. (1991) Putting our two heads together: A mainly women's research group looks at women's occupational health. In Wine, J. and Ristock, J. (Eds), *Feminist Activism in Canada: Bridging Academe and the Community.* James Lorrimer Press, Toronto. Reprinted in National Women's Studies Association Journal 3: 355–367, 1991.

38. Université du Québec à Montréal (1982) *Le protocole UQAM-Relais-femmes.* Côté, M.-H. (1988) Bilan des activités 1987–88 et perspectives pour la prochaine année. Both available from Services aux collectivités, Université du Québec à Montréal, CP 8888, Succ. Centre-ville, Montréal, Québec, H3C 3P8, Canada.

In this context, we have furnished some expertise to the local women's health center (Centre de santé des femmes) and to groups involved with employment access such as Action-travail des femmes. Our work with some predominantly male unions is described in two papers: Mergler, D. (1987) Worker participation in occupational health research: Theory and practice. International Journal of Health Services 17: 151–167. Messing, K. (1987) Union-initiated research on genetic effects of workplace agents. Alternatives: Perspectives on Technology, Environment and Society 15: 15–18.

39. Doctors testified otherwise, but the workers won their case.

Index

■ ■ ■